Typography
Essentials

Brimming with creative inspiration, how-to projects, and useful information to enrich your everyday life, Quarto Knows is a favorite destination for those pursuing their interests and passions. Visit our site and dig deeper with our books into your area of interest: Quarto Creates, Quarto Cooks, Quarto Homes, Quarto Lives, Quarto Drives, Quarto Explores, Quarto Gifts, or Quarto Kids.

Dedication

For my husband, Steven

First published in 2009; revised edition published in 2019 by Rockport Publishers, an imprint of The Quarto Group, 100 Cummings Center, Suite 265-D, Beverly, MA 01915, USA.
T (978) 282-9590 F (978) 283-2742 QuartoKnows.com

Rockport Publishers titles are also available at discount for retail, wholesale, promotional, and bulk purchase. For details, contact the Special Sales Manager by email at specialsales@quarto.com or by mail at The Quarto Group, Attn: Special Sales Manager, 100 Cummings Center, Suite 265-D, Beverly, MA 01915, USA.

10 9 8 7 6 5 4 3 2 1

ISBN: 978-1-63159-647-6

Digital edition published in 2019
eISBN: 978-1-63159-648-3

Originally found under the following Library of Congress Cataloging-in-Publication Data

Saltz, Ina.
  Typography essentials : 100 design principles for working with type / Ina Saltz.
     p. cm.
  Includes index.
  ISBN-13: 978-1-59253-523-1
  ISBN-10: 1-59253-523-2
1. Graphic design (Typography) 2. Type and type-founding. I. Title.
  Z246.S223 2009
  686.2'24—dc22
                                        2009001540
ISBN-13: 978-1-59253-740-2
ISBN-10: 1-59253-740-5

10 9 8 7 6 5 4 3 2 1

Design: Ina Saltz

Cover Design: Donald Partyka
Additional Design and Page Layout: Leslie Haimes

Printed in China

REVISED AND UPDATED

Typography Essentials

100 Design Principles for Working with Type

Ina Saltz

ROCKPORT

CON

> **"One of the principles of durable typography is always legibility; another is something more than legibility: some earned or unearned interest that gives its living energy to the page. It takes various forms and goes by various names, including serenity, liveliness, laughter, grace and joy."**
>
> –Robert Bringhurst, *The Elements of Typographic Style*

TENTS >>

INTRODUCTION

TO THE REVISED AND UPDATED EDITION OF TYPOGRAPHY ESSENTIALS

I am excited to have the opportunity to present this newly revised edition of *Typography Essentials,* which includes a wonderful selection of new design work by some of the top professionals in the field. I hope you will be inspired by these stellar examples of both print-based work and screen-based work: mobile, tablet, web, and environmental work, three dimensional and electronic.

Our eye for visuals and our swiftly advancing technology are ever changing and evolving. However, the typographic principles that govern all good design remain the same. The mission of *Typpography Essentials* is to distill, organize, and compartmentalize—but not to oversimplify—the many complex issues surrounding the successful and effective use of typography. It is for designers of every medium in which type plays a role.

A deep understanding of letterforms and knowledge of the effective use of letterforms develops over a lifetime of design practice and study. *Typography Essentials* is intended to advance the progress of designers seeking to deepen their typographic expertise; it is organized and designed to make the process enjoyable and entertaining, as well as instructional.

The typographic principles are divided into four sections: The Letter, The Word, The Paragraph, and The Page. Each of the 100 principles has a spread with an explanation and examples representing the principle in action.

You will notice that, in some cases, the principles will contradict one another. Contradiction is inherently necessary because many excellent typographic designs flout the basic rules of any Type 1 class. This is why it is so important to know the rules in the first place. As my calligraphy teacher, Donald Jackson, so eloquently observed: "All rules may be broken in divinely successful ways."

This sentiment has been expressed in many forms by prominent designers, yet it leads beginners to think that there really are no hard-and-fast rules. Nothing could be further from the truth. In fact, there are myriad rules that govern the use of type. As design schools and design students chafe under the yoke of teaching and learning those rules, type can be one of the most disliked (indeed, feared) components of design. And yet, it is the most crucial aspect of almost all design-related projects.

I believe that those who possess finely honed typographic skills have an enormous advantage in the workplace, whether they are newly graduated designers or mid-career professionals. Typographic skills are eminently transferable across all media, but few designers have a true grounding in typographic essentials. Those who do, immediately stand out.*

The number of available typefaces keeps expanding exponentially, but the essential principles of good typographic design remain largely unchanged. Whether in print, on computer screens, interactive interfaces, tablets, or mobile devices, designers must still respond to the same human factors that have always governed sound typographic choices. In fact, as baby boomers age and their eyesight degrades, and as smaller devices demand greater legibility under multiple viewing conditions, the challenges that must be considered have never been greater for designers.

Just as some principles may be contradictory, there is, inevitably, some overlap among the four sections of typographic principles in *Typography Essentials.* And, while there is no single volume that can convey the vast body of information about typography, I hope this book will play a significant role in continuing typographic education with clarity and easy comprehension for designers at all levels.

---

*In *Becoming a Graphic and Digital Designer*, by Steven Heller and Teresa Fernandez (Fifth Edition, Wiley, 2015), most prominent designers list "excellent typographic skills" or "superior typographic skills" as among the most important characteristics of job seekers. Also, an independent review of hundreds of job descriptions for designers lists "excellent typographic skills" as a major job requirement.

Project
Background Panels

Design Director
Donald Partyka

Designer
Donald Partyka

Client
LinkedInLearning

1 Using letter as form

EACH LETTER IS A SHAPE UNTO ITSELF, a shape that may serve as an illustration, as an icon, as a vessel, or as a graphic focal point, apart from its meaning as an alphabetic unit. Especially when used at very large sizes, the extreme proportions of letterforms can have exceptional impact—this technique has been exploited very effectively by many successful designers.

Letters can be expressive when used alone, as a simple silhouette, as an outline, or as a container for image, texture, or pattern. The beauty and power of the individual form may also be used partially: or a shape that is sliced and diced, cropped, or reversed horizontally or vertically. Because it is a letterform, it has a built-in relationship with any typeface that accompanies it. Its inherent integration unifies the design of the whole piece.

Project
Rebecca Minkoff Couture
Identity Concept

Design Studio
Remake

Art Director, Designer
Michael Dyer

Client
Rebecca Minkoff

This custom-lettered logo forms a discrete shape, but within its boundaries, each letter is delicate and leaf-like. The delicacy is further underscored by the pastel color gradation. The logo also appears with some of its counter spaces filled with a similar hue.

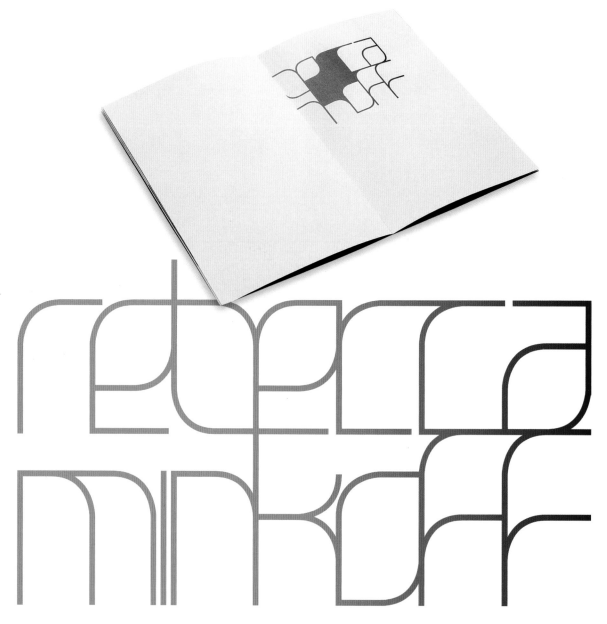

Project
Brooklyn Public Library
Branding

Studio
Eight and a Half

Art Director
Bonnie Siegler

Designer
Andrew James Capelli

Client
Brooklyn Public Library

The letters comprising the logo can accommodate images, textures, and colors to reflect different aspects of the organization's identity and a variety of events. It is a vessel made of the letters Bklyn, the common abbreviation for Brooklyn.

Project
Salute the Sound

Design Director
Paul Sych

Typographer
Paul Sych

Client
Bass the Beat Productions

These letterforms are beautiful abstractions, chunky ribbons of color. It is amazing that we can actually read this phrase, given how spare the forms are. The letterforms suggest the vinyl ridges of an album or LP.

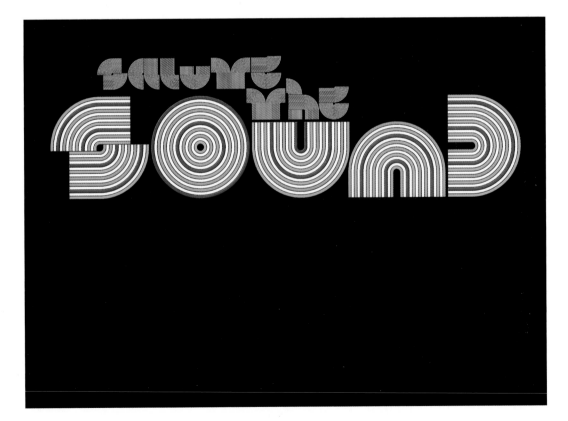

2 Using counter spaces as form

THE SPACES INSIDE AND AROUND the shape of a letter, called counter spaces, are often overlooked as design elements. Their shapes can be customized using color, pattern, or texture. The "bulk" of the counter spaces adds to the weight of the display and can provide a unique and memorable effect. Creative use of counter spaces may take many forms.

The beauty of counter spaces, sometimes called "negative" spaces, is that they are the jewels that are already tucked into the letters…using them well is like discovering buried treasure. They were there all along, hidden in plain sight.

Project
Poster

Design Director
Jeff Wall

Company
SFMOMA

Designers
Amadeo DeSouza,
Owen Hoskins, and
Jeremy Mende

Client
SFMOMA

An aggressively broad and linear display typeface provides ideal windows (counter spaces) that enclose and encapsulate intriguing glimpses of still film frames. Each group of letters assumes its own chunky shape within a field of gray, suggesting the half-light of the theater.

Project
The Brand Union identity

Creative Director
Wally Krantz

Designer
Jaime Burns

Client
The Brand Union

The logo of this multinational branding firm is "built" of counter spaces. They chose this direction because the counter spaces "reflect our position of being master brand builders … in the process of building (not built)."

thebrandunion.com

Project
Packaging

Design Director
Rick Davis

Designer
Louis Fishauf

Illustrator
James Marsh

Client
Niagara Vintners, Inc.

The image within the perfectly circular counter space of the zero allows us to enter a fantasy world of rolling hills inhabited by giant bees and tiny vintners.

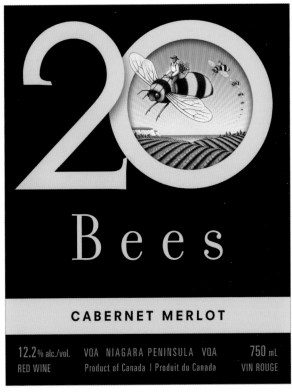

3 Letterform details

SPECIALIZED DETAILING CAN COMMUNICATE apart from the literal message; whether customized or built in as alternate characters within a typeface, even a simple swash or ligature can add an extra level of meaning or make the design more specific to the message. Making something more interesting to look at, however, may interfere with legibility, so there must always be a balance between adding effects and maintaining a comfortable level of reading.

Letterform details have never been easier to alter or create: many typefaces, especially in the OpenType format (which allows for unlimited glyphs), have alternative swash caps and ligatures. They also allow the designer to open the glyph as a vector and alter its outline, making customized letterform details easy to execute. However, this function may invite designers to "tamper" with the original designer's forms, and if they have not been trained in the rigorous and demanding specifics that good type design requires, the results may be unique but unfortunate to the trained eye.

Project
Identity

Creative Director
Matteo Bologna

Art Director, Designer
Andrea Brown

Client
Sant Ambroeus

Mucca's design for a new Manhattan restaurant based on Milan's patron saint (and with a history of almost seventy years in Italy) uses quirky custom typography to suggest an era. Odd widths (a lowercase m that is narrower than a lowercase s) and strange gaps (the capital A, combined with letters that tilt inconsistently) produce a charming eccentricity.

Project
Identity

Design Director
Paul Sych

Client
Gears Bike Shop

The letterform details of this customized logo suggest the turning of the gear shaft above the type. The simple device of a few curved lines within the letters adds a twisting motion effect.

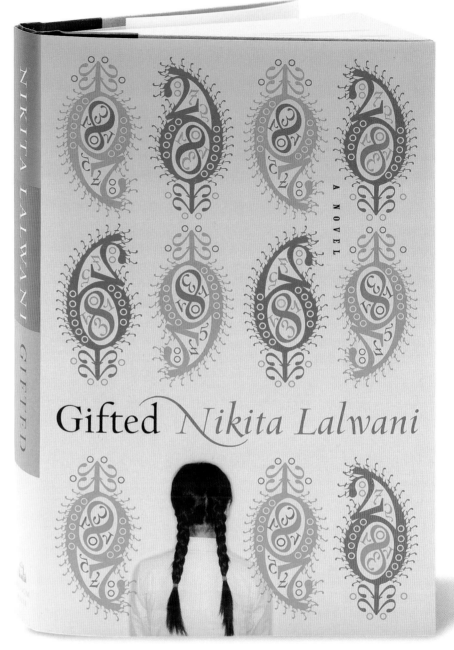

Project
Book cover

Art Director
Robbin Schiff

Designer
Roberto de Vicq

Client
Random House

The superextended swash of the capital *N* connects the author to the title, but also adds drama to the simple typography. This cover design also uses counter spaces creatively, creating nested numbers in feminine colors with ethnic ornament (this is the story of a young Indian girl's mathematical gifts).

4 Emotional content implied by the text

LETTERFORMS CAN AMPLIFY the emotional weight of the text. The delicate tracery of a flowing italic might best convey a poem about nature. The chest-thumping proclamations of a heavy slab serif might punch up a political pronouncement. The rational intellectualism of an old-style typeface might add credibility to a well-reasoned debate. The proper choice of typeface is therefore essential to the tenor of the message, and it may add to—or, if a poor choice, may detract from—the believability of the text.

Other factors play into emotional content. Rounded shapes and lighter weights might convey a more feminine touch, such as those used on most cosmetic packaging. The oppo-site is generally true for products appealing to a male demographic: these would typically have more weight, and be more squared off and "muscular" in appearance. The color of the type affects its emotional content, too. We think of warmer or more subdued shades as more feminine; primary colors as appealing to children; deep burgundies, forest greens, and navy blues as more masculine. Yes, these are stereotypes, but stereotypes exist for a reason and can be used very successfully to appeal emotionally to a specific audience.

Project
Feature spread

Design Director
Carla Frank

Designer
Kristin Fitzpatrick

Client
O, The Oprah Magazine

Six lightbulbs whose glowing filaments spell out the word *energy* embody the concept literally and figuratively. The colors and the approach used here give us a positive and warm feeling.

\ˈe-nər-jē\ *n, pl* -gies **1.** Available power. **2.** Force. Zip. we can do more, be more, live life to the fullest. 24/7. Not that way: Energy is a resource. It needs to be managed. Renewed. some sleep.) This month's *O* brings you both sides. Everything (emotional, sexual, spiritual). And something more precious— Get-up-and-go. That thing we're always trying to pump up so there's anything wrong with 24/7. Life *is* short. But look at it this (Here's a radical thought: If you're running on empty, try getting science can tell you about making the most of your energy the wisdom to know when it's time to turn off the lights.

Project
Feature spread

Design Director
Carla Frank

Designer
Kristin Fitzpatrick

Client
O, The Oprah Magazine

Enormity of scale, festive colors, a bouncing beach ball to increase the contrast in scale—this is an example of a word that says "fun" even if you can't read at all. Drop shadows add dimension, an *n* that is bouncing above the baseline, a tilted exclamation point—all of these details contribute to the lively effect. Here the counter spaces serve as vessels for introductory text.

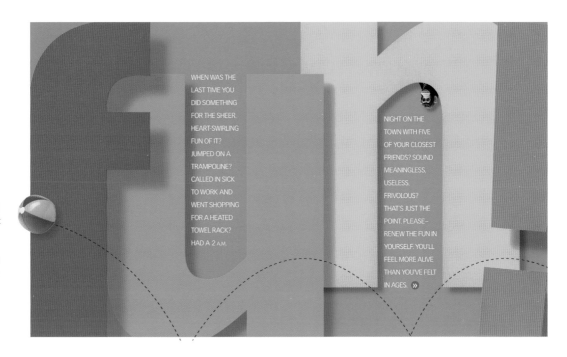

WHEN WAS THE LAST TIME YOU DID SOMETHING FOR THE SHEER, HEART-SWIRLING FUN OF IT? JUMPED ON A TRAMPOLINE? CALLED IN SICK TO WORK AND WENT SHOPPING FOR A HEATED TOWEL RACK? HAD A 2 A.M.

NIGHT ON THE TOWN WITH FIVE OF YOUR CLOSEST FRIENDS? SOUND MEANINGLESS, USELESS, FRIVOLOUS? THAT'S JUST THE POINT. PLEASE– RENEW THE FUN IN YOURSELF. YOU'LL FEEL MORE ALIVE THAN YOU'VE FELT IN AGES. »

Project
Website

Creative Director, Designer
Roberto De Vicq

Client
Roberto De Vicq

From the super friendly "hi!" in a charming spring green outlined typeface, to the designer's flourished logo at the upper left, to the active multicolored labels and dancing type on the package designs at the bottom, we are immediately uplifted to a happier place when we land on this home page.

5 Historical connotation

TYPEFACES ARE A PRODUCT OF THEIR ERA. A good design may be well served with a historically appropriate typeface choice when possible. For example, traditional or old-style typefaces imply timeworn wisdom, authenticity, integrity. Another example is the circles, squares, and triangles underlying the design of geometric sans serifs—a response to the revolutionary zeitgeist of the Bauhaus—convey a feeling that is modern and sleek. The historical implications of typographic forms remain part of their essential identity, though they may be used quite

effectively in a different era. The suggestion of a time period may be real or perceived. What matters most is how the reader will interpret the appearance of the type, and whether that interpretation will add to the reader's comprehension of the content.

It is not always possible or even desirable to "match" the historical time span of a typeface to the text—many other factors may be more important. But it is a factor that the designer should at least consider when choosing type.

Project
The High Style of Dorothy Draper exhibition

Exhibition Graphic Design
Pure+Applied

Exhibition Design
Pure+Applied and Jennifer Turner

Photographer
Harry Zernike

Client
Museum of the City of New York

The high-style '30s elegance of influential American interior designer Dorothy Draper is embodied in the faux-brush lettering of the exhibition title. A nice touch of italic on either side of the roman caps also reflects the style of the era.

TOWNLINE
BBQ

TOWNLINE
BBQ

CORNER OF
TOWNLINE
ROAD &
MONTAUK HWY.
SAGAPONACK, NY
631-537-2271
WWW.TOWNLINEBBQ.COM

CHRISTY COBER
TITLE

Project
Visual identity

Creative Director
Harry Segal

Art Director
Shamona Stokes

Client
Townline Barbecue

The slab serifs and "corny" script play off one another to give us a sense of the Old West, a time and a place where barbecue is eternal. The display type is deliberately distressed to suggest a low-tech printing process; the two-color approach adds to a down-and-dirty effect.

MENU

Texas Style Ribs

Pork Slab	
rack	$12
full rack	$24

Specialty Smoked Ribs

Brisket	$6
Texas Link	$6
Chicken	$8
Pork Chops	$12
Pulled Pork	$6
Rib Tips	$6 (as available)
Burnt Ends	$6

Sandwiches

Brisket	$8
Pulled Pork	$8
Texas Link	$8
Burnt Ends	$8 (as available)
Rib Tips	$8 (as available)

*Please call for our daily specials.

Sides

Baked Beans	$4/$8
Cole Slaw	$3/$6
Potato Salad	$3/$6
Greens	$3/$6
French Fries	$3/$6
Corn Bread	$2.50/$5.00
Texas Style Chili	$4/$8
Pickles	$1/$2

Dessert

Fried Cherry Pie	$2.50
Banana Pudding	$2.50

Beverages

Drink TK	$4/$8
Drink TK	$3/$6
Drink TK	$3/$6
Drink TK	$3/$6
Drink TK	$3/$6

CORNER OF
TOWNLINE
ROAD &
MONTAUK HWY.
SAGAPONACK, NY
631-537-2271
WWW.TOWNLINEBBQ.COM

Townline BBQ SAUCE

XX FL.OZ

TOWNLINE
BBQ

INGREDIENTS
KETCHUP, TOMATO JUICE, ONION, BROWN SUGAR, WORCHESTERSHIRE SAUCE, BUTTER, MOLASSES, LEMON, CHIPOTLE PUREE, CHILI POWDER, WHITE VINEGAR, GARLIC, SALT

QUESTIONS OR COMMENTS? CONTACT US AT WWW.TOWNLINEBBQ.COM

6 Considering the medium

HOW AND WHERE LETTERFORMS APPEAR should be a clue as to a designer's typographic decisions; the medium may dictate what constitutes a more legible type choice. Consider whether the text appears on a reflective surface (i.e., paper, billboard, environmental signage) or a light-emitting surface (i.e., a computer screen, a video screen, a tablet, or mobile device).

We can break it down further: if the medium is a reflective surface, is it designed to be viewed primarily while being held in the hand, at a typical reading distance, or is it intended to be viewed from a distance, and if so, what distance? Is the intended reader quite young, quite old, or visually impaired? (In these cases, a larger size and a highly legible typeface should be used—perhaps something with a larger x-height and more open counter spaces for increased legibility.) Is the surface glossy or matte or somewhere in between? If glossier, light reflections can interfere with reading, so the typeface might need to be larger or weightier.

If the medium is light emitting, there is typically a kind of "glowing" effect produced as a more pronounced light enters our eyes. This generally means that letterforms need to be sturdier and to have a bit more tracking applied to counteract the effects of the glow for optimum readability. As with reflective surfaces, the distance at which you intend the text to be viewed should be a factor in the type choice, as well as color, contrast with the background, size, and weight.

The medium may also be one in which the type is moving, and it may be moving in myriad ways: zooming in and out, fading in and out, flashing on and off, moving from one place to another, breaking up, reassembling—the options are endless. Here, timing plays a role, as well as all of the other factors mentioned. In any case, the medium must be considered when choosing all of the typographic aspects to best convey content.

Project
Tablet edition

Studio
TischenFranklin

Digital Design Director
Tischen Franklin

Creative Director
Keziah Makoundou

Client
Afropolitain

Text in relation to the tablet size must be considered when making typographic choices.

Environmental graphic identities must perform in all types of lighting conditions and even in all kinds of weather. Sturdy sans serif letterforms, illuminated from within and without, are a beacon for museum visitors.

Project
Brand Identity, Environmental Graphics, Digital Design

Studio
Pentagram

Art Director
Eddie Opara

Designers
Brankika Harvey and Pedro Mende

Web Designer and Developer
Chan Young Park

Web Developer
Jacob McDonald

Strategist and Writer
Rachel Abrams

Project Managers
Erin Wahed
Carrie Brody

Client
The Queens Museum

7 Honoring dignity

ONE OF THE MOST ELOQUENT DEFENDERS of excellence in typography is Robert Bringhurst. In his seminal text *The Elements of Typographic Style*, Bringhurst frames the notion of honoring the dignity of the text in a twofold manner; briefly, it is this: the text (the content) is paramount, and all else exists to honor it, but letters also have their own life and dignity. Clarifying and ennobling "important" text is an honorable goal, to be sure. And even simple informational texts such as bus schedules and telephone directories deserve to be handled with typographic care and attention.

In a perfect world, all content would be worthy of being honored, but we know too well that a great deal of content is trivial, redundant, badly composed, witless, even despicable. What, then, is our responsibility to the text? How often have we seen film credits that were beautifully done, for films with no artistic merit whatsoever? How often have we seen a well-designed book jacket and been utterly disappointed with its contents? Or enjoyed an elegantly presented menu before discovering that the restaurant's cuisine was inedible? As designers, we all make moral choices (is this worthy of my talent?) and practical decisions (will I lose my job/client if I turn down this assignment?), but one way to think about honoring the text is akin to the way defendants are treated under U.S. law: everyone is entitled to legal representation and a fair trial, innocent until proven guilty.

Project
Homepage

Company
FusionLab

Designer
Alon Koppel

Client
Architectural Digest

The simple geometric sans serif titling, isolated in its own stripe of tone, floats above the image much as the island of the image floats in the water. Its quiet forms act in harmony with the quietness of the sepia-toned image.

Cultural Reflections
Period Photographs Richly Document the Complexity of Chinese Life in the 19th Century

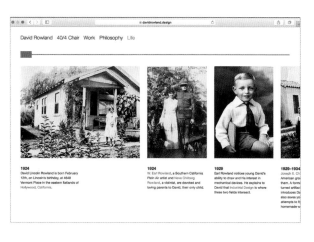

Project
David Rowland
Desktop and mobile website

Studio
Eight and a Half

Art Director
Bonnie Siegler

Designer
Kristen Ren

Client
Erwin Rowland

This historical tribute to the work of an innovative minimalist artist is typographically restrained and respectful, in keeping with his enduring designs.

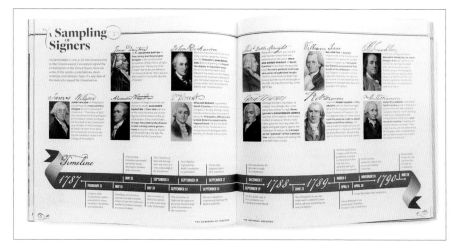

Project
Charters of Freedom
book design

Studio
Eight and a Half

Art Director
Bonnie Siegler

Designer
Bonnie Siegler

Client
National Archives

Documents of American history ask to be treated with dignity. This typographic treatment honors their importance and heritage.

8 The handmade solution

IN OUR INCREASINGLY TECHNICAL WORLD, there has been a huge backlash against the machine-made aesthetic. Handmade forms appeal to our humanity, and the enormous popularity of handmade objects reflects the do-it-yourself spirit of our times. Even large corporations are using hand-drawn letterforms (or typefaces that are designed to resemble hand-drawn letterforms, containing a panoply of alternate characters) to warm their chilly images. The MTV logo is an example of the renegade or counterculture aspect of hand-drawn letters, as is the psychedelic lettering that typified the '60s, or the deliberately rough and exuberant hand lettering of the *Moulin Rouge* posters.

The handmade solution is a display-only solution, for the irregularity and quirkiness of form and material inhibits the legibility of text passages. But when used judiciously and with restraint, handmade letterforms can infuse the content with emotion.

Irregularity of handmade and hand-drawn typographic forms can be particularly effective in conveying qualities such as playfulness, originality, authenticity, rebellion, and spontaneity, or to signal an organic nature. These forms suggest that they were customized, created for a singular purpose, not intended to be replicated. These "personalized" implied aspects add to the perception of the content as unique, appealing to the reader in a more visceral way than any out-of-the-box typography. Thus the reader may be made to feel that the act of reading is more satisfying and creative, more personally touching.

Project
Theater poster

Designer, illustrator
Bülent Erkman

Letterer
Bilge Barhana

Photographer
Fethi Izan

Client
Kum, Pan,
Ya Theatre Group

Rough script handwriting creates texture, shape, and "facial" framework for the images in addition to providing information. The hand-drawn lettering adds to the surrealist effect of the silhouetted eyes, lips, and eyebrows.

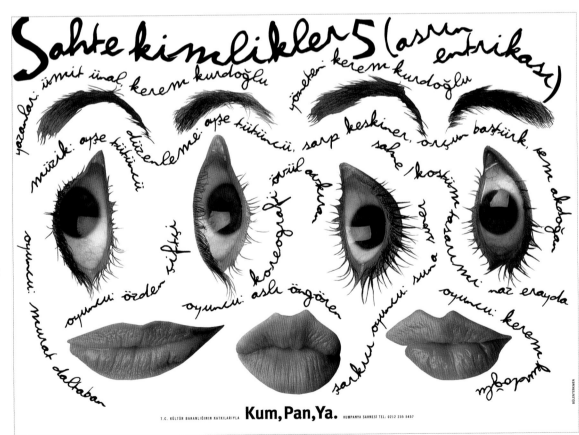

Project
Theater poster

Designer, illustrator
Eric Beloussov

Letterer
Dmitriev Nick

Client
Cultural Centre Dom

Flamelike hand-drawn typographic forms mass together in a red, white, and black palette to create an ominous and threatening look. A unified approach using scratchboard technique for both art and text offers a powerful example of how effective this approach can be; the intricately fitted, custom-shaped text blocks would have been impossible to create using conventional typography.

Project
Promotional poster

Designer
Norito Shinmura

Client
Yasei Jidai ("Wild Age")

Publisher
Kadokawa Shoten Co., Ltd.

From a series of promotional posters, these letterforms are delightfully playful, crafted from a traditional children's party entertainment of balloon toys. A careful examination reveals that the balloon forms are unique and varied, lending a charm and warmth that is appealing to one's inner child.

9 Being expressive

A STRONG TYPOGRAPHIC PERSONALITY can be a very effective showstopper, as over the top as a designer chooses to make it. Any and all effects can be used to express the spirit and meaning of the text, including hand-drawn lettering, modified typography, and distorted or manipulated letterforms, as long as they are created in service of the content or to amplify the meaning of the text. In this mode of typographic design, there is no limit to a designer's options (but this freedom can be dangerous in untrained hands!).

Like the handmade solution on the preceding pages, expressive typography is a display-only solution, because text type or body copy must be legible. Legibility is not as great a concern for expressive typography; however, depending on the solution, it most likely cannot be completely illegible, unless it is intended to stand solely as an image.

Project
Death from Above 1979

Company
Little Friends of Printmaking

Client
Wisconsin Union Directorate

Drawn in the same creepy-cartoon style as the illustration, the letterforms are squeezed within the mouth and teeth and become the focal point by playing off of the facial expression.

Project
Lemon Fresh Kids

Company
Alphabet Arm Design

Designer
Aaron Belyea

Client
Tim McCoy

The type is as "lemon fresh" as the title, with the added touch of the citrusy dingbats in the counter spaces.

Project
Cover story

Creative Director
Donald Partyka

Client
Americas Quarterly

The typographic treatment of the headline expresses disruption as the letters themselves are disrupted by coming apart. The effect is heightened by the strategic use of color.

DISRUPT LATIN AMERICA

HOW INNOVATIVE STARTUPS ARE DISRUPTING FINANCIAL SERVICES IN LATIN AMERICA BY JACKIE HYLAND

Microfinance revolutionized the financial services sector in Latin America over 40 years ago. Millions of individuals who were excluded from traditional financial institutions obtained access to a variety of financial products and services for the first time. Inevitably, there were gaps in coverage. In recent years, various players have been looking beyond microfinance to find ways to fill those gaps. Their main weapon has been the disruptive force of new technology.

10 Staying neutral

SIMPLICITY AND NEUTRALITY allow the text to visually say "no comment." The maxim "cleanliness is next to godliness" is the theory behind this approach; the classic Swiss school of design typifies it. Neutrality possesses a cool elegance, which may be either classical or modern, depending on whether serif or sans serifs typefaces are used, and, of course, how they are used to contain the content.

Some designers find staying neutral to be a boring and banal exercise. The recently released *Helvetica*, a documentary film by Gary Hustwit, addresses the controversy over whether neutrality is a desirable characteristic or whether neutrality simply propagates anonymity and blandness. Helvetica is a typeface that exemplifies neutrality; this allows it to be used in many different contexts and to assume the identity of the brand, project, or product. Designers such as Massimo Vignelli believe that in its very neutrality, Helvetica is infinitely malleable and useful, while other designers such as Paula Scher see Helvetica as a representation of the facelessness and soullessness of big corporations and government.

Project
Feature spread

Design Director
Carla Frank

Designer
Kristin Fitzpatrick

Client
O, The Oprah Magazine

The unfussy typography of the title provides perfect counterpoint to the ornate patterns of these decorative teapots.

Project
Brand identity, environmental graphics, website design

Studio
Pentagram

Art Director
Eddie Opara

Designers
Brankica Harvey, Ken Deegan, Pedro Mendes, Andrew Mbiam, Jacob MacDonald, Ben Leonard, and Taylor Childers

Client
Grace Farms

This quiet lowercase type treatment allows the lush landscape to be the star of the brand identity. The typography takes a back seat to the imagery.

Project
Brand identity

Studio
Pentagram

Art Directors
Emily Oberman and Michael Bierut

Designers
Elliott Walker
Deva Pardue

Client
The Minneapolis Institute of Art

Packed and superbold sans serif letters convey a sense of importance and authority. The neutrality of a sans serif allows for a broad interpretation of the collection.

11 Considering background contrast

THE DIFFERENCE BETWEEEN FOREGROUND and background totality is a key factor in legibility. The highest degree of contrast exists between black and white. Studies have shown that, while black type on a white background is highly legible, the same quantity of white type on a black background is harder to read. In large quantities, especially at text type sizes, there is a kind of "halo" or sparkle effect that impedes legibility and is actually uncomfortable to the eye.

As type color and background color come closer together in hue, saturation, and density, legibility is reduced. At a certain point where there is not enough contrast (and this point is a moving target, because it depends on many other factors, including letter weight, set width, stroke width, slope, and point size), legibility may be significantly impaired. The amount of text is a factor (a few lines might be less of a problem), the length of the lines or "measure" may be a factor, and the light conditions and paper surface may also be factors (see "Theory of Relativity I" on page 56).

Project
Feature spread

Design Director
Carla Frank

Designer
Kristin Fitzpatrick

Photographer
Gentl & Hyers

Client
O, The Oprah Magazine

The opening spread has the same type style and size under the title, but the tint changes as the type position grows lower in the page. This is a graphic demonstration of the decrease in contrast and how it can affect legibility. In this case, legibility is not an issue because the type size is still sufficiently large (but if the page were viewed from a distance, the difficulty in legibility would be apparent).

Project
Feature spread

Art Director
Donald Partyyka

Designer
Donald Partyka

Client
Americas Quarterly

Black body copy on a white background is always highly legible. The byline of bold red sans serif text at a larger size on a white background is also highly legible. The deck, using the same size and weight of red sans serif, this time on a black background, is also quite legible, precisely because of its weight and size. Red text on black, or black on red, can be hard to read depending on its size and weight because they have a similar level of saturation.

by Antonio de Aguiar Patriota

The end of the unipolar world is creating opportunties for diplomacy and greater respect for international law. But it won't happen on its own. The world's new emerging powers have to act in concert to reform multilateral institutions.

A redistribution of global power is underway. Emerging countries are playing increasingly significant roles in the global economy, trade, investment, as well as in diplomacy and in multilateral decision-making on issues of global interest.

At some point in the next few years, we will witness an historically rare phenomenon: a new country taking on the mantle of the world's largest economy. China's gross domestic product (GDP) will become the largest in the world, overtaking the United States. The last time the world's number one economic changed was in the nineteenth century, when the U.S. economy surpassed the United Kingdom's.

These changes are accompanied by the unprecedented reduction of poverty on a global scale, witnessed most dramatically in the decline of social inequality in Brazil, and making the eradication of extreme poverty now an attainable goal. It is possible that, by 2030, a majority of the world's population will be able to enjoy a middle class standard of living, an achievement unprecedented in human history.

However, this will not eliminate the significant gap in living standards that will continue to exist between the developed countries and developing countries such as China and India, even though the latter two will probably become the first and second largest world economies in terms of GDP by 2050.

The growing role of emerging countries as new centers of world power does not mean that Western countries, or the so-called "established powers," are "submerging." On the contrary, they will continue to have diversified economies, formidable technological capacity and, in some cases—particularly that of the U.S.—the ability to maintain military power far superior to that of any other country for decades to come. Nevertheless, there is no question that the relative power of the G7 countries has declined and, with it, their capacity for global leadership.

The Loss of Economic and Moral Leadership

The decline of the "developed" powers—in particular, of the U.S.–is the result not only of measurable, long-term trends, such as the size of the econ-

Project
Tablet app

Studio
TischenFranklin

Design Director
Thomas Alberty

Digital Art Director
Tischen Franklin

Client
New York magazine

This screen-based tablet app uses the classic technique of black text on a white background for high contrast, ensuring legibility. It also employs some strong blue typography to pop out key phrases; this dark blue against a white background adds visual variety, adds entry points for the reader, and is also easy to read.

12 Emphasis using weight

STAYING WITHIN THE SAME TYPE FAMILY and simply varying the weight of the family member can signal a shift in hierarchy, even when the point size is unchanged. Changing the weight allows two words to be melded together, yet still retain their own identity without the use of a word space. Changing the weight within a single word can indicate a shift in hierarchy. Or, most commonly, heightening emphasis by using a heavier weight in a list, in a paragraph lead-in, or within the text without changing size is a simple yet effective tool. Depending on the typeface used, the point size may need to be slightly reduced to maintain an even typographic color of a passage of text. (See "Hierarchy using weight" on page 66.)

Project
Freestyle—The Free Word

Creative Director, Illustrator, Designer
Donald Beekman

Client
GRAP—Amsterdam foundation for pop music

Weight emphasis keeps this piece visually stimulating despite its monotone palette. The justified block of typography indicates hierarchy with size changes in a few places, but also with a shift in weight where size remains the same.

Project
Phone app

Studio
TischenFranklin

Design Director
Thomas Alberty

Digital Art Director
Tischen Franklin

Client
New York magazine

This phone app screen makes good use of typographic weight to differentiate content. This principle is demonstrated both in the underlined text and in the emphasis of the headline over the subhead. They are the same size and style; the weight is the factor that creates emphasis.

CRITICS

POP / LINDSAY ZOLADZ

Good Girl Gone Indifferent

Rihanna probably doesn't care what you think about her new album.

13 Emphasis using contrasting weights

A BROAD FAMILY OF TYPE affords a wider range of options. Levels of hierarchy can be more subtle; this is sometimes necessary depending on content. A variety of weights can enable multiple entry points and offer more opportunities to establish hierarchy (order of importance).

Typefaces that are flexible because their families offer many weights are most often sans serif, but modern type designers have developed serif and sans serif type families with an extensive range of weights. New releases of older typefaces often include a greater breadth of weights.

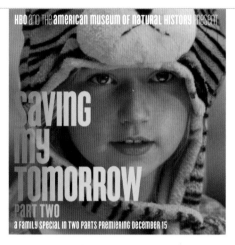

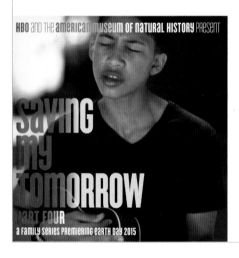

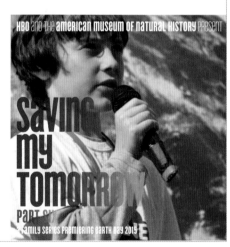

Project
Saving My Tomorrow

Studio
Eight and a Half

Art Director
Bonnie Siegler

Designer
Andrew James Capelli

Client
HBO

Two weights of a single typeface at several different sizes allow the design to emphasize key information.

Project
Type specimen

Art Director, Designer
Charlie Nix

Client
Terminal Design, Inc.

Regular, medium, bold, and
heavy weights are commonly
found in recently designed
typefaces, such as Alfon by
James Montalbano.

Project
Type specimen

Company
Hoefler & Frere-Jones

Designer
Jonathan Hoefler

Client
Hoefler & Frere-Jones

Whitney, a sans serif typeface,
has six weights of roman with
italic counterparts, and a full
range of small caps.

14 Emphasis using size

BIGGER ISN'T ALWAYS BETTER, but it does get more attention. Size, especially when combined with a more prominent position (i.e., top), is a simple but effective way to emphasize a letterform. Even a modest change in scale can make a big difference. It is best to start small and scale gradually to see the effect the change makes, unless your goal is to shout very loudly (visually speaking) or to use the letterform as a design element that is not intended to function as a piece of text.

Project
Blow-Up: Photography, Cinema and the Brain

Company
Pure+Applied

Client
Distributed Art Publishers (D.A.P)

The effect of oversized text filling the entire frame of the cover is even stronger when using an extended set width and a slight color overlap. The text is bleeding off the edges and tightly leaded to maximize the text size.

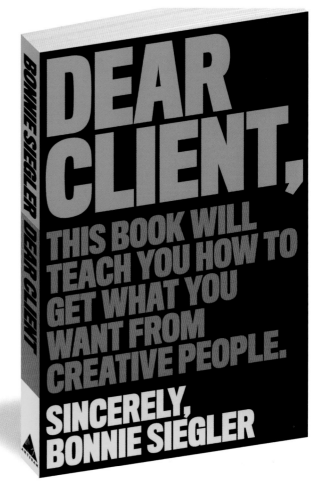

Project
Single page

Consulting Design Director
Luke Hayman

Designers
Rami Moghadam and Mark Shaw

Client
Vibe

The combination of the large text *V STYLE* and the image create one strong, unified graphic.

Project
Book cover

Studio
Eight and a Half

Art Director
Bonnie Siegler

Designer
Bonnie Siegler

Client
Artisan Books

Using the full surface of the cover, the headline, subhead, and author's name are magnified to fill the cover surface vertically and horizontally for maximum impact. The impact is further emphasized by using superbright colors (cyan, magenta, and yellow) on a black background, a nod to the CMYK printing process.

15 Emphasis using contrasting sizes

A BROAD RANGE OF SIZES is an easy way to indicate emphasis; however, other factors come into play (see "Theory of Relativity I" on page 56). Weight, size, and character width (compressed versus expanded, for example) can affect the level of emphasis as well.

Project
Cover

Art Director
Arem Duplessis

Art Director, Designer
Gail Bichler

Designer
Gail Bichler

Client
The New York Times Magazine

The contrasting sizes of the words of the headline highlight the *Why*, the key word in the title.

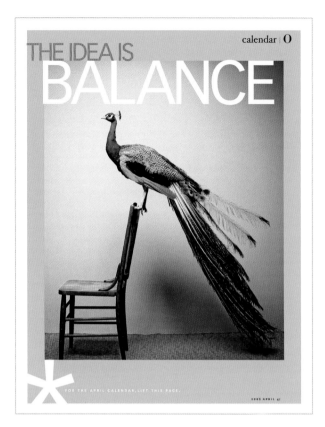

Project
Single page

Design Director
Carla Frank

Designer
Chloe Weiss

Client
O, The Oprah Magazine

The emphasis is on *BALANCE* with a larger
size of caps. The airy composition allows
the shape of the artwork to hold court and
to maximize the impossible balance of the
peacock on the chair.

Project
Back, Back, Back

Company
SpotCo

Designer
Gail Anderson

Client
Manhattan Theater Club

The headline treatment of receding
sizes of the same word creates a three-
dimensional illusion of the ball traveling
through space.

16 Proper smart quotes

THE INCORRECT SUBSTITUTION for typographers' marks or "smart" quotes is probably one of the most irritating offenses in the world of digital typography. It seems to proliferate everywhere: the appearance of "dumb" quotes or prime marks in places that otherwise display high (or at least reasonable) standards of design. It is simple enough to correct, so we can only conclude that the neglect of smart quotes stems from a lack of understanding or poor typographic training. Smart quotes (sometimes called "curly quotes," though they are not always curly) can be selected in the preferences menu of most design-related software. They are the quote marks (and apostrophes) that have been designed by the type designer to accompany the typeface. The only appropriate use of the default glyphs (dumb quotes) is to indicate the measurements of feet and inches.

Project
Feature spread

Creative Director
Donald Partyka

Photographcer
Keith Dannemiller

Client
Americas Quarterly

The opening quote marks serve as art and, by overlapping the photo, serve to connect it with the text across the spread.

Victor Leonel Juan Martínez is a lawyer and journalist and is currently deputy director of the magazine, *En Marcha*, published Oaxaca, Mexico.

Victor Leonel Juan Martínez

:Reform
The Immigration
System.

smart quotes

no. bad. very bad.

Project
Feature spread

Creative Director
Carla Frank

Junior Deputy Art Director
Jana Meier

Photographer
Robert Maxwell

Client
O, The Oprah Magazine

Smart quotes in display sizes are combined with brackets and a question mark to shape a lively ornate frame for the opening spread of an interview with an author.

Project
Opener

Creative Director
Donald Partyka

Client
Americas Quarterly

Proper smart quotes have been enlivened by changing color within the glyph.

17   The hyphen, the en dash, and the em dash

THESE THREE HORIZONTAL MARKS are often misunderstood and confused. The hyphen connects linked words and phrases and also may be found when a word breaks from one line to the next. An en dash (slightly longer than a hyphen but shorter than an em dash) is used to connect a range of numbers (i.e., 20–30). An em dash, the longest of these horizontal marks, is used to set off a separate thought or grammatical break within the text, and it is often used in tandem with another em dash at the end of the break. This is a generally recognized standard; however, Robert Bringhurst advises a more refined version of these rules: using spaced en dashes rather than em dashes (reserving em dashes to introduce speakers in a narrative dialogue) and using close-set en dashes to connect a range of numbers.

When a hyphen is not a hyphen

a—b   em dash

a--b   indication of em dash in html text not to be used in final typesetting

a–b   en dash

a-b   hyphen

Project
Feature spread

Art Director
Arem Duplessis

Art Director, Designer
Gail Bichler

Client
The New York Times Magazine

The em dashes set off a separate thought; they look best with a generous space on either side.

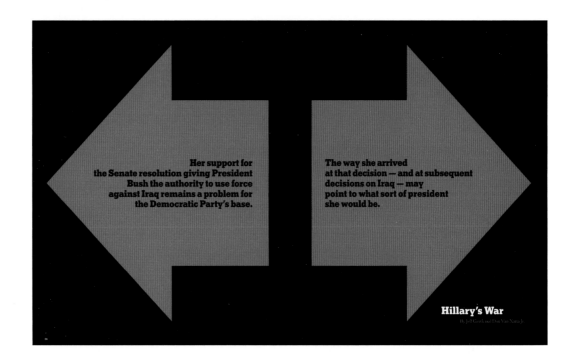

Her support for the Senate resolution giving President Bush the authority to use force against Iraq remains a problem for the Democratic Party's base.

The way she arrived at that decision — and at subsequent decisions on Iraq — may point to what sort of president she would be.

Hillary's War

By Jeff Gerth and Don Van Natta Jr.

Project
Stats spread

Redesign Art Director
Francesca Messina

Co-Designer
Amy Rosenfeld

Client
Businessworld

Number ranges show the proper use of en dashes, and word breaks show the proper use of hyphens. Em dashes are used to indicate a lack of data in the chart.

STATS — the numbers you need to know now

Given the population of **India and China**, even if **5-10%** of people can can afford pharma products, the market will grow at an annual rate of **7-12%** to

$10 billion

0.80%
JAPAN's INFLATION RATE
After years, prices have begun rising again in Japan. If inflation continues to pick up, the Japanese Central Bank may have to raise interest rates

7.60%
US CURRENT ACC. DEFICIT
The US current account deficit is rising again hitting new highs despite hopes that it might perhaps fall in the last quarter of this year

SINCE THE 1960s India has become self sufficient in foodgrains like wheat and rice. However for the first time since 1997-98 we have had to import large quantities of wheat. Is this an indicator of the future? The graph below shows that India's consumption of wheat is likely to rise sharply into the future. However, our production is likely to remain fairly constant since yields and the area covered by wheat is not expected to rise too much into the future. This means that some future imports of wheat from the international markets are likely to be even higher than they are currently.

THE LATEST CREDIT POLICY released by the Reserve Bank of India (RBI) on 25 June talks about inflation being fuelled by rising food and oil prices. But as the continued rise in petroleum prices takes on a 'permanent' nature (something the RBI has already acknowledged), could it, in turn, propel food prices even higher?

Here's how such an effect might work. As petroleum prices continue to rise across the globe, the search for alternative fuels, including biofuels, can only increase. And as the demand for biofuels increases, an increasing proportion of crops that would otherwise have found their way into the kitchen would be diverted towards biofuel production. If that proportion is large enough, the effect

on the prices of foodstuffs made from basic commodities such as corn, oilseeds and sugar could be very noticeable indeed.

Take a few examples. The Indian sugar crop this year is expected to be quite good. But if the Centre gets its biofuel policy in place, a big chunk of the sugar crop could be diverted towards production of ethanol. That could affect the amount of crop available for human consumption and other uses. (For the US, one could replace sugar with corn.) The same could hold true for vegetable oils, of which India is a big importer.

Of course, any such spike in global sugar or oilseeds prices might be temporary as farmers, attracted by the higher prices, start devoting increasing acreage towards such crops. Almost every economic

CAPITAL IDEAS
by Niranjan Rajadhyaks

mist bewails the large US current account deficit and wants it to contract. Whole forests have been felled to provide newsprint to write why and how the "global imbalances" need to be rectified, and the chief imbalance is the US current account deficit.

Not so, says Gavekal Research, famed for their out-of-the-box articles, in a recent report

titled The Leverage in the System and the Weak US Dollar, they point out that the US has had a current account deficit for most of its history, except for a few years after World War II. This has not stopped the US from having good growth and a relatively stable currency. Also, in the past 15 years, they "find that the best performing OECD economies (UK, US, Australia, Spain) have run large deficits while the model students with the current account surpluses (Germany, Switzerland, Japan) have been economic laggards."

Instead, Gavekal says that since oil is priced in dollars and since most countries are short of oil, they need to hold more dollars to pay for their oil now that the price has increased. In short, the transaction demand for dollars has increased. That is why the dollar has continued to be relatively strong. The US consumer has to some extent supplied these dollars outside of the US through the current account deficit.

The upshot: "In recent

years, we have seen large amounts of dollar borrowing taking place outside of the US. This means that an improvement in the US current account deficit could trigger a massive economic crisis; all the guys who are short

would find themselves unable to earn the dollars to service their debt. So policy-makers should be careful about what they wish for...!"

How 'adequate' are India's foreign exchange reserves? That might seem like a bizarre

THE BW WEEK 3.12.06 A BREAKDOWN IN NUMBERS							
PRODUCTION AND TRADE	UNIT	PERIOD	LATEST DATA		YEAR AGO	% CHANGE	% PREDICTED
1 GDP growth quarterly	%	April 2006	7.9		7.2	3%	3%
2 Industrial production growth monthly	%	April 2006	7.9		7.6	6%	4%
3 Export growth monthly	$ million	April 2006	8,347	YoY change 9.4%		8%	8%
4 Import growth monthly	$ million	May 2006	12,561	YoY change 16.7%		10%	8%
5 Trade deficit is monthly	Rs/crore	April 2006	-4,214.14		-3854.55	3%	6%
6 Trade deficit as % of GDP	—	April 2006	4.1		4.1	5%	6%
7 Current account deficit in $ bn*	—						
8 Current account deficit as % of GDP*	—	April 2006	-3.0		-3.0	-15%	6%
MONEY AND PRICES							
10 FX Reserves weekly	$ million	July 14 2006	1,62,659		1,37,561	12%	8%
11 M3 Growth weekly	Rs / crore	July 7, 2006	28,20649		23,73,397	4%	6%
13 WPI weekly		July 1,2006	203.3		193.7	6%	6%
14 CPI for non manual urban workers		May 2006	465		445	.03%	.06%
FINANCIAL MARKETS							
15 Market indices		July 21, 2006	BSE Sensex 10,085.91	BSE Sensex -7,304	NSE	-30%	-20%
			NSENifty 2945	Nifty 2,230.50		-8.4%	6%
16 Short term interest rates end of the week	%/ annum	July 7,2006	6.00		6.00	0%	6%
17 Long term interest rate-end of the week	%/ annum	July 1,2006	10.75 - 11.25		10.25-10.75	-.05%	6%
18 Gold end of the week		July14, 2006	582.15		437.55	-3%	8.4%
19 Rupee end of the week		July 14 2006	46.42		43.52	-.06%	.01%
20 Six month forward cover on the rupee	%	July 2006	0.97		1.50	4%	6%

SECOND PICK

Sliding Down
The demand for wheat lessens

Legend: FRANCE, GERMANY, ITALY, UK, US, BRAZIL, CHINA, INDIA, JAPAN

1964 1974 1984 1994 2004

Demand For Wheat
million tonnes

70 75 80 85 90 95

08/2008	78.28
09/2009	80.24
10/2009	82.02
11/2010	83.65
12/2011	85.35
13/2012	87.02
14/2013	88.68
15/2014	90.34

DATA: KISHORE DAS

18 High contrast in reverse

REVERSING OUT OR "DROPPING OUT" type may be used to great effect, but it must be done with care at small sizes and with regard for the printing process of the final piece. Very fine serifs or hairline flourishes may "disappear" if over-inked on press, and the smaller the point size, the more likely this is to occur. Use high contrast in reverse sparingly with text type, as it can be difficult to read. Monoline typefaces (those with no variation between thicks and thins) and those which have at least a moderate stroke weight, with little or medium contrast between thicks and thins, work best in reversed-out type.

Project
The Mythic City:
Photographs of New York
by Samuel H. Gottscho,
1925–1940 exhibition

Exhibition Graphic Design
Pure+Applied

Exhibition Design
Pure+Applied and
Jennifer Turner

Photographer
Agatha Wasilewska

Client
Museum of the
City of New York

On the dark wall, light or
white text stands out.

Project
Cover

Design Director
Scott Dadich

Photographer
Michael Crichton

Food Stylist
Nancy Midwicki

Client
Wired magazine

On a black background, all white type (and some pale green type), is eminently legible, even at small sizes. There are no fine serifs in this reversed-out typography and the weight and stroke width of the text holds its own.

Project
Sportdesign

Designer
Martin Woodtli

Client
Museum für Gestaltung Zürich

High contrast (and a large size) allows the foreground text to be readable despite overlapping a complex background.

19 Extreme scaling

IF YOU LOVE TYPE, YOU LOVE TO SEE IT writ large. Extreme scaling (especially when very large elements are used in contrast with normally scaled typographic elements) is a powerful tool in the designer's arsenal. Almost every typeface assumes a whole new identity when used in gargantuan ways; like the faces on Mount Rushmore, the scale alone is so impressive that we don't always stop to think about whether it is well-crafted artwork. Its size is enough to seize our attention.

Project
Thalia Theater media

Designers
Friederike Kuehne, Jana Steffen, Martin Jahnecke, and Bastian Renner (students), Burg Giebichen-stein University of Art and Design Halle

Professor
Anna Berkenbusch

Assistant Professor
Manja Hellpap

Client
Thalia Theater

The large number adds visual drama while also serving as an anchor for the black text.

DER SKANDAL BERUHT AUF DER VERABREDUNG ZUM SKANDAL.

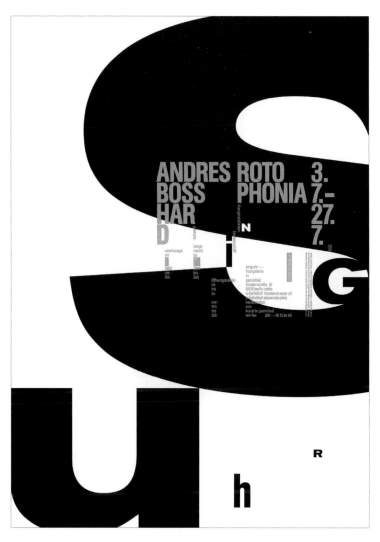

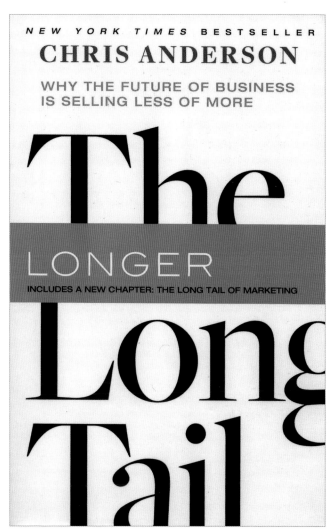

Project
"Singuhr" — Sound Art Gallery
at Parochial Church

Company
Cyan

Client
Kunst in Parochial E.V.

This poster for a jazz sound installation
used large type forms to convey the idea
of clear, distinct sound.

Project
Cover

Designer
Scott Dadich

Client
Hyperion Books

The book title does double duty as art;
additional drama is created by bleeding
the type off the edges (the parts of the
letterforms that are cut off are not
critical to legibility).

20 Heavy flourishes

WHEN USED IN MODERATION, such as a single letter or mark, elaborate flourishes create an effect of complexity, luxury, antiquity, or timelessness. Flourishes work best when paired with very simple typographic elements or design to counterbalance their ornate character. In expert hands, heavy flourishes, such as those shown here, can work well. If inexpertly overused, heavy flourishes can create spaghetti-like visual confusion.

Project
A Beautiful Addiction logo

Design Directors
Paul Sych and Sam O'Donahue

Client
Established

This logo's tight flourishes draw the viewer into a hypnotic spiral, visually reinforcing the word *Addiction*.

Project
Descendants cover

Art Director
Robbin Schiff

Designer
Roberto de Vicq

Client
Random House

This clever use of flourishes representing the "roots" of the letterforms amplifies the book's theme of the family tree.

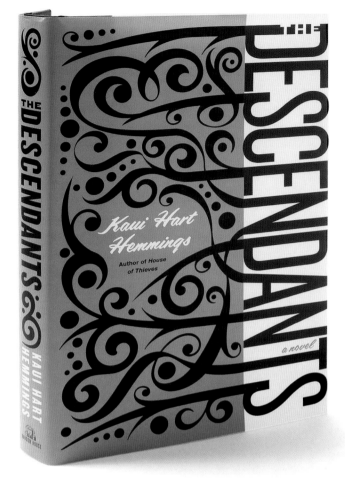

Project
Feature spread

Art Director
Arem Duplessis

Designer
Nancy Harris Rouemy

Photographer
Daniel Jackson

Client
The New York Times Magazine

The flourishes in the lettering reflect the shapes of the materials used in the dress opposite the headline.

21 Thinking like a typesetter

ALL TOO OFTEN, in today's production-streamlined world, designers are also required to be editors and typesetters. So they must be extra vigilant about rooting out double spaces, especially after periods (these introduce unsightly gaps in the text); the use of spaces instead of tabs; extra tabs; and the incorrect use of the hyphen, en dash, and em dash (the use of the double hyphen as a substitute for the em dash is an all-too-common occurrence). Pesky "invisible" or "hidden" characters like paragraph returns, soft returns, and the like can cause untold misery if not discovered before style sheets are applied.

Project
Mobile app

Company
Joe Zeff Design

Client
National Geographic

Under each drop-down menu, apps like this one often contain a great deal of text material that must be free of common errors like those described above. If text is improperly formatted, production time will be affected.

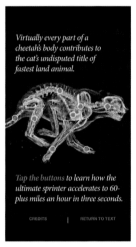

Project (below)
Infographic

Creative Director
Robert Priest

Designer
Jana Meier

Illustrator
John Grimwade

Client
Condé Nast Portfolio

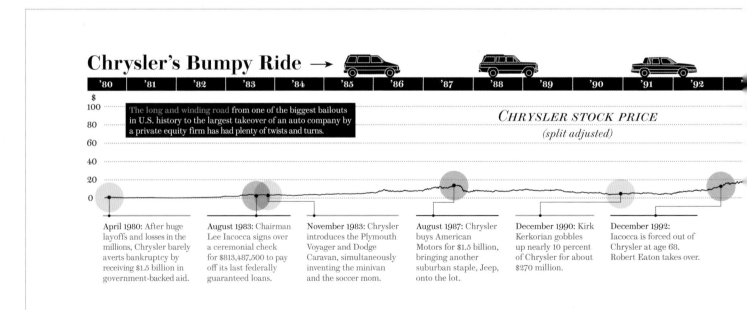

Chrysler's Bumpy Ride →

| '80 | '81 | '82 | '83 | '84 | '85 | '86 | '87 | '88 | '89 | '90 | '91 | '92 |

CHRYSLER STOCK PRICE
(split adjusted)

The long and winding road from one of the biggest bailouts in U.S. history to the largest takeover of an auto company by a private equity firm has had plenty of twists and turns.

April 1980: After huge layoffs and losses in the millions, Chrysler barely averts bankruptcy by receiving $1.5 billion in government-backed aid.

August 1983: Chairman Lee Iacocca signs over a ceremonial check for $813,487,500 to pay off its last federally guaranteed loans.

November 1983: Chrysler introduces the Plymouth Voyager and Dodge Caravan, simultaneously inventing the minivan and the soccer mom.

August 1987: Chrysler buys American Motors for $1.5 billion, bringing another suburban staple, Jeep, onto the lot.

December 1990: Kirk Kerkorian gobbles up nearly 10 percent of Chrysler for about $270 million.

December 1992: Iacocca is forced out of Chrysler at age 68. Robert Eaton takes over.

Project
Book design

Studio
Eight and a Half

Art Director
Bonnie Siegler

Designers
Andrew James Capelli and Kristen Ren

Client
Blue Man Group
Black Dog & Leventhal

These text blocks and sections can be streamlined if style sheets have been properly created and applied.

Below: This complex infographic containing stock prices, dates, and tightly tailored text blocks requires a great deal of typesetting skill to render the data clearly for the reader's comprehension. When importing the text, it is imperative that the file be free from unnecessary tabs and spaces. Note the use of old-style numbers with upper- and lowercase text.

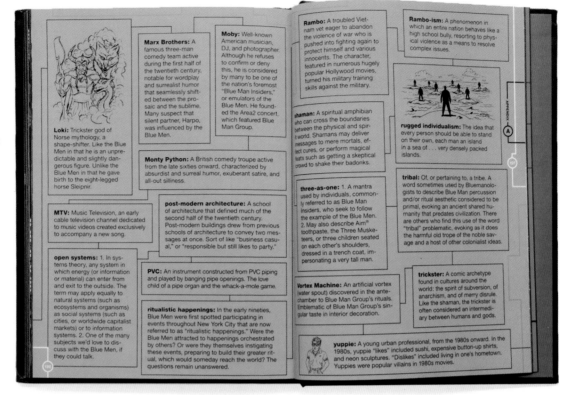

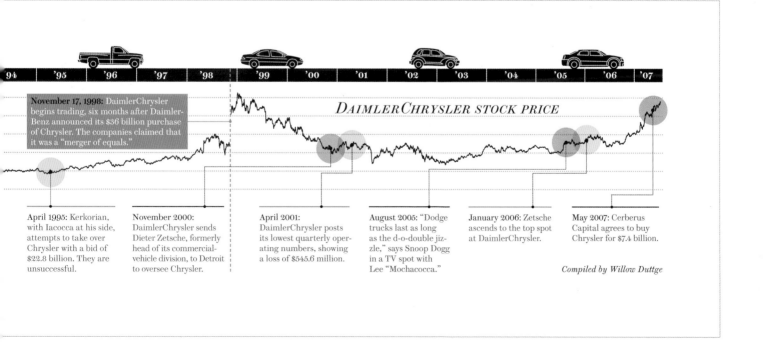

November 17, 1998: DaimlerChrysler begins trading, six months after Daimler-Benz announced its $36 billion purchase of Chrysler. The companies claimed that it was a "merger of equals."

DAIMLERCHRYSLER STOCK PRICE

April 1995: Kerkorian, with Iacocca at his side, attempts to take over Chrysler with a bid of $22.8 billion. They are unsuccessful.

November 2000: DaimlerChrysler sends Dieter Zetsche, formerly head of its commercial-vehicle division, to Detroit to oversee Chrysler.

April 2001: DaimlerChrysler posts its lowest quarterly operating numbers, showing a loss of $545.6 million.

August 2005: "Dodge trucks last as long as the d-o-double jizzle," says Snoop Dogg in a TV spot with Lee "Mochacocca."

January 2006: Zetsche ascends to the top spot at DaimlerChrysler.

May 2007: Cerberus Capital agrees to buy Chrysler for $7.4 billion.

Compiled by Willow Duttge

22 Using display versions

TITLING AND DISPLAY VERSIONS of text type have been designed to look good at display sizes (i.e., above 14 or 16 point); specifically, they have been refined in their details, especially in the design and weight of their serifs. Text typefaces, when enlarged to display sizes, will have thicker details; this is because the letterforms need to hold their own in body type sizes. Thus (depending on the typestyle), they may not translate especially well when enlarged beyond their intended size range. Use titling and display versions whenever possible.

Project
Cover

Company
Hopkins/Baumann

Creative Directors
Will Hopkins and
Mary K. Baumann

Images
Corbis, Historical Picture
Archive

Client
Kids Discover magazine

This condensed version of Bodoni would be inappropriate if used at text sizes; its tight counter spaces would make it difficult to read. This holds true for the sans serif type: it is too condensed for body copy, but fine for display.

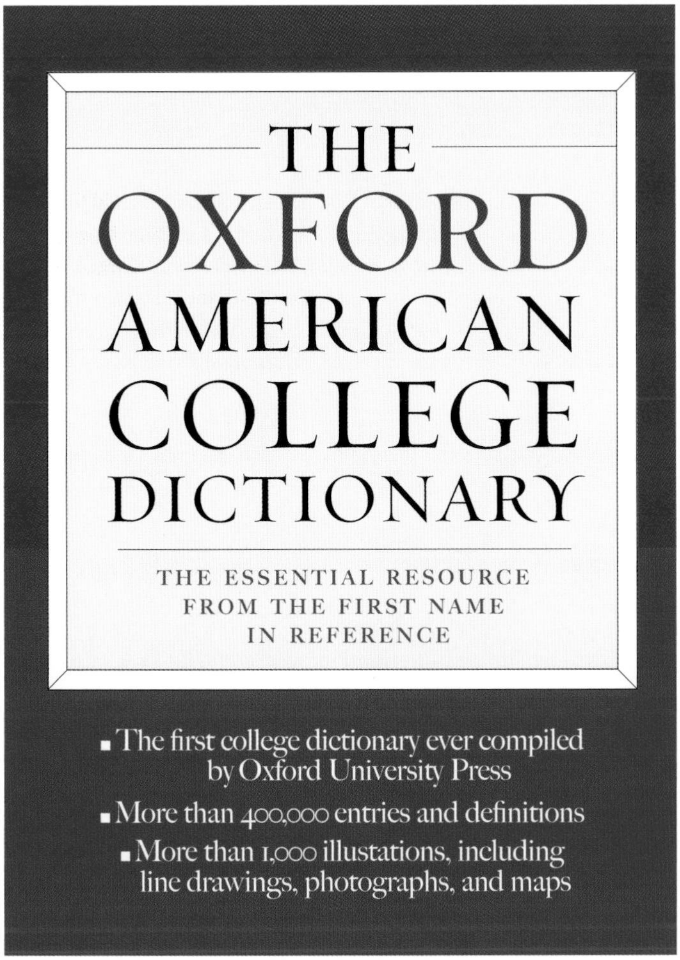

THE OXFORD AMERICAN COLLEGE DICTIONARY

THE ESSENTIAL RESOURCE FROM THE FIRST NAME IN REFERENCE

- The first college dictionary ever compiled by Oxford University Press
- More than 400,000 entries and definitions
- More than 1,000 illustations, including line drawings, photographs, and maps

---

The Essential Resource from the First Name in Reference

THE Oxford AMERICAN COLLEGE Dictionary

THE FIRST COLLEGE DICTIONARY EVER COMPILED
BY OXFORD UNIVERSITY PRESS

MORE THAN 400,000 ENTRIES AND DEFINITIONS

MORE THAN 1,000 ILLUSTRATIONS,
INCLUDING LINE DRAWINGS, PHOTOGRAPHS, AND MAPS

Project
Book cover

Creative Director
Donald Partyka

Client
Barnes & Noble

The delicate terminal strokes of this headline would disappear at text sizes. The typeface has been tailored for display usage.

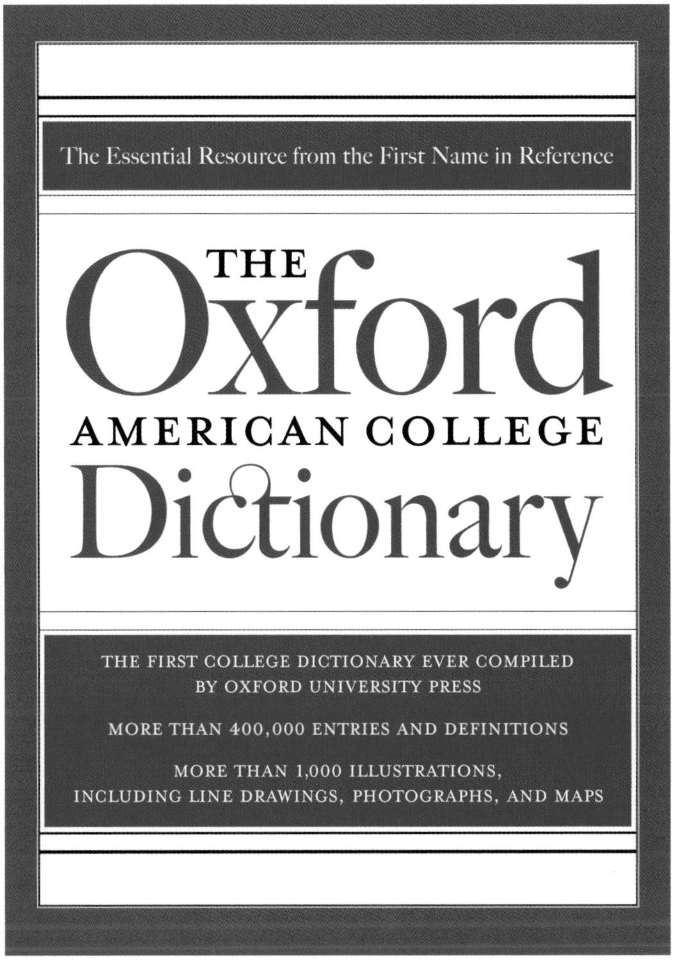

Project
Book cover

Creative Director
Donald Partyka

Client
Barnes & Noble

The finely wrought ligature between the *c* and the *t* of this headline would not be visible at text sizes. The typeface has been tailored for display usage.

MODERATO
Samuel Rogers
Die Fledermaus
RALLENTANDO
Ernest Schelling

CONTINUO
Das Rheingold
Antonio Salieri
FOUR SEASONS
String Quartets

Well Tempered Clavier
Russian Easter Overture
SERGEI RACHMANINOV
Complete Violin Sonatas

Project
Type specimen

Company
Hoefler & Frere-Jones

Designer
Jonathan Hoefler

Client
Hoefler & Frere-Jones

Hoefler Titling is the accompanying display type for Hoefler Text, an old-style typeface with a very broad range of weights.

23 Using numbers

NUMBERS NEED SPECIAL ATTENTION. Numbers (more correctly called numerals or figures) often require extra spacing; this need increases as the point size and the length of the string of numbers grows. As to how much extra spacing, let visual harmony and consistent typographic color with the surrounding letterforms be your guide. You should also understand the difference between lining figures (or titling figures) and old-style figures (or lowercase figures). The former align with the capital letters and are therefore best used when the surrounding text is all uppercase. The latter are of mixed sizes (some with the equivalents of ascenders and descenders), the better to coexist harmoniously with surrounding text type in lowercase or with small caps.

Project
Identity program

Company
Mucca Design

Creative Director
Matteo Bologna

Art Director, Designer
Christine Celic Strohl

Client
Butterfield Market

The numbers in these business cards have been kerned in mixed ways (tight and open) in order to form columns; also, different weights and sizes have been mixed to create visual interest.

MH
Special Section

Part 1
WHAT WE LEARN
FROM THE DYING
page 190

Part 2
50 WAYS TO BEAT
THE REAPER
page 198

Part 3
THE HIDDEN COST
OF HEROISM
page 204

A MATTER OF DEATH... AND LIFE

How to ensure you'll live to fight another day

and not end up like one of these guys

NUMBER OF MEN IN THE UNITED STATES WHO WILL DIE IN 2008 AS A RESULT OF...

CANCER (all types):
307,655

SKIN CANCER:	COLON CANCER:	PROSTATE CANCER:
7,258	21,289	26,987

BRAIN CANCER: SIX THOUSAND EIGHT HUNDRED AND TWELVE

| LUNG CANCER: 96,835 | PANCREATIC CANCER: 16,785 | HEART DISEASE: 316,968 |

| HYPOTHERMIA: 449 | HEAT-STROKE: 207 | FIREWORKS ACCIDENT: 5 | FIRE: 1,737 |

CAR ACCIDENT: 17,463

FALLING FROM A CLIFF: 57

SHARK ATTACK: ONE

LIGHTNING STRIKE: 40

FOREIGN OBJECT LEFT BEHIND DURING SURGERY: 2

ALCOHOL POISONING: 270

BEE, HORNET, OR WASP STING: 43

FALLING DOWN STEPS: 1,062

MOTORCYCLE ACCIDENT: 4,624

COLLISION WITH OR BLOW FROM SPORTS EQUIPMENT: SEVEN

ELECTROCUTION: 374

FALLING FROM A BUILDING: 504

| SUICIDE: 26,132 | LOU GEHRIG'S DISEASE: 3,420 | ALZHEIMER'S DISEASE: 23,898 | BEING HIT BY A CAR: 3,920 |

HOMICIDE: 12372

STROKE: 55,105

THE FLU: 469

EARTHQUAKE, AVALANCHE, OR LANDSLIDE: TWENTY-EIGHT

DIVING INTO SHALLOW WATER: 47

HIV/AIDS: 8,423

SPIDER BITE: FIVE

Numbers are projected estimates based on mortality figures from the Centers for Disease Control and Prevention WONDER database and the FARS Encyclopedia.

Chart illustration by JULIA HOFFMANN

Project
Feature spread

Design Director
George Karabotsos

Art Director, Designer
John Dixon

Illustrator
Julia Hoffman

Client
Men's Health

Numbers (of deaths) and supporting text cleverly form the shape of a skull; contrasts in scale and color have been used to enliven the page's design. Note the arrow as navigational aid and the mini table of contents at the top left. This fantastic construction of a skull created from multiple statistics employs numbers in a range of weights and sizes, along with dingbats and typographic "furniture," to achieve its sepulchral effect.

The Case for Loyola

1 Sense of Community
With 1,300 students, 35 student groups and a steady stream of activities, it's student life at its fullest.

2 Breadth and Depth
16 curriculum tracks, specialty programs and real-world experience. Because one size does not fit all.

3 Experienced and Accessible Faculty
Learn from some of the greatest minds in the profession.

4 Invested Alumni
From mentoring to externships, they help students succeed.

5 Learning Outside the Classroom
Real experience with real clients turns eager students into better lawyers.

6 Dynamic Location
In the heart of the largest government district outside of D.C. And there's the beach.

7 Commitment to Diversity
With a campus full of diverse perspectives, interests, attitudes and experience, we've been walking the talk for 90 years.

8 More than One Path
Accelerated tracks, dual degrees, evening and summer programs, and overseas study. It's all here.

9 Focus on Social Justice
Students donate over 40,000 public service hours a year.

10 Hit the Ground Running
Interview support, career services and networking. You'll be ready.

Ten Reasons to Choose
Loyola Law School · Los Angeles

Project
Admission brochure

Studio
Pentagram

Art Director
DJ Stout

Designer
Daniella Floeter

Client
Loyola Marymount University
Law School

Numbers in a variety of styles, weights, colors, and sizes are used here as graphic elements to compartmentalize and enliven a simple list. Changes of orientation add to the energy of the page.

24 Dingbats and pictograms

THE DERISIVE TERM *DINGBATS* refers to typographic glyphs or symbols that have no relationship to a typeface (unlike analphabetic symbols such as an asterisk or a dagger). Dingbats are often pictograms that represent pointing fingers, scissors, checkmarks, and symbols for objects such as a telephone, plane, church, etc. A font of dingbats functions as a typeface does—they flow with the text as it is moved or edited (which is why dingbats can be more useful than simple vector-based illustrations).

Project
Kay Hanley "Weaponize"

Company
Alphabet Arm Design

Art Director
Aaron Belyea

Designer
Ryan Frease

Client
Kay Hanley

Dingbats form the wings and tail of the militaristic logo.

Project
Poster

Art Director
Michael Walsh

Designer
Gail Anderson

Client
School of Visual Arts

An unusual pattern of dingbats creates a mosaic background surrounding the text.

Project
Canadian Gala

Company
Hammerpress

Client
Bungalow Creative

Dingbats are used decoratively as a framing device in a monochrome palette and with display typestyles suggesting the Old West.

25 Theory of Relativity I

LETTERS EXIST IN RELATION to other letters. Therefore, every design decision is dependent on the specific set of circumstances governing the letter's context. In other words, it reacts to, and should be considered in relation to, its design environment. This is what makes it so difficult to provide an immutable set of rules about type usage—every set of circumstances is different, if only slightly. Moreover, there are often many successful ways to get it right, but usually even more ways to get it wrong.

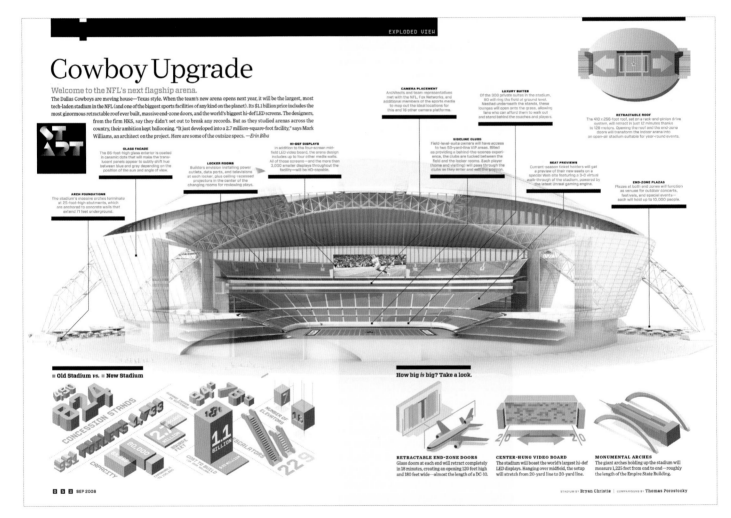

Project
Feature spread

Creative Director
Scott Dadich

Designer Director
Wyatt Mitchell

Designer
Christy Sheppard

Illustrators
Bryan Christie and Thomas Porostocky

Client
Wired

This complex spread contains a large amount of content; the text is carefully balanced with the other visual elements to fill the space comfortably, but not too tightly. Multiple levels of information hierarchy have been carefully tailored to keep the text distinct yet harmonious with the whole. Of particular interest are the centered captions sitting on a black bar, which point to elements in the center visual.

Project
Package design

Company
Mucca Design

Creative Director
Matteo Bologna

Art Director, Designer
Andrea Brown

Client
Sant Ambroeus

The centered text on these labels has many levels of information; the size, weight, and contrast of the levels of information have been carefully calibrated, and the spaces between the lines have been subtly manipulated to create separation while maintaining a cohesive vertical column of text.

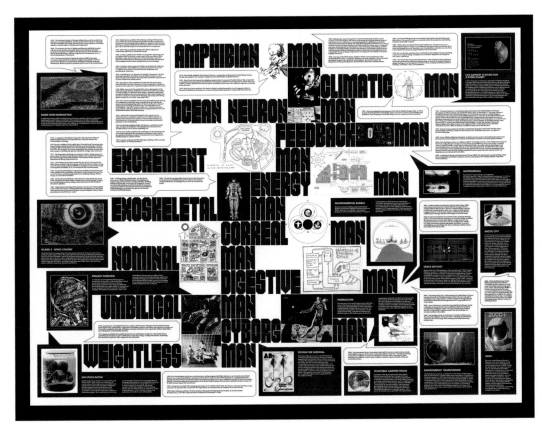

Project
Exhibition design, film and motion graphics

Studio
Pentagram

Art Director
Natasha Jen

Designers
Graphic Designer and Type Design: Jang Hyun Han, Exhibition Designer: Melodie Yashar

Client
Storefront for Art and Architecture

This content-packed poster (one component of an exhibition design project) engages the reader with accessible and organized "info-bites." The energetic presentation uses high contrast bold key words, a few images, and tons of text type contained in outlined "talk bubbles," some of which are reversed out (white type on a black background). Note the many line spaces within the talk bubbles that break up large swaths of text type. All of the elements are carefully calibrated not to overwhelm the viewer, and to make serious material look almost playful.

26 A "bad" typeface?

THERE IS EASY ACCESS to font creation tools, so anyone who has a mind to try his or her hand at type design can do so. That said, it is surprising that almost all of the 90,000 or so typefaces that are digitally available today (and the vast majority of these are display typefaces) are useful for some purpose, even if it is an obscure one. There are many typefaces that are deliberately amorphous or naive or do not follow the niceties of traditional type design. But if a typeface has qualities that make it fit for even one situation, can it be considered a "bad" typeface? Type is a matter of taste; in the ninth century, uncials were descried as ugly; in the eighteenth century, Bodoni was ridiculed.

Project
Weirdo Deluxe (cover, artist spread)

Company
Studio of ME/AT

Art Director
Brett MacFadden

Designer
Mike Essl

Illustrator
Brian Romero

Client
Chronicle Books

Playful novelty faces are often deliberately ugly (but beauty is in the eye of the beholder). Here, the word *weirdo* is emphasized by a "weird" letterform and mismatched letterforms in the ribbon of text, appropriate for a book on lowbrow art.

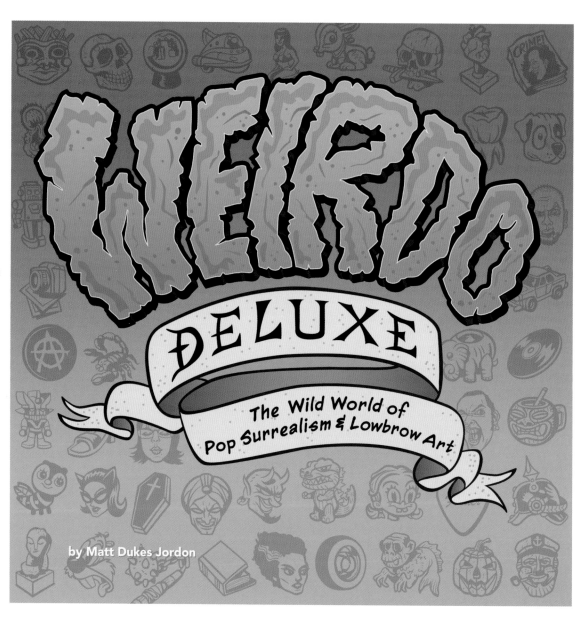

CAMILLE ROSE GARCIA

WHERE DOES SHE LIVE?
She lives in Glassell Park on the east side of Los Angeles with her husband.

WHAT DOES SHE COLLECT?
"My main collection is my ugly doll collection—the orphaned dolls that no one else will buy. I collect anything pirate-themed, especially from the golden age of piracy. Also obscure comic books that are independently published. Animal books from Germany. I love any kind of book."

MATERIALS: Acrylic and glitter on wood panels.

ON HER WORK:
"Usually most of my work is social-political commentary. It's based in current affairs. It's critical of the military-capitalist machine. It's done in storybook ways, through squirrels and storybook things. I like to think it's slightly subversive. I'm influenced by whatever horror is happening in the world currently. I try to talk about these issues in ways people can understand."

FIRST SHOWS
"I had my first shows right out of grad school in 1994 in San Francisco. I moved to L.A. and was in a punk-rock band and didn't paint for a while. Later I did a lot of street shows and made my own flyers. I'd have shows at friends' houses. Merry Karnowsky in L.A. is where I show now, and I've been there since 2000."

DID SHE WORK AS AN ILLUSTRATOR?
"I went to school for fine art and wasn't trained in illustration, but when I got out I did illustrations for all kinds of magazines and record covers. I did a lot of stickers and posters for a pirate radio station in L.A. called KBLT, which was based in Silverlake."

INFLUENCES:
"A lot of writers. Philip K. Dick is a big influence because of his sort of schizophrenic narrative. It's narrative but also comments on capitalist culture. Burroughs. Jello Biafra and Noam Chomsky. Definitely R. Crumb. The Clayton Brothers. Disney. The Clash. Henry Darger. Dame Darcy. Georganne.

77

CAMILLE ROSE GARCIA
Pharmaceuticools, Panel 1, 2003
12" × 12"

Serpentine letterforms with uneven weights and vaguely sinister flourishes are oddly squashed together. They form a medallion, the appearance of which mirrors the artwork on the facing page.

27 Typographic abominations

THERE ARE SOME TYPOGRAPHIC FORMS that can be considered abominations: chief among these are any forms that have been manipulated or distorted for no good creative reason. This often happens unintentionally; inexpert users may not know how to constrain proportion using the resizing tools within their software when working with type.

Or it may happen intentionally when users are not educated enough about type and try to squash or stretch type to fit into a particular space; this subverts the proportions crafted by the typeface's creator and always results in ugly, mismatched forms.

Project
Baggataway

Company
Alphabet Arm Design

Designer
Aaron Belyea

Client
Rocky Batty

The logo shape is a container, which the text is shaped to fit inside. This modest distortion is deliberate and specific to this situation.

Project
Beyond the Red Horizon

Designer
Jakub Stepien

Client
Center for Contemporary
Art in Warsaw

Similarly, although more simply, the type is used as art to suggest a sunset using depth, therefore the distortion serves a purpose and is executed skillfully. The small informational text supports the illusion, also receding into the distance.

Project
Poster

Company
Studio of ME/AT

Designer
Mike Essl

Client
Cranbrook Academy of Art

The key is the designer's intention: stretching type to fit into a shape serves the design in this poster.

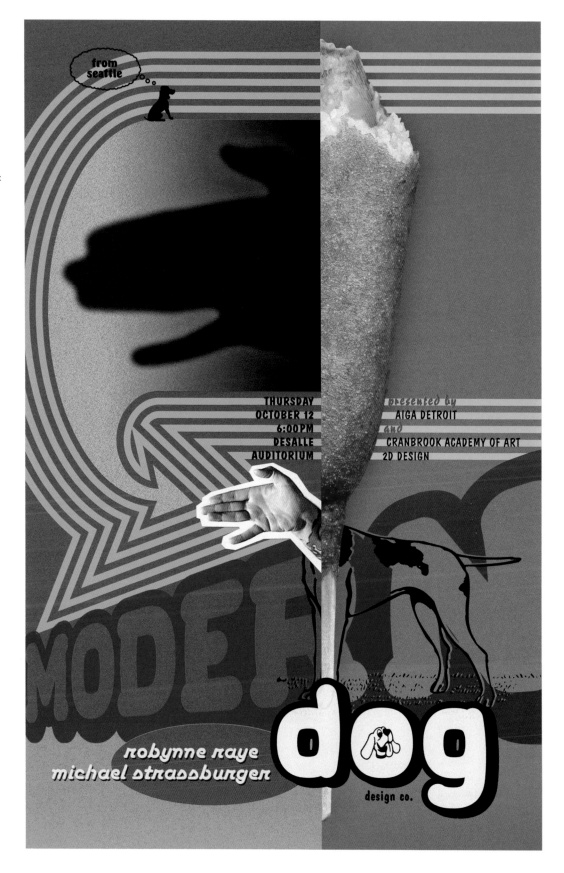

28 Hierarchy using position

LETTERS IN "PRIMARY" LOCATIONS receive visual priority. Upper areas are most prominent—the higher the better. With respect to horizontal positioning, statistics have demonstrated that focus groups have a slight preference for the right-hand side of the visible area over the left-hand side. So assuming all point sizes are equal, a higher-priority position indicates a higher level of importance.

Project
Inside page

Consulting Design Director
Luke Hayman

Designers
Rami Moghadam
and Mark Shaw

Client
Vibe

The headline is very low in the page but because of its size, its position in the hierarchy is evident. Its placement also serves as an anchor for the truncated photo, a reason for their tight proximity. Note the prominent typographic "furniture" of vertical lines, which also contain text. This device runs throughout the multipage section and acts as a branding device, as does the small, stacked section logo in the upper left-hand corner of the page. Also note three different levels of emphasis and separation in the headline using color shifts.

STYLE Goods

Toner shell jacket by **The North Face** ($249; *thenorthface.com*)

Basic denim like these from DKNY jeans ($60; *dknyjeans.com*) helps tone down the bright look

SIX MORE HIGHLIGHTS

Cashmere watch cap by **J.Crew** ($62; *jcrew.com*)

Wool ribbed scarf by **DKNY** ($125; *dkny.com*)

Lightweight hoodie by **H&M** ($20; *hm.com*)

Logo thermal by **Juicy Couture** ($98; 202-337-4131)

Nylon gloves by **UNIQLO** ($20; *uniqlo.com*)

Borealis SE backpack by **The North Face** ($99; *thenorthface.com*)

THE NORTH FACE HELPS YOU STAND OUT **IN THE COLD**

Summer's over, but that doesn't mean you have to retire the brights. This winter, anyone with even a penny of fashion sense will flock to new collections of outerwear designed to carry the fluorescent look of '08 well into the colder months. Take the toner shell jacket pictured above. It's engineered by The North Face, so you know it's warm. And it looks like an explosion of highlighters, so you know it's cool. Young Dro (and Ghostface Killah) would be proud.

JANELLE GRIMMOND

62 VIBE OCTOBER 2008

*Photographed by **Brian Pineda** in New York City, April 13, 2008*

Project
Covers

Art Director, Designer
Adam Fulrath

Client
Time Out New York

In this series (all on the newsstand simultaneously), the typographic elements are
in identical positions and sizes on each;
only the content and color differ. Though
the headlines are vertically centered (i.e.,
not positioned at the top), their large size
and boldness prioritize them over the
mastheads and all other text.

29 Hierarchy using size

BIGGER IS BETTER. That is, size is a very important indicator of hierarchy. A major shift in size can trump position, if the point size is big enough. But point size is only one factor; another is weight (see following principle). A cautionary note: when layering type over image, texture, or other type, be very aware of the need to preserve legibility.

Project
Feature spread

Creative Director, Designer
Dirk Barnett

Photographer
Ben Watts

Client
Blender

The same display type used in the headline is used much smaller in the subhead; the remainder of the text in the opening spread is neatly tucked into the remaining space.

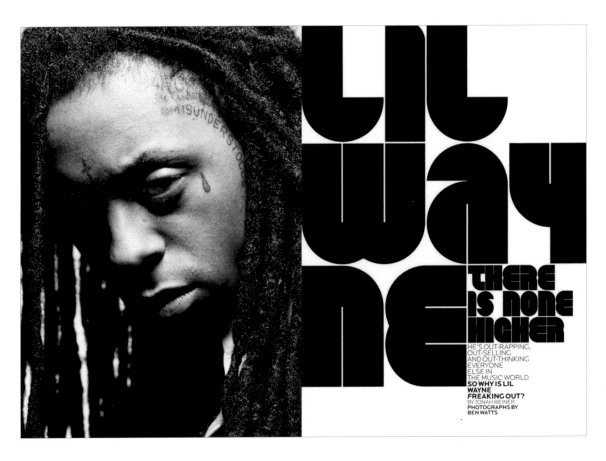

Project
Venture Crush
website and branding

Studio
Eight and a Half

Art Director
Bonnie Siegler

Designer
Kristen Ren

Client
Lowenstein Sandler

Strong shifts in weight and size give the viewer a clear sense of informational hierarchy. Note how the words *VENTURE* and *CRUSH* collapse down when scrolling to remain onscreen yet preserving display space beneath.

Project
Book cover

Studio
Eight and a Half

Art Director
Bonnie Siegler

Designers
Andrew James Capelli,
Kristen Ren, and Anthony Zukofsky

Client
Black Dog & Leventhal

Dramatic title display, followed by a much smaller subhead and author name, and a still smaller third line, use size effectively to indicate hierarchy. The shift in color from subhead to author name allows for a shift in content while the size, weight and style remain the same.

30 Hierarchy using weight

FATTER IS MORE VISIBLE. Letters that have wider stems and stroke widths have a stronger presence on the page. Weightier forms may supersede position and size as a determinant of hierarchy; however, typographic hierarchy is relative, therefore it depends on how weighty versus how big versus how prominently positioned (see "Theory of Relativity II" on page 106).

Project
Environmental graphics and digital design for MahaNakhon

Studio
Pentagram

Art Director
Eddie Opara

Designers
Brankica Harvey and Pedro Mendes

Developer
Kiattiyot Panichprecha

Architect
BuroOS

Client
Pace Development Co., Ltd.

The electronic signage changes second by second but always retains a sense of hierarchy using typographic weight.

Project
*What's Out There: Images from
Here to the Edge of the Universe*

Company
Hopkins/Baumann

Creative Directors
Will Hopkins and Mary K. Baumann

Images
Nasa/JPL/Space Science Institute

Client
Duncan Baird Publishers

The stacked title employs weight as well
as width to create a justified block of text;
the word *OUT* is emphasized by its weight,
though the letters are much smaller.

Project
Avoid One Thing

Company
Alphabet Arm Design

Designer
Aaron Belyea

Client
SideOneDummy Records

The logo and its legend both use a weight
shift (and a shift in width) to separate and
emphasize. Interestingly, the wider word
ONE appears more prominent than the
weightier words on either side, though
the point size is the same, perhaps partly
because it is centered.

31 Hierarchy using color

STRONG COLOR CREATES "POP." While black and white provide the highest level of contrast, a piece of text in a burst of color can become more prominent in the hierarchy of elements that are present (depending on other factors such as size, weight, typestyle, and position).

Paul Morrison.
Black Dahlias (detail). 2002.
One from a portfolio of
twelve screenprints
COMP.: 28⅓ x 38¼" (71.3 x 98.5 cm).
PUBLISHER: The Paragon
Press, London, PRINTER:
Coriander Studio Ltd., London.
EDITION: 45. The Museum of
Modern Art, New York. Gift of
Charles Booth-Clibborn and
The Paragon Press, 2000

///// **deborah wye & wendy weitman** ////////////
//////////////// **extending a heritage** ///
// **european prints, books, and multiples** ////////////////
///////////////////////// **and their institutional network** //////

In a period of instant communication

and growing interdependence throughout the world, there is undoubtedly a need for greater knowledge and understanding of cultural similarities and differences. It is remarkable that the contemporary art history of Europe, surely the continent with the closest ties to the United States, has not been more widely exhibited and understood outside the realm of specialists. There was a time, beginning in the late 1940s and reaching into the 1970s, when American art, and particularly that created in New York, was at the forefront of critical and popular artistic thinking, with scant attention paid to work produced elsewhere. American art was not only widely seen in European museums and galleries but also had an impact on European artists. This represented a shift following the end of World War II, as Europe rebuilt and America's economic and political structures dominated. The capital of the art world was said to have moved from Paris to New York, and artists such as Jackson Pollock and Andy Warhol became first American and then international art stars. But as recent decades have unfolded, more contemporary art from Europe has been shown in the United States, particularly since the 1980s, and it has become clear that its rich history and contributions deserve further attention.

As radical voices emerged from Paris to Turin, Brussels to Düsseldorf, artists from the 1960s to the present overturned accepted notions of artistic practice. Painting and sculpture took on new subjects and new structures; art began demanding new kinds of participation from the audience; and longtime traditions were reinvigorated. As artists expanded their creative visions, printed and editioned formats, with their inherent properties of transference, reproduction, sequencing, and multiplicity, were essential vehicles for enhancing and further articulating their practices. This study examines 118 artists, collectives, and journals from twenty countries with an inclusive approach to these mediums that reflects the inventive choices made by leading figures of the period. Artists from Richard Hamilton and Gerhard Richter through Daniel

15

Project
Eye on Europe

Company
Pure+Applied

Client
Museum of Modern Art

The modest typography adds just a bit of color for emphasis; this is very effective because of the restrained palette of the spread.

Project
Great British Food

Design Director
Joseph Luffman

Designer
Joseph Luffman

Client
British Food Fortnight /
The Type Museum

The entire joke rests
upon the selective use
of color in this poster
to "reveal" a hidden
message.

32 Hierarchy using contrast

HIGHER CONTRAST SEPARATES background from foreground. Separation can also be emphasized using outlines, hard drop shadows, soft drop shadows, and any combination of these effects. Especially when there is a complex background, whether an image or typographic texture, extra care must be taken to create sufficient contrast between the type and what is behind it.

Project
Show poster

Company
Alphabet Arm Design

Art Director
Aaron Belyea

Designer
Ryan Frease

Client
The Boston Conservatory

A "faux" sign provides a strong background contrast for the text; an interesting mix of styles uses outlines and drop shadows to stand out.

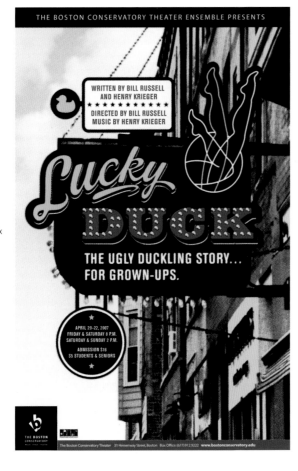

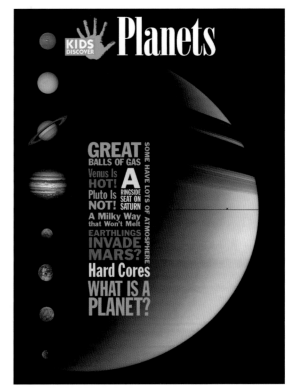

Project
Cover

Company
Hopkins/Baumann

Creative Director
Will Hopkins and
Mary K. Baumann

Designer
Wenjun Zhao

Images
Saturn: Nasa/JPL/
Space Science Institute
Planets: Medialab, ESA

Client
Kids Discover

Hierarchy is created here using size and weight, but moderated by color. For example, though some of the text in blue is larger, the smaller text, some of which is in shades of gold and yellow, stands out more because its relative contrast against the background is greater.

Project
Brand identity

Studio
Pentagram

Art Director
Harry Pearce

Designers
Johannes Grimmond
and Alex Brown

Project Manager
Tiffany Fenner

Client
The Old Vic

A single typeface with a single weight and width varies by three characteristics in this series of theater posters (part of a larger identity project): size, color, and outline. These factors determine the hierarchy of information. The type color contrast with the backgrounds are highest for the names of the productions, with "The Old Vic" always in white, against a strongly saturated background.

33 Hierarchy using orientation

DEVIATION FROM THE STANDARD BASELINE introduces the impression of motion and imparts dynamism to type. However, there should always be a design rationale for simply tilting a baseline; this technique alone is not a substitute for good design.

Project
Espresso mug set

Design Director
Sandro Franchini

Designer
Sam Becker

Client
Crate and Barrel

There is a feeling of playfulness in the swooping letters on this series of coffee mugs, each which change size as well as orientation, creating a sensation of depth and motion.

Project (opposite)
Book series

Art Director
Lauren Panepinto

Designer
Lauren Panepinto

Client
Orbit Books

The powerful use of bold sans seif stands out, despite the vertical orientation of the titles. Running the titles and authors vertically allows space for a more powerful use of the artwork on this series of book covers.

Project
Feature spread

Design Director
Amy Rosenfeld

Art Director
Douglas Adams

Illustrator
John Hendrix

Client
This Old House

Bumps and lumps in the remodeling process are the subject of this story, and the typography reflects the chaotic voyage in its off-kilter title treatment.

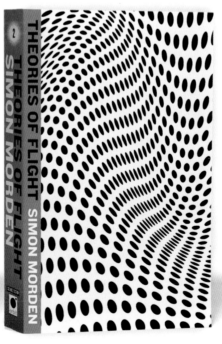

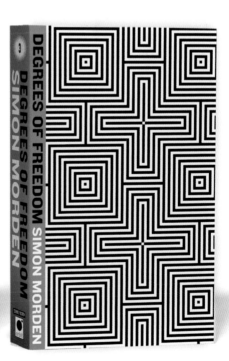

34 Hierarchy using special effects

WITH THE ADVENT of easy-to-use effects palettes in commonly available design software, it was inevitable that the result would be the overuse of special effects in typographic design. However, when properly deployed, these special effects (such as beveling, debossing, glows, feathering, etc.) may be very useful and striking, elevating a simple typographic design into memorable imagery.

Project
Transformers

Designer
Jakub Stepien

Client
Center for Contemporary
Art in Warsaw

The concept of "transform-ing" for an art exhibition, reflecting political, cultural, and economic transformation in Russia and Poland, finds its visual solution in the realm of special effects; the typo-graphy is bursting forward from the perspective of a deep central point.

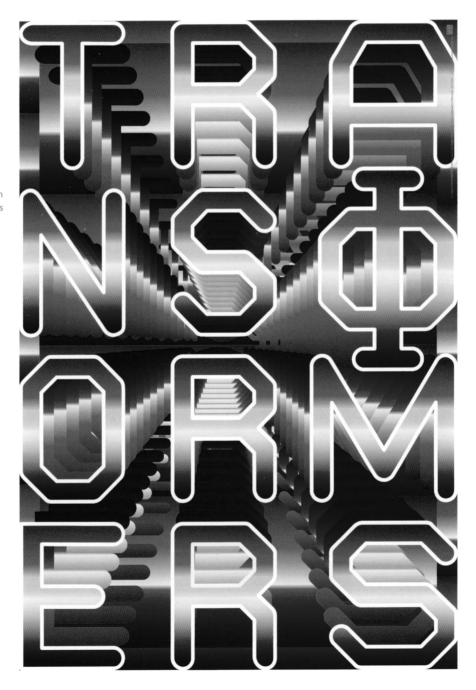

Project
Cover

Creative Director
Donald Partyka

Client
Americas Quarterly

A layered 3D rendering visually represents high technology. It is clearly the most prominent headline on the cover; the subhead is dimensionalized but much smaller and positioned lower. The letters *TECH* are deeply dimensionalized and highlighted, each is unique, which suggests that a variety of technologies will be addressed inside.

Project
All About the Money

Company
Thirst

Designer
Rick Valicenti

Client
ESPN/Thirst

Bling carried to an extreme and dizzying digitally enhanced degree is the force behind this "diamond-encrusted" headline.

35 To kern or not to kern

THE SHAPES OF LETTERS come from a variety of sources (Greek, Roman, Phoenician, Hebrew) and therefore are not inherently designed to fit together. In our digital world, type designers embed kerning pairs in their typefaces, which usually work well at the text type level (subject to adjustments to the hyphenation and justification settings, which can be customized by the designer). When type is used at a size larger than text size (above 14 point), small disparities and deviations in the spaces between the letters become more evident, and it is the designer's duty to rectify these by adjusting the kerning manually. Certain combinations of letters require more adjustment than others. In every case, the object is to create optically consistent kerning.

Project
Cover

Creative Director
John Klenert

Art Director
Christine Bower

Designer
Greg Gradbowy

Illustrator
National Forest

Client
Billboard

Going against the conventional expectation of optical consistency (where extra space would have been added between narrow vertical letters), the *Billboard* logo has been tightened instead, even touching the rounded shapes and tucking the *d* under the *r*. This tight kerning makes for a unique mark and has the added advantage of allowing the long word to be as large as possible, bounded only by the cover's border.

Project
Nectar Wine Bar

Company
Alphabet Arm Design

Designers
Aaron Belyea and Ira F. Cummings

Client
Jai Jai Greenfield and Eric Woods

Very open kerning of this logo suggests the spaciousness of open flowers, supporting the hummingbird illustration.

Project
Cover

Creative Director
Donald Partyka

Client
Americas Quarterly

The letters of the headline have been customized to allow super-tight kerning for a powerful and punchy effect.

36 Type as image

ONE OF THE JOYS of working with letterforms is their uncanny ability to be shaped into images. For designers who enjoy "playing," typographic forms in all of their infinite variations are like a gigantic set of Legos, building blocks that allow us to create images that speak to viewers both as visuals and as text.

Project
Men of Letters & People of Substance

Creative Director, Designer
Roberto de Vicq de Cumptich

Client
David R. Godine, Publisher

Likenesses built from characters using a single font are a charming use of type as image.

Project
Stacked cover

Art Director
Amy King

Designer
Roberto de Vicq

Client
Bloomsbury

For this book cover title, text and image become one as the customized letterforms are tucked together to form the shape of a brassiere.

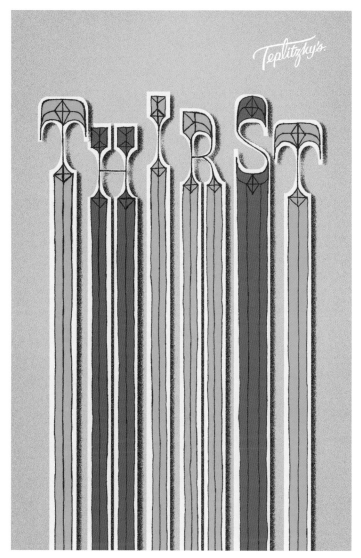

Project
Restaurant identity

Company
Mucca Design

Creative Director
Matteo Bologna

Designer, Illustrator
Steve Jockisch

Client
Teplitzky's

Customized letterforms have been stretched and lit (parts of a series of restaurant menus) to make them function as illustrations as well as literal text.

37 Three-dimensional type

WHETHER BUILT IN A DIGITAL 3D environment such as Maya, or whether hand-drawn, physically constructed, or implied by drop shadows, three-dimensional type lends extra weight and impact to a typographic design. Depth and bulk help type stand out in three-dimensional spaces such as those in environmental and exhibition graphics, but they can also enhance print and digital projects.

Project
Liquid Stone: New Architecture in Concrete

Exhibition Graphic Design
Pure+Applied

Exhibition Design
Tod Williams Billie Tsien Architects

Photographer
Frank Oudeman

Client
National Building Museum

Exhibition signage for concrete in new architecture has depth and shadow; the segmented letterforms represent the forms built to shape poured concrete.

Project
The College Issue opener

Art Director
Arem Duplessis

Deputy Art Director
Gail Bichler

Designer
Hilary Greenbaum

Illustrator
Emily Dwyer

Client
The New York Times Magazine

Stacked textbooks form the title; a few extras are scattered about for scale; they also suggest the clutter of a typical dorm room.

Project
Single page: The Sixth Annual Year in Ideas

Art Director
Arem Duplessis

Art Director, Designer
Gail Bichler

Client
The New York Times Magazine

Three-dimensional type from *A* to *Z* serve as illustrations for this annual round-up of the year's most innovative ideas, those that have "shaped" our world.

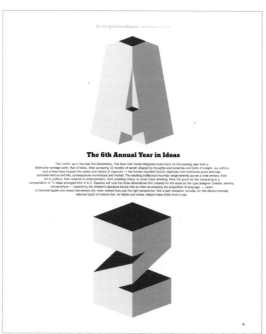

38 Repetition

A POWERFUL WEAPON in every designer's arsenal, repetition works equally well using typographic form. Repetition creates emphasis and mass; it can be used for pattern or texture as well as for impact.

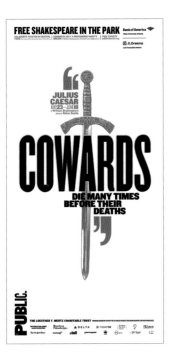

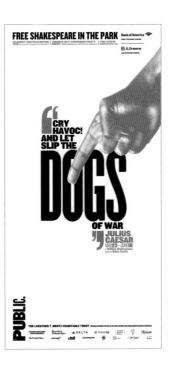

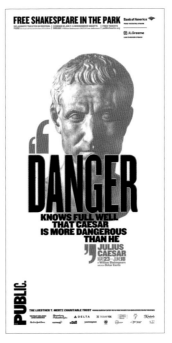

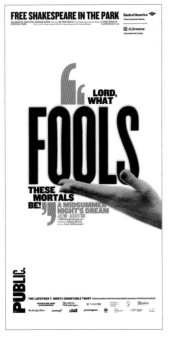

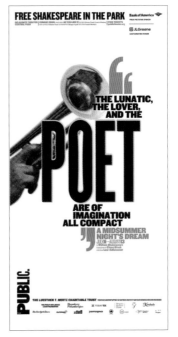

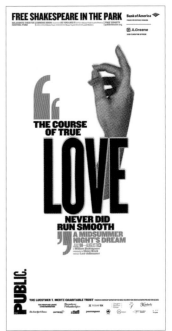

Project
Environmental graphics and campaign for Shakespeare in the Park

Studio
Pentagram

Art Director
Paula Scher

Designers
Tammy Shell, The Public Theater
Kameron Neal
Margalit Cantor (this page)
Dora Godfrey (opposite page)
Collaborator: Kirstin Huber

Client
The Public Theater

The most recent project in a decades-long partnership between Paula Scher and The Public Theater, these graphics make the most of heavy repetition of critical design elements: typography, color, imagery, and supporting graphic elements. They are instantly identifiable both as an annual iteration of the Shakespeare Festival's identity and as a long-running series.

39 Deconstructed type

PIECES OF TYPOGRAPHIC FORMS have a beauty all their own. They can be used as ornament, as navigational devices, as pattern. Something old may attain an entirely new look when its parts are disassembled, reassembled, or partially assembled.

Project
Identity

Design Director
Domenic Lippa

Client
London Design Festival

A design festival was branded with a deconstructed pattern of letterforms in vermillion and reversed bold lowercase type.

Project
Identity

Company
Pentagram

Designer
Michael Bierut

Client
Saks Fifth Avenue

Splitting apart the long-standing script
logo of the legendary department store,
varying iterations of black-and-white
patterns were applied to every possible
surface, including store awnings and
window displays.

40 Vertical stacking

OFTEN DONE FOR THE SAKE OF CONVENIENCE or because of ignorance, vertical stacking is generally inadvisable. Because different letters have significantly different widths, centered vertical stacking creates ugly shapes with neither vertical nor horizontal alignment. A much better solution is simply to turn the type on its side so that its baseline remains intact (this helps the reader, too). However, as with all rules, this rule, too, can be successfully broken.

give your grill the works

Turn your burger-flipping station into an outdoor kitchen where you can prep, cook, and clean up all in one place. Here's how

NOTHING DRAWS A CROWD LIKE THE KITCHEN, but who wants to hang out—never mind cook—indoors on a gorgeous summer day? Not us. The solution: Move the kitchen outside. But simply plunking a grill on the patio really doesn't do the trick. What you want is a workstation that's practical enough to turn out a meal and attractive enough to bring cook and guests together to share a drink and shoot the breeze—just like your indoor kitchen, but with a better view.

Industrial designer Ed Potokar, a grill master who much prefers outdoor cooking to the indoor variety, designed the outdoor kitchen shown at left for the Accord, New York, house he shares with his wife, *This Old House* design director Amy Rosenfeld. But when grilling season arrived this year, Potokar was still charring chops and brats on the gas grill he had propped on a makeshift restaurant-cart stand—and longing for more room to prepare food and place platters. "If the meat's done and you want to take it off the fire," he says, "where do you put it down while you wait for the peppers to finish cooking?"

BY AMANDA LECKY
PHOTOGRAPHS BY WENDELL T. WEBBER
STYLING BY DONALD LA PERA

BEFORE | AFTER

UPGRADES WITH IMPACT

Project
Feature spread

Design Director
Amy Rosenfeld

Art Director
Hylah Hill

Photographer
Wendell T. Webber

Client
This Old House

This clever headline treatment vertically "skewers" letters colored to look like vegetables ready for the backyard barbecue.

Project
Book design and exhibition design for
"Revolution of the Eye"

Studio
Pentagram

Art Director
Abbott Miller

Designers
Jesse Kidwell, Yoon-Young Chai,
and Jaeyoon Kim

Client
The Jewish Museum

Taking artistic license to create a tall
shape works here because, even though
the word *Revolution* has been broken
up, it is the only possible interpretation
of the word fragments.

41 See the shape

WITH CENTERED ALIGNMENT, or with any ragged edge, "bad rags" can be a problem. Always look for a balanced rag, one that does not inadvertently create a shape. When deliberately creating a shape from type, a skilled designer will fill the shape with type in such a way that its texture is consistent, without gaps or heavy spots. (See "Theory of Relativity II" on page 106.)

age: You're 22. (Will you ever get a job you really like?) You're 32. (If only you'd known then what you know now.) You're 50. (Wait a minute... that can't be right.) This month we take a look at the Ages of Woman— the good, the bad, and the...no, honey, you can't wear Lycra anymore. Forty may be the new 30, but getting older still has an image problem. Why, we asked ourselves, should everyone be selling youth? Why not commission a few ads for maturity? Which we did. So read. Reap wisdom. Live joyously. You're only (fill in the blank) once.

Project
Feature spread

The sands of the hourglass, shaped by using letters as sand, illustrate a story on aging.

Design Director
Carla Frank

Designer
Kristin Fitzpatrick

Client
O, The Oprah Magazine

Project
Poster

Design Director, Designer
Joseph Luffman

Client
Carluccio's

A map of Italy for a food purveyor is built
from the names of Italian dishes. Because
the letters are all caps, they can be tightly
stacked; a compressed letterform creates
visual bulk; different sizes and orientation
are used to vary the texture and create
separation without extra spaces, so the
shape can be tightly constructed.

Project
Poster

Art Director
Gabriel Benderski

Designer
Gabriel Benderski

Client
Gabriela Pallares

The 3-D effect of this poster
typographically reflects the subject
of the documentary, the British
architect Norman Foster.

42 Using cases

MAJUSCULES ARE MAJESTIC. Minuscules are modest. Uppercase and lowercase letters (so called because they were kept in separate drawers of the typographer's "case," or cabinet) have distinct purposes. Capital letters, as they are also known, speak loudly, while small letters are quieter.

Again, everything is relative; very lightweight uppercase letters in a simple sans serif might speak more quietly than a chunky slab serif lowercase. Everything depends on proportion and the mix.

Project
Identity and packaging for a boutique condiment company

Company
Mucca Design

Creative Director
Matteo Bologna

Art Director, Designer
Andrea Brown

Client
The Gracious Gourmet

These completely lowercase labels in playful colors are warmly appealing. The lowercase is informal and approachable.

Project
Tablet edition

Creative Direction
Joe Zeff Design

Client
Kids Discover

Cases are flipped here, as the enormous bold sans serif headline clearly dominates all other text in caps in the left panel.

Project
Cover

Creative Director,
Designer
Vanessa Holden

Photographer
Ellen Silverman

Client
Real Simple

Though the magazine's logo is in caps, the cover employs simple, modestly sized lowercase cover lines; unlike many magazines, it does not wish to "shout" visually. The core of its mission is to calm and reassure the reader.

43 The rule of three typefaces

CONVENTIONAL WISDOM HOLDS that most projects require only three typefaces, or, more precisely, three type families. All situations may be handled quite thoroughly with good compatible choices of the following: a good legible serif, a simple sans serif, and a display typeface (usually a serif typeface that has the refinements not usually found in a serif text type). The available variations in weight, slope, and width should be more than adequate to handle the needs of the content. The primary benefit in this approach is the likelihood that, by limiting the typefaces, compatibility and harmony will be maximized.

Project
Single page

Redesign Art Director
Francesca Messina

Co-Designer
Amy Rosenfeld

Client
Businessworld

This complex page of type creates a compatible whole by using a serif appropriate for body copy, a condensed sans serif for contrasting body copy, and a slab serif for display. Each of these serves its own purpose, yet is harmonious with the whole.

THINK BIG

ideas lab

New York's garment districe is the thread that ties this small business together.

1 Set Up Your Offices Abroad

With quotas going away, how can small garment manufacturers tap global markets? The best way, according to Bharat Vedant,

managing director, Ashapura Garments, a Rs 106-crore denim company, is to set up your own offices abroad. He opened an office in New York's Garment District at a monthly cost of Rs 3.5 lakh. This includes the office space, two local employees (with salaries of $2,000 and $1,500) and two employees from India. He set up a similar base in Cologne, Germany, at a cost of Rs 2.5 lakh a month. "This is better than using agents. They charge a huge mark-up and push up retail prices. But by selling directly, we enjoy better margins and offer lower retail prices," says Vedant. Ashapura has already bagged a few small orders through its New York and Cologne offices. And a large 500,000 is.

M. Anand

2 Hire A Pool of 250 Women Managers

FINDING good talent to recruit, especially at middle and senior levels, can be difficult for small and medium enterprises. Hiring experienced and skilled staff for these positions can sometimes be uneconomical for such businesses. Hiring a part-time manager could be the way to balance costs without compromising on the required skills.

Chennai-based recruitment firm Avtar's I-WIN (Interim Women managers' Interface Network) division provides precisely this option. It has more than 250 women managers available for recruitment on its network, across various sectors. And at least 40 per cent of them are senior managers with over five years of post-qualification experience. These are women who have chosen not to continue at a full-time job, but are willing to work part-time or flexible hours.

Depending on your requirements, you can hire a part-time professional in two ways. One, you can hire a person to work for lesser hours in a day, say from 9 a.m. to 2 p.m. Or you could hire the person for an interim period, where a particular task needs to be taken care of. For instance, an IT firm could take on an interim project manager for a particular project for, say, six months. The manager would then be paid on the basis of the projects she implements. Thus, a company can set the terms based on productivity, instead of simply the number of hours put in.

M. Anand

Rajesh hires women who want to work part time or flexible hours.

3 Recruit students to work offsite

A key charge a huge mark-up and push up retail prices and something about students. But by selling direct-ly, we enjoy better margins and offer prices," says Vedant. Ashapura has already bagged a few small orders as a through its New York and Cologne offices. A 500,000 pieces order is in the final stages of some this dealing.

A student or an employee?

M. Anand

 # IN EARLY

SEPTEMBER 2006, a vice president of Wal-Mart sent a highly personal email to his boss through what he thought was a safe email account. "My Gmail is secure," Sean Womack assured Julie Ann Roehm, the company's senior vice president for marketing communications. "Write to me. Tell me something, anything…. I feel the need to be inside your head if I cannot be near you."

Roehm had persuaded the company to hire Womack only three months before. "I hate not being able to call you or write you," she replied. "I think about us together all of the time. Little moments like watching your face when you kiss me. I loved your voicemail last night and love the idea of memory and kept thinking/wishing that it would have been you and I there last night." Then she signed off, saying she had to take her two children to the park.

Unfortunately for Roehm and Womack, who were both married to other people, their intimate email exchanges would become public in a legal dispute between Roehm and their employer. Wal-Mart learned about the relationship while investigating Roehm for accepting gifts from an ad agency that received a huge contract with the retailer. Ultimately, Wal-Mart fired both execs for violating company policy and later accused them of carrying out a love affair on company time.

Largely overlooked in the furor was the role that Wal-Mart's internal security department had played in digging up the salacious details. This department, a global operation, was headed by a former senior security officer for the Central Intelligence Agency and staffed by former agents from the C.I.A., the Federal Bureau of Investigation, and other government agencies. A person familiar with the episode said in an interview that an ex-C.I.A. computer specialist was involved in piecing together the email evidence—which included copies of Womack's private Gmail messages, provided by his estranged wife—and that another former government agent had supervised the overall investigation.

COMPANY MAN
After 16 years in the C.I.A., Mike Baker redirected his skills toward corporate espionage, co-founding the investigation firm Diligence. *Photographed in New York on November 16.*

Project
Feature spread

Creative Director
Robert Priest

Designer
Jana Meier

Photographer
Matt Hoyle

Client
Condé Nast Portfolio

A finely detailed serif designed for display is used with a serif typeface for body copy, accented with a limited use of sans serif. All of the needs of this content are adequately served by these three choices.

44 Mixing many typefaces

TYPOGRAPHIC CACAPHONY CAN BE APPEALING when in the hands of a skilled designer (otherwise, it can be a nightmare of conflicting forms). Mixing many typefaces works best when there are extreme differences in the type choices; this implies intent and control underlying the mishmash. When mixing typefaces within a document, bear in mind that, as always, each choice should serve a specific need and must exist in a harmony and balance with other typefaces. It is never a good idea to use different typefaces for no good reason.

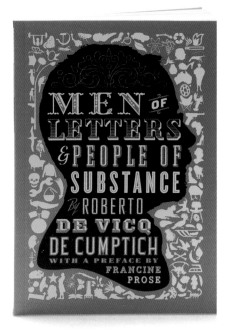

Project
Men of Letters & People of Substance

Creative Director, Designer
Roberto de Vicq

Client
David R. Godine, Publisher

The title, encapsulated within the silhouette of a head in profile, alludes to the content: this book contains portraits of literary figures made entirely from type characters, one font per portrait. A mosaic of dingbats surrounds the silhouette; these, too, are used for portraiture in the book.

Project
Acoustic Showcase poster

Designer
Lauren Panepinto

Client
Electric Plant

An irregular collection of pencils serves as text placeholders for an invitation; because each pencil is different in function and style, the typeface used on each pencil is different. The multiplicity of typefaces works because each is confined in its own space and shape.

Project
Special section opener

Company
The New York Times

Art Director
Wayne Kamidoi

Illustrator
Lorenzo Petrantoni

A highly organized cacaphony of typography, tiny shapes and images form a tightly crafted whole. This image is deliberately intense. It's typographic nuances invite and reward deep inspection.

45 Mixing type using contrast, weight, or color

BUTTING LIGHTWEIGHT LETTERS up against heavyweight ones, or changing color, while using one size within a single type family allows words to be combined that might otherwise need a letter space. Within a single word, two (or more) ideas can coexist yet also be separate, with distinctly different emphasis. This is a display-only design solution that has been used successfully in many arenas.

If the needs of the content can be served with the use of different members of a broad-based type family, it is almost always better to do so. If the content requires something more for its full expression, then and only then is it desirable to introduce additional faces; as they like to say in government, it is on an "as-needed basis."

Project
Cover

Art Director
Arem Duplessis

Designers
Arem Duplessis and Leo Jung

Photographer
Horacio Salinas

Client
The New York Times Magazine

Although a single weight of display type is used for the cover lines, emphasis and levels of hierarchy are achieved through variations in color and size. Despite the light weight of the type, the high contrast with the background ensures legibility.

Project
Advertising campaign

Creative Director
Johanna Savad

Art Directors
Michi Turner and Shamona Stokes

Client
The Netherlands Board of Tourism and
Conventions

The two title words can coexist without
a word space because they are dif-
ferentiated by weight. These ads have
a great deal of visual energy; a single
type family is employed.

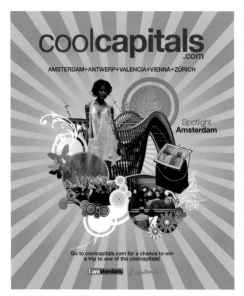
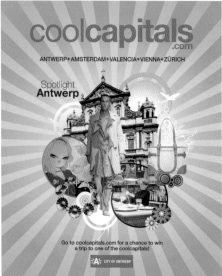
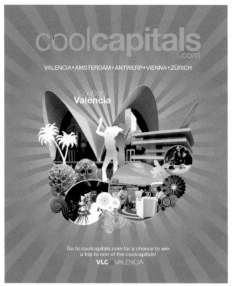
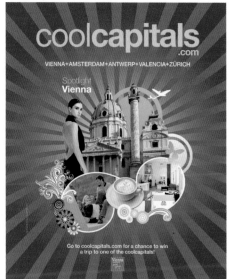
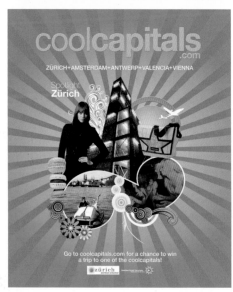

46 Mixing typefaces using historical compatibility

TYPE DESIGN REFLECTS ITS ERA, so multiple typefaces within a single project should be historically compatible, i.e., designed within a similar time frame, or a revival from that time frame. Another method for choosing typefaces that are historically compatible might be to choose from the designs of a single type designer. As with all type choices, the faces should work with the content; historical considerations are not the only factor.

Project
Package

Art Director, Designer
Louise Fili

Client
Bella Cucina

Dolci Biscotti packaging was designed using various Victorian-era typefaces that were scanned from old type books and redrawn.

Project
Package

Art Director
Louise Fili

Designers
Louise Fili and Chad Roberts

Illustrator
Graham Evernden

Client
Late July

The Late July package was
inspired by early twentieth-
century cracker packaging.
Everything was hand lettered,
including the net weight copy.

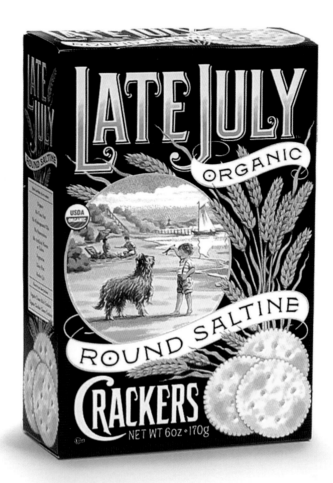

Project
Barker & Mills
cocktail cherries

Art Director
Lauren Panepinto

Designer
Lauren Panepinto

Photography
Lauren Panepinto

Client
Ryan Barker

A wonderful mix of vintage
typefaces, this package
design perfectly evokes a
golden age of mixology.
The crosshatched sans
serif type and classic red-
and-black-on-ivory palette
hearkens back to the era of
the general store.

47 Familiarity breeds legibility

LEGIBILITY IS PARAMOUNT in most type-driven projects, so be careful to choose typefaces with design elements that are easy for the reader to grasp immediately. Many typefaces, because of their frequent usage and wide availability, have especially recognizable features and proportions. Readers should be able to "decipher" the letterforms within a split second. As with all things, our comfort level is determined by previous experience.

Project
Feature spread

Art Director, Designer
Louis Fishauf

Illustrator
Anita Kunz

Client
Toronto Life

Clarity in text and display type, combined with spacious margins, make this an easy read.

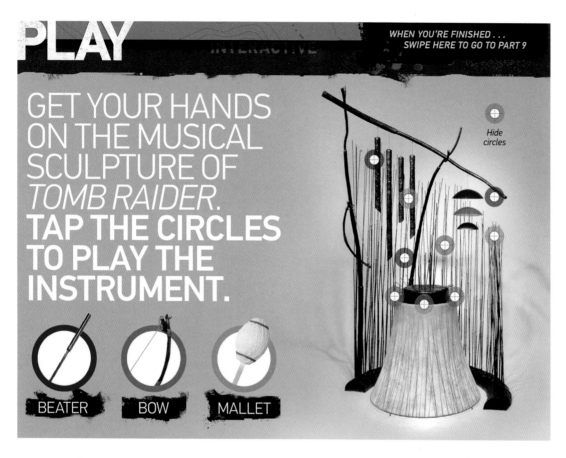

PLAY INTERACTIVE

GET YOUR HANDS ON THE MUSICAL SCULPTURE OF *TOMB RAIDER.* **TAP THE CIRCLES TO PLAY THE INSTRUMENT.**

WHEN YOU'RE FINISHED . . .
SWIPE HERE TO GO TO PART 9

Hide circles

BEATER   BOW   MALLET

Project
Tablet app

Studio
Joe Zeff Design

Client
The Final Hours of Tomb Raider

This screen of The Fall of Tomb Raider's tablet app uses a highly legible sans serif typeface to convey clear on-screen instructions for usability and play.

Project
Phone app

Studio
Brobel Design

Client
UCLA Anderson

This phone app (there is also a tablet app) for Admit Preview Day at UCLA Anderson has text in bright color-coded bars that are consistent throughout the app, thus easy to navigate.
A clean and legible sans serif completes the ease of use.

48 Properly weighted small caps and fractions

PROPORTION IS KEY when using small caps and fractions. Shortcuts to their creation provided by design software may seem easy, but any comparison of "fake" small caps or slapped-together fractions with the real thing will immediately reveal the difference. Properly weighted small caps are slightly wider and slightly weightier in addition to being shorter; this allows them to exist harmoniously within the tonal density of the surrounding text. Similarly, properly weighted (and constructed) fractions are also slightly wider and slightly weightier, and the spaces on either side of their slashes are calibrated by the type designer to match the spacing in text type.

Project
Feature spread

Creative Director
Dean Markadakis

Designer
Jana Meier

Photographer
Howard Cao

Client
Fast Company

Small caps in the gray subhead match the weight of the surrounding lowercase text. Note the use of the em dash, with a comfortable space on either side of it, to set off the final thought. Also note the levels of emphasis created by an italicized name (the subject) and a roman name (the author), as well as the shifts of slope, size, and color in the all-lowercase headline. The shape enclosing the headline is a "devilish" play on the lowercase *g* of the word *green*, with its tail and horns (and halo).

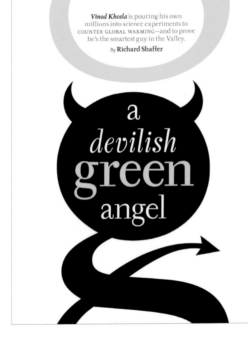

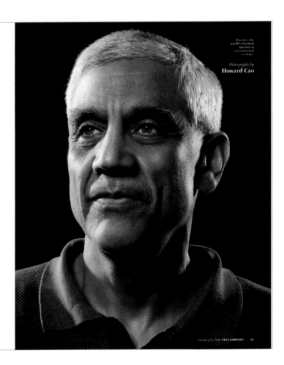

MERCURY NUMERIC GRADE 1		
Operating cash	$	390,563
Deposits		1,373,050
Receivables		121,537
Equipment		*247,158*
Investments		1,143,771
Property		124,092
8½ PT		

Paris	**74 55 T**	**63 42 C**
Prague	68 55 s	77 62 s
Rio de Jan	71 61 R	73 64 T
Riyadh	99 67 c	96 68 c
Rome	**82 65 s**	**83 65 s**
Santiago	72 41 s	78 42 s
San Salvador	91 66 c	91 68 s
8 PT		

BalancedA ♣	14.39 -1.7	-0.8
BondA ♣	31.77 -2.9	-1.4
CapGrowA	15.46 +0.2	+0.1
CapGrowB	17.77 -1.0	-0.3
CapGrowM	**55.67 +2.8**	**+1.9**
EqIncA	12.79 +0.1	+0.1
HiYldA ♣	9.25 -2.0	-1.0
8½ PT		

MERCURY NUMERIC GRADE 2		
Operating cash	$	390,563
Deposits		1,373,050
Receivables		121,537
Equipment		*247,158*
Investments		1,143,771
Property		124,092
8½ PT		

Paris	**74 55 T**	**63 42 C**
Prague	68 55 s	77 62 s
Rio de Jan	71 61 R	73 64 T
Riyadh	99 67 c	96 68 c
Rome	**82 65 s**	**83 65 s**
Santiago	72 41 s	78 42 s
San Salvador	91 66 c	91 68 s
8 PT		

BalancedA ♣	14.39 -1.7	-0.8
BondA ♣	31.77 -2.9	-1.4
CapGrowA	15.46 +0.2	+0.1
CapGrowB	17.77 -1.0	-0.3
CapGrowM	**55.67 +2.8**	**+1.9**
EqIncA	12.79 +0.1	+0.1
HiYldA ♣	9.25 -2.0	-1.0
8½ PT		

MERCURY NUMERIC GRADE 3		
Operating cash	$	390,563
Deposits		1,373,050
Receivables		121,537
Equipment		*247,158*
Investments		1,143,771
Property		124,092
8½ PT		

Paris	**74 55 T**	**63 42 C**
Prague	68 55 s	77 62 s
Rio de Jan	71 61 R	73 64 T
Riyadh	99 67 c	96 68 c
Rome	**82 65 s**	**83 65 s**
Santiago	72 41 s	78 42 s
San Salvador	91 66 c	91 68 s
8 PT		

BalancedA ♣	14.39 -1.7	-0.8
BondA ♣	31.77 -2.9	-1.4
CapGrowA	15.46 +0.2	+0.1
CapGrowB	17.77 -1.0	-0.3
CapGrowM	**55.67 +2.8**	**+1.9**
EqIncA	12.79 +0.1	+0.1
HiYldA ♣	9.25 -2.0	-1.0
8½ PT		

MERCURY NUMERIC GRADE 4		
Operating cash	$	390,563
Deposits		1,373,050
Receivables		121,537
Equipment		*247,158*
Investments		1,143,771
Property		124,092
8½ PT		

Paris	**74 55 T**	**63 42 C**
Prague	68 55 s	77 62 s
Rio de Jan	71 61 R	73 64 T
Riyadh	99 67 c	96 68 c
Rome	**82 65 s**	**83 65 s**
Santiago	72 41 s	78 42 s
San Salvador	91 66 c	91 68 s
8 PT		

BalancedA ♣	14.39 -1.7	-0.8
BondA ♣	31.77 -2.9	-1.4
CapGrowA	15.46 +0.2	+0.1
CapGrowB	17.77 -1.0	-0.3
CapGrowM	**55.67 +2.8**	**+1.9**
EqIncA	12.79 +0.1	+0.1
HiYldA ♣	9.25 -2.0	-1.0
8½ PT		

Those who had learned to sail by dead reckoning
MERCURY TEXT ROMAN, GRADE 2

Captain Wessex was the first to chart the coast
MERCURY TEXT SEMIBOLD, GRADE 2

Nearly two centuries since the first explorers
MERCURY TEXT BOLD, GRADE 2

It was the discovery of the Americas that ultimate
MERCURY TEXT ITALIC, GRADE 2

Worked well in the early days when the colonies
MERCURY TEXT SEMIBOLD ITALIC, GRADE 2

Due to mercantile rivalry among the seafaring
MERCURY TEXT BOLD ITALIC, GRADE 3

THEY FIERCELY DEFENDED THEIR PACIFIC TRADE
MERCURY TEXT ROMAN SMALL CAPS, GRADE 2

BEFORE EACH GALLEON WAS HEAVILY ARMORED
MERCURY TEXT SEMIBOLD SMALL CAPS, GRADE 2

COOPERATION OF THE TWO MAJOR MARITIME
MERCURY TEXT BOLD SMALL CAPS, GRADE 2

98.76 1_23_4 $1/2$ $1/3$ NRs
MERCURY TEXT NUMERIC ROMAN, GRADE 2

10.98 0_01_1 $2/5$ $3/5$ NRs
MERCURY TEXT NUMERIC SEMIBOLD, GRADE 2

32.10 6_67_7 $3/8$ $5/8$ NRs
MERCURY TEXT NUMERIC BOLD, GRADE 2

54.32 7_78_8 $1/4$ $3/4$ NRs
MERCURY TEXT NUMERIC ITALIC, GRADE 2

76.54 3_34_4 $1/6$ $5/6$ NRs
MERCURY TEXT NUMERIC SEMIBOLD ITALIC, GRADE 2

98.79 9_90_0 $1/2$ $1/3$ NRs
MERCURY TEXT NUMERIC BOLD ITALIC, GRADE 3

MERCURY TEXT NUMERIC, GRADE 2

Old style numbers and groups of capitals can disrupt the consistent typographic color of a body of text. By reducing their point size slightly, consistent color can be restored.

small caps
old style
numbers
lining figures

Four score and seven years ago our fathers brought forth on this continent, a new nation, conceived in Liberty, and dedicated to the proposition that all men are created equal.

Now we are engaged in a great NASA esting whether that nation, or any nation so conceived and so dedicated, can long endure. We are met on a great battlefield of that war. We have come to dedicate a portion of that field, as a final resting place for those who here gave their lives AIDS that that nation might live. It is altogether fitting and proper that we should do this.

But, in a larger sense, we can not dedicate—we can not consecrate—we can not hallow—this ground. The brave men, living and dead, who struggled here, have consecrated it, far above our poor power to add or detract. The world will little note, nor long remember what we say here, but it can 1492 never forget what they did here. It is for us the living, rather, to be dedicated here to the unfinished work which they who fought here have thus far so nobly advanced. It is rather for us to be here TWA dedicated to the great task remaining before us—that from these honored dead we take increased 1654 devotion to that cause for which they gave the last full measure of devotion—that we here highly resolve that these dead shall not have died in vain—that this nation, under God, shall have a new birth of freedom—and that government of the people, by the people, for the people, shall not perish from the earth.

Four score and seven years ago our fathers brought forth on this continent, a new nation, conceived in Liberty, and dedicated to the proposition that all men are created equal.

Now we are engaged in a great NASA esting whether that nation, or any nation so conceived and so dedicated, can long endure. We are met on a great battlefield of that war. We have come to dedicate a portion of that field, as a final resting place for those who here gave their lives AIDS that that nation might live. It is altogether fitting and proper that we should do this.

But, in a larger sense, we can not dedicate—we can not consecrate—we can not hallow—this ground. The brave men, living and dead, who struggled here, have consecrated it, far above our poor power to add or detract. The world will little note, nor long remember what we say here, but it can 1492 never forget what they did here. It is for us the living, rather, to be dedicated here to the unfinished work which they who fought here have thus far so nobly advanced. It is rather for us to be here TWA dedicated to the great task remaining before us—that from these honored dead we take increased 1654 devotion to that cause for which they gave the last full measure of devotion—that we here highly resolve that these dead shall not have died in vain—that this nation, under God, shall have a new birth of freedom—and that government of the people, by the people, for the people, shall not perish from the earth.

Four score and seven years ago our fathers brought forth on this continent, a new nation, conceived in Liberty, and dedicated to the proposition that all men are created equal.

Now we are engaged in a great NASA esting whether that nation, or any nation so conceived and so dedicated, can long endure. We are met on a great battlefield of that war. We have come to dedicate a portion of that field, as a final resting place for those who here gave their lives AIDS that that nation might live. It is altogether fitting and proper that we should do this.

But, in a larger sense, we can not dedicate—we can not consecrate—we can not hallow—this ground. The brave men, living and dead, who struggled here, have consecrated it, far above our poor power to add or detract. The world will little note, nor long remember what we say here, but it can 1492 never forget what they did here. It is for us the living, rather, to be dedicated here to the unfinished work which they who fought here have thus far so nobly advanced. It is rather for us to be here TWA dedicated to the great task remaining before us—that from these honored dead we take increased 1654 devotion to that cause for which they gave the last full measure of devotion—that we here highly resolve that these dead shall not have died in vain—that this nation, under God, shall have a new birth of freedom—and that government of the people, by the people, for the people, shall not perish from the earth.

Project (left)
Type specimen

Company
Hoefler & Frere-Jones

Designer
Jonathan Hoefler

Client
Hoefler & Frere-Jones

This type family from Hoefler Frére-Jones was designed with a broad spectrum of properly weighted small caps and fractions for the specific tabular uses that require them, such as stock quotes.

49 Using the right type

FINDING THE RIGHT TYPE is just as important as finding the right soul mate. Every project embodies a spirit, and choosing the right type for the project will amplify and clarify its spirit as well as its message. Depending on the design challenge, there may be more than one or even many "right" choices. Understanding what is to be communicated and to whom should help to navigate the vast universe of available typefaces.

Project
Les Liasons Dangereuses

Company
SpotCo

Art Director
Gail Anderson

Designer
Darren Cox

Photographer
Christopher McLallen

Client
Roundabout Theatre

Wispy, ornate ribbons of text, smoky and indistinct, strike the right emotional notes for this sexually charged play; they provide a literal counterpart to the illustration and are gesturally linked by the uplifted arm and the downward sloping *D.*

Project
Package

Company
Mucca Design

Creative Director
Matteo Bologna

Art Director
Andrea Brown

Designers
Andrea Brown and Ariana Dilibero

Client
Domaine de Canton

The ribbed container and the bamboo-inflected type details suggest the ethnic origins of this product: Indochina.

Project
Cover

Creative Director
Scott Dadich

Design Director
Wyatt Mitchell

Art Director
Carl DeTorres

Illustrator
Yoichiro Ono

Client
Wired

The cover art and display type are the right pop-culture approach to depict Manga, the graphic cult of Japanese comics.

50 Theory of Relativity II

WORDS EXIST IN RELATION TO OTHER WORDS. Therefore, every decision that is made, whether style, size, weight, width, color, or contrast, must take into consideration all of the other words (and all of the other elements) on the page or screen. Every design decision, no matter how small, has an effect on every other aspect of the design.

Changing the scale of one word may necessitate adjusting the scale of another, and not necessarily by the same percentage. The more elements there are, the more complex the equation becomes (but unlike mathematics, where there is only one answer to an equation, designers may find many successful answers to the same problem).

Project
Riefenstahl/Astaire

Company
SFMOMA

Design Director
Jennifer Sonderby

Designers
Amadeo DeSouza, Steven Knodel, and Jeremy Mende

Client
SFMOMA

Theoretically, this design violates many rules, especially type overlapping complex images and the ninety-degree type rotation, but because of the delicate balance of elements, it is an elegant piece of design.

Project
The Frank Lloyd Wright Foundation
desktop and mobile website

Studio
Eight and a Half

Art Director
Bonnie Siegler

Designer
Kristen Ren

Client
The Frank Lloyd Wright Foundation

A precise balancing of typographhic elements overlays images of Frank Lloyd Wright's work. The site's logo acts as an anchor to the pull-down menu at the left of the screen and the horizontal copy extending from it at the top. There is a sense of structural elegance, appropriate for an architect's site. Each typographic element exists in a clear relationship to the other elements.

Project
Thalia Theater media

Designers
Friederike Kuehne,
Jana Steffen, Martin Jahnecke,
and Bastian Renner (students),
Burg Giebichenstein University
of Art and Design Halle

Professor
Anna Berkenbusch

Client
Thalia Theater

The raw energy of this design uses effects that might not work elsewhere to its advantage: the lack of margin and gutter spaces, overlong lines of dense text overlaid on a strong field of color cutting though the lines, and text covering the eyes of the image. It is clear that these choices have been made intentionally, and that they support one another.

51 Invisible typography

SPEAK SOFTLY AND CARRY A BIG STICK.
Teddy Roosevelt's philosophy of governing can also be applied to type usage: sometimes the best way to emphasize the content visually is with "quiet" typography. At other times, the nature of the content calls for a low-key treatment. "Softness" can be accomplished in a variety of ways: choosing a typeface with a thin stroke width, or choosing to keep contrast to a minimum. Using a small point size is another method for "invisible" typography, but remember that legibility may be impaired if these techniques are not properly executed.

Project
Cover

Design Director, Designer
Chris Dixon

Client
New York

This is a brave design for a magazine cover, though not the first to use white-on-white (that was a legendary *Esquire* cover). The subject matter—how to find peace and quiet and achieve serenity in a frenetic city—is perfectly addressed and supported by the logo in its near invisibility.

Project
Brand identity, digital design, product design

Studio
Pentagram

Art Director
Marina Willer

Designers
Hamlet Auyeung, Leon Hapka, Cleber de Campos, Ana Estrougo, and Jessica Samuel

Client
Vibia

The whisper of type on this logo suggests the subtleties of illumination for this lighting company.

52   Highly evident typography

HIGH-IMPACT TYPE is like high-impact aerobics: it gets your heart rate pumping, and fast. Type can be aggressive, loud, and even harsh; it screams out for attention. One of the attributes of highly evident typography is its ability to create balance when paired with a strong image; together, they send a powerful message.

Project
Feature spread

Creative Director
Scott Dadich

Design Director
Wyatt Mitchell

Art Director, Designer
Carl DeTorres

Client
Wired

Highly geometric and abstract letter shapes cluster and overlap, filling the title page and providing an exuberant counterpoint to the supporting text elements. Their bulky strength balances the powerful monochrome silhouetted figure on the opposite page.

Project
Calea Nero d'Avola

Art Director
Louise Fili

Designers
Louise Fili and Jessica Hische

Hand Lettering
Jessica Hische

Client
Polaner Selections

Referencing early twentieth-
century Italian poster design,
the typography was used
to convey a lively mood. Its
ornate forms push up to the
very edges of the label and are
tightly surrounded by a vaguely
floral ornamental border.

Project
Can't Jump Rope

Company
Studio of ME/AT

Designer
Mike Essl

Client
Grand Valley State University

Muscular forms heavily outlined
and shadowed in black pack even
more of a punch than the images.

53 Less is more

SIMPLICITY HAS AN UNDENIABLE APPEAL to a time-pressured and overworked reader. A type treatment that promises to be "quick and easy" is just what the doctor ordered. Type that has minimal detail, has highly legible letterforms, and is floating in a good-sized space feels like a breath of fresh air even before we choose to read it.

Project
Cutthroat: Native Trout of the West

Art Director
Charlie Nix

Designers
Charlie Nix and Gary Robbins

Client
University of California Press

The exquisitely rendered image is clearly the star of this jacket; the headline quietly allows the fish to take center stage. Even the choice of black for the text is restrained.

Project
Life at These Speeds book cover

Art Director
Henry Sene Yee

Designer
Lauren Panepinto

Images
Imagebank, Getty

Client
Picador Books

Floating in the blank space between two images and tracked out to feel airy, the type on this book cover is deceptively simple. It sucks us into its "black hole" while simultaneously reassuring us that we will be safe.

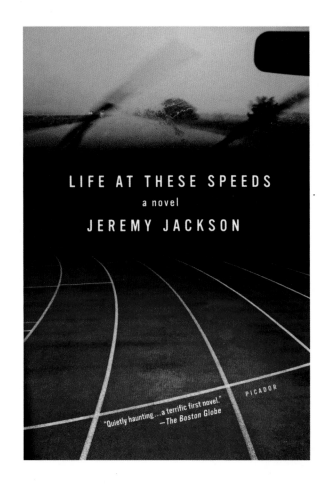

Project
Feature spread

Design Director
Carla Frank

Designer
Randall Leers

Client
O, The Oprah Magazine

Floating calmly in a sea of bright yellow, the text is low-key lowercase with a twist: a typographical wink at sex.

54 More is more

A SMORGASBORD OF CONTENT served up to the reader feels bountiful, and the urge to overstuff ourselves is ever so tempting. A plethora of choices competing for attention may deter timid or tired readers, but its main advantage is that this approach offers many opportunities for the reader to find something of interest. This is the theory behind magazine covers with many layers of cover lines, and newspapers that display as many stories as possible on their front pages.

Project
Cover

Design Director, Designer
David Curcurito

Photo Editor
Nancy Jo Lacoi

Photographer
Mark Hom

Client
Esquire

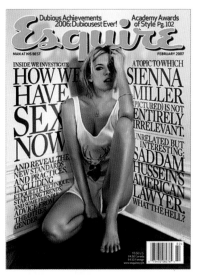

Photographer
James White

Photo Editor
Michael Norseng

Photographer
Jake Chessum

Esquire's jam-packed cover typography treatment was almost revolutionary when it first appeared; because it is so typographically different from all of the other covers on the newsstand, it defined its own niche and became an instant classic.

Project
Covers

Art Director, Designer
Donald Beekman

Illustrator
Donald Beekman

Client
APE

A lively and intense mix of stories fight for attention on these charmingly illustrated magazine covers. While staying within a limited color and typographic palette, these jostling and unconventional cover lines convey a sense of youthful fun, and the idea that a great deal of content is waiting inside for the reader.

Project
Blue Man World
book design

Studio
Eight and a Half

Art Director
Bonnie Siegler

Designers
Andrew James Capelli and
Kristen Ren

Client
Blue Man Group,
Black Dog & Leventhal

A mass of words covering the surface of the spread and bleeding off the edges, combined with an electric palette, sweeps over the viewer like a saturated force of nature.

55 Letter spacing and word spacing

THE INTERTWINED RELATIONSHIP of the letter and the word dictates that any decision to alter spacing between letters requires a similar adjustment in the spaces between words. In almost all software programs, this proportional relationship is automatically accomplished. There is also a relationship between the width of letters and the word spaces required for the eye to distinguish the end of one word from the beginning of the next; the narrower the letterform, the less space the eye requires.

Columns of type that are set justified will have uneven word spacing in order to accomplish the alignment; good typesetting will minimize that disparity as much as possible. At text-type size settings (up to 12 or 14 points), preset kerning pairs and automatic word spacing will look fine. But at display type sizes, word spacing and letter spacing (kerning) will most likely need additional small but critical manual adjustments to look optically correct.

Project
Cover

Company
Hopkins/Baumann

Creative Directors
Will Hopkins and
Mary K. Baumann

Illustrator
John Baxter

Client
Kids Discover

The condensed letterforms used here don't require much space between words in order to be legible.

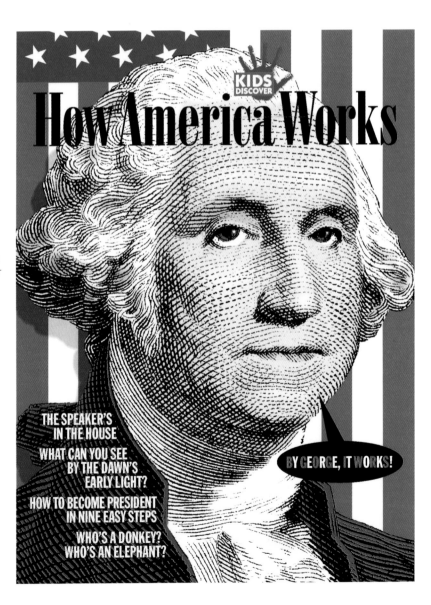

33

THE MOST OVERRATED PEOPLE, PLACES, TRENDS AND OTHER JUNK IN ROCK
FROM YOUR FAVORITE BAND IN HIGH SCHOOL TO THE MOST REQUESTED SONG IN THE WORLD. *BLENDER* CALLS B***S**T ...
ILLUSTRATION BY SERIAL CUT

/ SEXIN' ALL NIGHT LONG
Usher, Keith Sweat, AC/DC, Prince ... we could go on and on about the mack daddies who brag about going on and on—hittin' it, workin' it and doing other stuff to it—until the break of dawn. Even Dokken even have a song about all-night boning. Two words for all these guys: *Shyeah, right!* Have you actually ever tried sexin' it for more than, like, two hours? You get bored. You get sores. You get tired. Call us square, but unless you're Sting or a crystal-meth addict, an all-night sex marathon sounds about as fun as an all-day *Friends* marathon.
Underrated alternative: **Sexin' for 45 minutes and getting 10 hours of sleep**

32/ KISS
Memo to Gene Simmons: Either take your shirt off or put your pants on. As a band, they're about as perfunctory as Gene's sex tape—they're a tiresome, bickering circus act with a few decent glam songs.
Underrated alternative: **Cheap Trick**

31/ THE *IN RAINBOWS* MODEL
Record industry: evil! Paying what you want: good! But even in the "intellectual property wants to be free" age, a glorified tip jar isn't going to work for most bands—Girl Talk notwithstanding, if the act doesn't have a pretty huge fan base already, they can basically forget it. And if you look a little more closely at what Radiohead did, they actually made a lot of their money from *In Rainbows* the old-fashioned way: selling physical copies, including fancy, limited-edition versions with premium price tags.
Underrated alternative: **Tour-exclusive CDs**

30/ "FREEBIRD"
If Lynyrd Skynyrd's Ronnie VanZandt were alive today, he'd be rolling from town to town, beating the crap out of every last d-bag who feels the need to scream, "Freebird!" from the back row at a concert. We've got news for you, buddy, "Freebird" wasn't even Skynyrd's top six-string epic. That honor would have to go to "I Need You," from side one of *Second Helping*, highly recommended the next time you get the urge to blow your child-support check guzzling fifths of Jim Beam, playing air guitar and humping cattle. The South's gonna do it again, baby!
Underrated alternative: **"I Need You"**

29/ GETTING RICK RUBIN TO PRODUCE YOUR RECORD
It's not 1986, you're not the Red Hot Chili Peppers and Johnny Cash is dead.
Underrated alternative: **Getting Rick Rubin to produce your beard**

28/ MAKING MUSIC. AND CLOTHES. AND ENERGY DRINKS
Man, this Young Jeezy single is great! You know what would make it even better? If we could listen to it while drinking some Fergie-brand taurine-infused wine coolers and wearing a Jonas Brothers sweatband! Come on, pop stars of the world, we know no one's buying CDs and you gotta make your Maybach payments somehow, but we wouldn't wear those velour jogging pants with Nelly's name emblazoned on the ass if they came free via BitTorrent.
Underrated alternative: **Making music. And music. And music**

27/ GETTING BACKSTAGE
What you are expecting: free Jäger, bowls of pills, babes by the couchful, getting to play beer pong with your favorite rock god. What you actually get: free Dasani, a suspect-looking fruit plate and three sorta-babes who take a look at the couchful of shlumpy industry types and split for the after party. Oh, no one told you about that? It's not in a carpeted closet here at the hockey rink; it's at a loft across town, where your favorite rock god is actually playing beer pong. Sorry!
Underrated alternative: **Getting White Castle**

26/ TIMBALAND
A genius, obviously. A producer gifted beyond all comprehension. In his late-1990s prime, he reinvented the sound of hip-hop radio on a monthly basis, making avant-garde notions of rhythm and noise bounce, pop and swing. But that was 10 years ago. Lately, dude has been coasting—even as his legend (and producing fee) inflates. That Nelly Furtado album? Eh. The Madonna single? We can't actually remember how that one goes. His solo set, *Timbaland Presents Shock Value*? *Bleeeeuuuuhh*—and it gave the world OneRepublic. The last Justin album stands alone as a recent Timbo triumph, and his upcoming collaboration with Chris Cornell isn't going to change that.
Underrated alternative: **Switch**

BY JON DOLAN, JOSH EELLS, JOE LEVY, ROB SHEFFIELD, ROB TANNENBAUM, JONAH WEINER AND DOUGLAS WOLK

Project
Feature spread

Creative Director, Designer
Dirk Barnett

Illustrator
Serial Cut

Client
Blender

Tight overall tracking and minimal word spacing is fairly common (especially in design aimed at young adult readers), so very minimal word spacing is enough to separate words sufficiently for quick comprehension of text type.

word spacing

Fourˌscoreˌandˌsevenˌyearsˌago
ourˌfathersˌbroughtˌforthˌon
thisˌcontinent,ˌaˌnewˌnation,

Four score and seven years ago
our fathers brought forth on
this continent, a new nation,

56   Hyphenation and justification

H&J, AS IT IS ALSO KNOWN, is one of the more complex areas of typesetting, and much greater detail about this topic can be found in technical manuals and online. Suffice it to say that today's page layout programs contain sophisticated hyphenation and justification controls, which can be adjusted to suit the end user's preferences. The goal is to have a texture and "color", or overall tonal weight of type, that is easy to read, invites the reader to read, and is pleasant to behold, without excessive or repetitive hyphenation.

**Justified
Hyphenated
2 columns**

Four score and seven years ago our fathers brought forth on this continent, a new nation, conceived in Liberty, and dedicated to the proposition that all men are created equal.

Now we are engaged in a great civil war, testing whether that nation, or any nation so conceived and so dedicated, can long endure. We are met on a great battlefield of that war. We have come to dedicate a portion of that field, as a final resting place for those who here gave their lives that that nation might live. It is altogether fitting and proper that we should do this.

But, in a larger sense, we can not dedicate—we can not consecrate—we can not hallow—this ground. The brave men, living and dead, who struggled here, have consecrated it, far above our poor power to add or detract. The world will little note, nor long remember what we say here, but it can never forget what they did here. It is for us the living, rather, to be dedicated here to the unfinished work which they who fought here have thus far so nobly advanced. It is rather for us to be here dedicated to the great task remaining before us—that from these honored dead we take increased devotion to that cause for which they gave the last full measure of devotion—that we here highly resolve that these dead shall not have died in vain—that this nation, under God, shall have a new birth of freedom—and that government of the people, by the people, for the people, shall not perish from the earth.

**Flush Left
No Hyphenation
2 columns**

Four score and seven years ago our fathers brought forth on this continent, a new nation, conceived in Liberty, and dedicated to the proposition that all men are created equal.

Now we are engaged in a great civil war, testing whether that nation, or any nation so conceived and so dedicated, can long endure. We are met on a great battlefield of that war. We have come to dedicate a portion of that field, as a final resting place for those who here gave their lives that that nation might live. It is altogether fitting and proper that we should do this.

But, in a larger sense, we can not dedicate—we can not consecrate—we can not hallow—this ground. The brave men, living and dead, who struggled here, have consecrated it, far above our poor power to add or detract. The world will little note, nor long remember what we say here, but it can never forget what they did here. It is for us the living, rather, to be dedicated here to the unfinished work which they who fought here have thus far so nobly advanced. It is rather for us to be here dedicated to the great task remaining before us—that from these honored dead we take increased devotion to that cause for which they gave the last full measure of devotion—that we here highly resolve that these dead shall not have died in vain—that this nation, under God, shall have a new birth of freedom—and that government of the people, by the people, for the people, shall not perish from the earth.

Flush Left
Hyphenation
2 columns

Four score and seven years ago our fathers brought forth on this continent, a new nation, conceived in Liberty, and dedicated to the proposition that all men are created equal.

Now we are engaged in a great civil war, testing whether that nation, or any nation so conceived and so dedicated, can long endure. We are met on a great battlefield of that war. We have come to dedicate a portion of that field, as a final resting place for those who here gave their lives that that nation might live. It is altogether fitting and proper that we should do this.

But, in a larger sense, we can not dedicate—we can not consecrate—we can not hallow—this ground. The brave men, living and dead, who struggled here, have consecrated it, far above our poor power to add or detract. The world will little note, nor long remember what we say here, but it can never forget what they did here. It is for us the living, rather, to be dedicated here to the unfinished work which they who fought here have thus far so nobly advanced. It is rather for us to be here dedicated to the great task remaining before us—that from these honored dead we take increased devotion to that cause for which they gave the last full measure of devotion—that we here highly resolve that these dead shall not have died in vain—that this nation, under God, shall have a new birth of freedom—and that government of the people, by the people, for the people, shall not perish from the earth.

How many letters should be before or after the hyphen?
How many hyphens should appear in a row?
What do you consider a ladder?
Should you break proper names or other capitalized words?
Should you hyphenate copy that isn't justified?
Should you hyphenate hyphenated words or conjunctions?

does-n't

Edit Hyphenation & Justification

Name:
sabon justified

☑ Auto Hyphenation
Smallest Word: 5
Minimum Before: 3
Minimum After: 3
☑ Break Capitalized Words

Hyphens in a Row: 2
Hyphenation Zone: 0p

Justification Method

	Min.	Opt.	Max.
Space:	85%	110%	250%
Char:	0%	0%	4%

Flush Zone: 0p

☑ Single Word Justify

Cancel   OK

57 Tracking guidelines

NOT TOO LOOSE AND NOT TOO TIGHT: tracking should feel "just right" (in the words of Goldilocks as she fell asleep in the baby bear's bed). Tracking refers to the overall or global adjustment of letter spacing within a word, a line, a paragraph, or a passage of text. As in all things typographic, the goal is consistency in the appearance of the text. Therefore, it is generally best to practice restraint in tracking, so that there appears to be little difference between the text that has been altered (tracked in or tracked out, as the case may be) and the text that surrounds it.

Poverty, Inequality and Economic Growth

Back to Basics **Jose Antonio Ocampo**

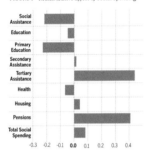

FIGURE 1 *Redistributive Effect of Social Spending*

water and sewage). In this case, spending is progressive in some countries and, on average, is not too far from equi-distribution among the whole population, as reflected in quasi-gini coefficients close to zero. Health spending lies between the first two categories. The third category includes tertiary education and pensions, where spending to a larger extent benefits high income groups.

Only social assistance programs confirm the view that targeting is the best instrument to enhance the redistributive effects of social spending; others can achieve close to the same level of redistribution. As we have seen, the best examples are the recent conditional cash transfer programs but there are also highly redistributive programs, such as nutrition programs and those that focus on early childhood development. However, the total redistributive effect of such spending is limited, given the fact that it concentrates only a small proportion of total social spending (less than a fifth).[9] Thus, according to existing studies, the most important redistributive effect of social spending is associated with education and health programs that have universal or quasi-universal coverage. And increasing coverage can turn any social program into a highly redistributive one. One example: increased coverage of secondary education from 1974 to 1992 turned this spending from being a regressive into a highly progressive social spending program in Colombia.[10]

One implication of this is that the traditional estimates of the impact of universal programs, such as the estimates reproduced in **FIGURE 1**, do not effectively capture the actual redistributive effects of additional social spending. So, an increase of spending to increase the coverage of secondary education and housing programs may be as redistributive as the targeted program. For the same reasons, additional spending on university education will also be much less regressive than it looks in **FIGURE 1**.

Furthermore, in the case of pensions, there are significant measurement problems that tend to give a wrong indication of their distributive impact. Measurements of payouts on pensions are generally estimated on a gross basis; thereby they do not net out social security contributions (past and present). If contributions are made by high income groups, they are by definition progressive. Furthermore, such contributions should include those made by the state as an employer. If one were to measure the net payout by the state, also netting out the contributions made by the state as an employer, the distributive impact of pension payments would look much better than it does in **FIGURE 1**.

Even here, though, there is a strong case to be made for expanding the coverage of pension systems. Retirement benefits in many Latin American countries are related to formal employment, thus severely limiting their progressiveness. A truly progressive pension system lies in the design of a program financed by the government that provides pensions for informal sector workers.[11] Such a pillar would be highly progressive, as reflected in those countries that have some basic pensions that are universal in character or some form of non-contributory pension system (Argentina, Bolivia and Brazil).

Compare the overall contribution of social spending to improving income distribution with the human development index of the United Nations Development Program and you see that the most effective form of targeting is, in fact—and, for some, perhaps ironically—a universal social policy. The two are highly correlated as demonstrated in **FIGURE 2** below. The largest redistributive effect of social spending is achieved in those countries that had an early development of more universal systems of social policy: Argentina, Chile, Costa Rica, and Uruguay (Cuba should be added to this list but is generally excluded from this type of estimates.) Countries with an intermediate level of development—Brazil, Colombia and Panama—have intermediate levels of redistribution associated with social spending, and the lowest level occurs in countries that have a lower level of development of their social policy instruments: Bolivia, El Salvador, Honduras, and Guatemala. In three countries—Ecuador, Mexico and Peru—the redistributive effects of social spending should be higher given their level of human development.

Targeting alone has a relatively limited impact. But it can play a subsidiary role in three specific areas. First, social assistance (conditional subsidies, nutrition programs, pension transfers for poor old people) can serve as a pillar of a broader universal system. But even in these cases these programs must aim for the eventual universal coverage of the targeted population. Second, targeting can also enhance the access of the poor to universal social programs. This is indeed a particular advantage of the recent conditional transfers; they tie the assistance to access of the population to universal programs of education and health. And third, targeting can also be used to differentiate the programs for specific groups of population, particularly indigenous peoples. In the last two cases, targeting must serve as an instrument of universalism and not as its substitute.

THE EFFECTS OF SOCIAL SPENDING ON INCOME DISTRIBUTION

The evidence indicates indeed that social programs with universal or close-to-universal coverage make the best contribution to improving income distribution. **FIGURE 1** summarizes the redistributive effect of social spending drawn from studies conducted by ECLAC in 2000, 2006 and 2007.[8] This shows the quasi-gini coefficient of social spending, which fluctuates between -1 (perfect targeting of spending to the poor) and 1, with zero representing a situation in which spending is equally distributed among all social groups. While some programs have a more direct redistributive effect, measurement problems in several hid their progressiveness.

We can distinguish three categories of spending according to their effect on distribution. The first covers the more redistributive areas of spending, which include social assistance as well as those programs that have achieved universal or quasi-universal coverage, particularly primary education and some basic health programs. The second category includes services with an intermediate level of coverage, such as secondary education and housing (which includes

THE PARADOX OF REDISTRIBUTION

UNIVERSAL SYSTEMS are associated with a better primary distribution of income across the population. In the industrial countries of continental Europe more universal welfare systems have gone hand-in-hand with a better distribution of income compared to countries that use more means testing (targeting) in their social policy, such as the Anglo-Saxon countries.[12] Causality goes both ways in this case: more equal societies demand more universal systems of social policy, but the latter contribute in turn to equality. In contrast, the extensive use of

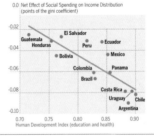

FIGURE 2 *Links Between Human Development and the Distributive Effect of Social Policy*

Project
Feature spread

Creative Director
Donald Partyka

Illustrator
Jared Schneidman

Client
Americas Quarterly

The even and highly legible tonality of the text columns look consistent throughout; this is the gold standard of well-set body copy.

Project
Visual identity

Company
Alphabet Arm Design

Art Director
Aaron Belyea

Designer
Ryan Frease

Client
Tennessee Hollow

This logo has tight tracking of its wide letterforms and is slightly curved; its strong horizontality provides a counterpoint to the (vertical) plant above it and the roots below it.

58 The "color" of the text type

TYPOGRAPHICALLY, the word *color* describes the density or tonal weight of the text type as a texture on the page. It is the goal of all good typographic designers to create an even or "smooth" texture. There should be no bits of text that stand out, either because they are too gappy (too loose) or overly dense (too tight). Watch out for irregularities in typographic color that may occur due to many long words within a line, type measures (line lengths) that are too narrow, when overzealous tracking has been applied, or some combination of these situations.

Project
Capabilities brochure

Company
Ross Culbert & Lavery, Inc.

Design Director
Peter Ross

Designer
Michael Aron

Client
Hughes Hubbard & Reed LLP

The color of this text is affected by the airier than usual leading and the relatively heavy vertical strokes of the typestyle. Its color is even throughout; especially because it is set rag right, the word spacing is consistent.

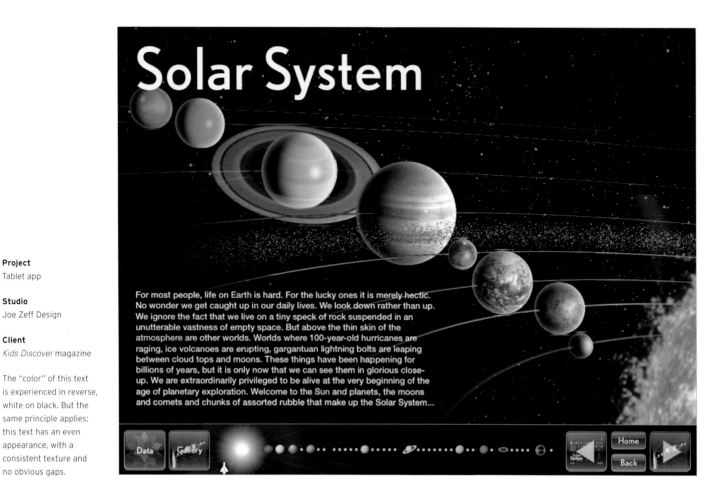

Solar System

For most people, life on Earth is hard. For the lucky ones it is merely hectic. No wonder we get caught up in our daily lives. We look down rather than up. We ignore the fact that we live on a tiny speck of rock suspended in an unutterable vastness of empty space. But above the thin skin of the atmosphere are other worlds. Worlds where 100-year-old hurricanes are raging, ice volcanoes are erupting, gargantuan lightning bolts are leaping between cloud tops and moons. These things have been happening for billions of years, but it is only now that we can see them in glorious close-up. We are extraordinarily privileged to be alive at the very beginning of the age of planetary exploration. Welcome to the Sun and planets, the moons and comets and chunks of assorted rubble that make up the Solar System...

Project
Tablet app

Studio
Joe Zeff Design

Client
Kids Discover magazine

The "color" of this text is experienced in reverse, white on black. But the same principle applies: this text has an even appearance, with a consistent texture and no obvious gaps.

I began to think about what I would see if I were in an airplane. You look down on things. You streak through the clouds so fast you don't know whether the flower below is a violet or what. You see only streaks of color.

–Alma Thomas, 1978

Alma Thomas lived through both the Wright brothers' first airplane flight and man's first steps on the moon. Many of her paintings are speculations of what flowers, gardens or the earth as a whole would look like from an airplane or spaceship. News and media sources expanded at almost the same rate as flight and space exploration, and Thomas primarily listened to reports of space travel on the radio. It gave her the freedom to sketch as she heard the stories unfold. Therefore, these imagined cosmic scenes are structurally similar to the rest of the artist's oeuvre. In 1971, she wrote, "My space paintings are expressed in the same color patterns as my earth paintings with the canvas forming intriguing motifs around and through color composition."

In *Snoopy Sees Earth Wrapped in Sunset* (1970), Thomas takes the colors and experience of a brilliant sunset to an imaginatively distant viewpoint, while also showing her increased use of the circle as an organizational tool in her compositions. However, *Starry Night and the Astronauts* (1972) gives Thomas the freedom to take her signature "Alma Stripe" out into the expanse of space, the glimpse of the warm yellow, red and orange horizontals disrupting the cool, dark verticality. Thomas believed in scientific progress and in many of her interviews she stated that since we no longer lived in the "horse-and-buggy" days, it was important to embrace and respond to new discoveries and technologies.

Project
Book design for 'Alma Thomas'

Studio
Pentagram

Art Director
Eddie Opara

Designers
Brankica Harvey and Shannon Jager

Client
The Studio Museum in Harlem

The spread demonstrates typographic "color" in both the larger text at left and the two paragraphs on the right.

59 Considering typographic mass

WALLS AND BLOCKS OF TYPE can be assembled to great effect: discrete units of type look organized and have heft within their design environment. The text within the blocks may vary in size, weight, width, and even typestyle, as long as the mass looks intentionally assembled.

Arman / John Armleder / *Art-Language* / *Art & Project Bulletin* / Atelier Populaire / Fiona Banner Georg Baselitz / Christiane Baumgartner / Carole Benzaken / Joseph Beuys / Jean-Charles Blais / John Bock / Christian Boltanski / KP Brehmer / Marcel Broodthaers / Joan Brossa Günter Brus / Daniel Buren / Rafael Canogar / Patrick Caulfield / Jake and Dinos Chapman Christo / Carlfriedrich Claus / Francesco Clemente / Claude Closky / Michael Craig-Martin Adam Dant / Hanne Darboven / Tacita Dean / *Décollage* / Peter Doig / Helen Douglas Olafur Eliasson / Equipo Crónica / Öyvind Fahlström / Hans-Peter Feldmann / Stanisław Fijałkowski / Robert Filliou / Ian Hamilton Finlay / Sylvie Fleury / Lucian Freud / Katharina Fritsch / Hamish Fulton / *futura* / Gilbert & George / Liam Gillick / *Gorgona* / Richard Hamilton Mona Hatoum / Juan Hidalgo / Damien Hirst / David Hockney / Peter Howson / Jörg Immendorff *Interfunktionen* / IRWIN / Kassettenkatalog / Ivana Keser / Anselm Kiefer / Martin Kippenberger Per Kirkeby / Yves Klein / Milan Knížák / Peter Kogler / *Krater und Wolke* / Langlands & Bell Maria Lassnig / Paul Etienne Lincoln / Richard Long / Sarah Lucas / Markus Lüpertz Mangelos / Piero Manzoni / Wolfgang Mattheuer / Chad McCail / Annette Messager / *Migrateurs* Jonathan Monk / François Morellet / Paul Morrison / Otto Muehl / Antoni Muntadas Museum in Progress / Olaf Nicolai / Hermann Nitsch / Paul Noble / OHO / Julian Opie / Blinky Palermo / Eduardo Paolozzi / *Parkett* / Simon Patterson / A. R. Penck / Giuseppe Penone Dan Perjovschi / Grayson Perry / Pawel Petasz / Jaume Plensa / *Point d'ironie* / Sigmar Polke / Markus Raetz / Arnulf Rainer / Gerhard Richter / Bridget Riley / Dieter Roth / Niki de Saint Phalle / David Shrigley / Daniel Spoerri / Telfer Stokes / Joe Tilson / Leonid Tishkov / Endre Tót Rosemarie Trockel / Ben Vautier / Wolf Vostell / Gillian Wearing / Franz West / Rachel Whiteread

Project
Eye on Europe

Company
Pure+Applied

Client
Museum of Modern Art

A list of names is separated by slashes to form a textured block balanced opposite a textured block of op art.

Project
Brand Identity and exhibition design for "Ferrari: Under the Skin"

Studio
Pentagram

Art Director
Marina Willer

Designers
Hamlet Auyeung, Stuart Gough, Ian Osborne, Jake Clewis, Marta Gaspar, Sthuthi Ramesh, Leon Hapka, James Falconer, and George Edwards

Collaborator
Paul Zak

Client
The Design Museum

Tightly stacked typographic mass creates high drama for this exhibition at London's Design Museum celebrating the 70th anniversary of Ferrari.

60 Pattern, gradation, and texture

TYPE INVITES INTERVENTION and experimentation. With sophisticated software, patterns, gradations, and textures are all relatively simple to try. Layered type has a fascination all its own, even if it is completely unreadable. It's reminiscent of everyone talking at once. Because we know there are thoughts, words, and phrases, it seems more meaningful than a pattern of any other kind, even if we can only glean a snippet of meaning here and there. Gradations offer another method to dimensionalize type.

Project
Cover

Company
Hopkins/Baumann

Creative Directors
Will Hopkins and
Mary K. Baumann

Illustrator
John Baxter

Client
Kids Discover

The cover lines form a block of '60s-style groovy letterforms; behind Shakespeare's (hipster-modified) head is a wonderful pattern of "psychedelic" text.

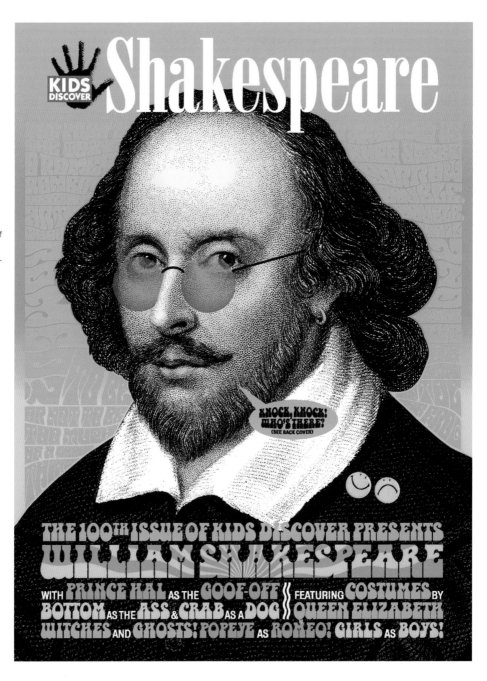

Project
Illustration

Art Director
Jennifer Daniels

Company
Studio of ME/AT

Designers
Mike Essl and Alexander Tochilovsky

Client
The New York Times

The word is formed as a pattern of computer icons.

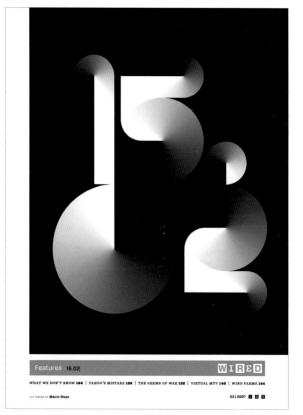

Project
Double Take

Design Director, Designer
Quentin Walesch

Client
Royal College of Art, London

Layered, reversed, translucent text areas are interleaved with highly legible information.

Project
Single page

Creative Director
Scott Dadich

Art Director
Carl DeTorres

Illustrator
Mario Hugo

Client
Wired

Large and small gradated and highly abstract text blocks appear throughout the magazine and contribute to its visual identity. When so many magazines tend to look alike, this typographic device is one element that separates *Wired* from its competitors.

The Paragraph 127

61 Basic leading principles

A GOOD RULE OF THUMB FOR TEXT TYPE is to add two extra points of leading. This creates a good comfort level for extended reading. However, when the typeface has strong verticals in relation to its horizontals and serifs, it will do better with a bit more leading. Extra leading adds some air between the lines and allows the eye to more easily distinguish the end of one line from the beginning of the next. The best way to determine how much leading you need for a particular passage of text is to set a good chunk of it with slight variations in leading. Even an extra quarter of a point can make a difference.

Project
Feature spread

Creative Director
Donald Partyka

Client
Americas Quarterly

Whether two or three columns, this format has sufficient leading for good legibility. This text is also highly legible due to its size, stroke width, and weight (strong typographic color).

A comparison of these two columns of text makes it clear at a glance that extra leading, especially when lines are long, makes for a more comfortable reading experience. Tight leading makes it more difficult for the eye to return to the next line from the end of the line above.

Project
Editorial spread
(shown here as a vertical
image)

Design Director
Blake Taylor

Designer
Blake Taylor

Client
Inc.

Each text block is fairly short
and self-contained, so a standard leading treatment (two
points more than the point
size) is fine. Look closely and
you will see that in a few
instances the leading is more
compressed, however,
legibility is not a problem
since the text blocks are fairly
narrow and have a limited
number of lines.

Not-So-Human Resources

From sleuthing candidates not actively on the job market to stripping
unconscious bias from your search, these new artificial intelligence tools will give
your HR department a high-tech upgrade. BY KATE ROCKWOOD

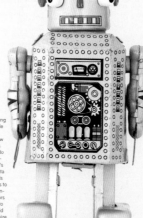

We Need More Interested Applicants!

Try an A.I. Matchmaker

► Two ex-Google engineering execs built Leap.ai, a platform that uses machine learning to analyze résumés, personal values, and job descriptions to suggest perfect-fit candidates for open roles. More than 70 percent of the people Leap puts forward make it past the first-round interview.

► Vettery's algorithms—used by companies like Peloton, Netflix, and ESPN—suggest matches from the thousands of candidates in its database. Thanks to machine learning, the more hiring managers interact with it, the smarter its A.I. gets about what your company wants.

FROM LEFT: GETTY/ISTOCK

CLOCKWISE FROM TOP LEFT: GETTY, ISTOCK (2)

Advertise the Opening

In years past, advertising a position on multiple job boards was a manual slog. But now PandoLogic makes predictive analytics do the hard work: Algorithms use a decade's worth of historical data on millions of job ads and thousands of sites to create a targeted campaign. Then it monitors the ads in real time to tweak budget and bid rate in order to maximize views and applications.

Look to the Past On average, companies receive 250 résumés for each opening—and many of those hopeful hires who don't land that gig could be a great fit for another role.
► *In April, Google started beta testing a tool called Candidate Discovery in its Hire by Google recruiting application, aimed at small and medium-size businesses. It uses intuitive search to scan past résumés and other data to rank which past applicants might be a match for the current role.*

▶ **Hunt for Passive Candidates** The unemployment rate is near its lowest level in 17 years, but more than 70 percent of employees say they are either actively looking for or are open to a new gig, according to a recent Indeed survey.

Finessing That Cold Call

Successfully cold-messaging a passive candidate takes skill, and most outreach falls on deaf ears. Just 5 percent of Americans have responded to a recruiter message in the past three months, according to a Textio survey.

Talenya

For those unable to fill a role, Talenya references hundreds of websites, including LinkedIn, GitHub, Stack Overflow, and Dice, as well as other public pages, to build rich candidate profiles. Then it compares those CVs with open positions—and scores the likelihood of a match.

Engage Talent

Wouldn't it be nice to know who is likely to jump at a job opportunity? A.I. platform Engage Talent uses "predictive availability signals"—like company performance, personnel changes, and news data—to calculate the odds that passive candidates might soon be dusting off their résumés.

Textio Hire's augmented writing platform uses millions of data points on previous messages—which words and phrases worked and which didn't—to offer real-time suggestions and red flags as you type. When Zillow tested the tool, the company says the response rate for its recruiting mail climbed 16 percent.

WE NEED TO MAKE HIRING LESS OF A TIME SUCK!

Employ a Chatbot Built with natural language processing and machine learning, a chatbot can field the repetitive questions candidates have, screen for basic qualifications, and schedule interviews.

Meet Mya
AUTOMATE THE COURTSHIP

► Mya chats up interested and passive candidates, and then screens, qualifies, and sends a conversation transcript to your applicant tracking system. If you greenlight an interview (or she does), she'll find a time that works for everyone on the team, coordinate with the hopeful hire, and update everyone's calendar.

S'Up, Ari?
WOO VIA TEXT

► IBM's Watson technology drives TextRecruit's chatbot Ari. But humans can also step in and send personalized text messages at scale. More than a third of applicants respond to the texts within 12 minutes.

Hi, Rai
GET YOURSELF AN HR ASSISTANT

► HiringSolved's Rai app, still in beta mode, currently communicates with recruiters, which means your hiring team can put it to work—finding candidates, refining your search, and interfacing with your email for outreach.

Hello, Olivia
LET YOUR BOT ROAM FREE

► What sets Paradox's Olivia chatbot apart is that people don't have to be in the applicant tool to engage with her. They can lob questions her way— *Why should I work at your company? What's the culture like? How's the vacation policy?*—through web, mobile, or social channels.

We Need a Better Way to Size Up Talent!

Put on Your Bias Blinders Many hiring managers default to Ivy Leaguers, or weed out those with attributes not similar to the age or ethnic makeup of their company. Don't leave incredible talent on the table just because they don't look like you.

Blendoor
GO COLORBLIND

► Airbnb and Twitter, among others, have tested Blendoor, which captures candidate data from whatever applicant tracking system you're using, and then removes info such as names, photos, and dates. This strips out details like race, age, and gender.

Interviewing.io
MASK ACCENTS

► Does a female voice or a foreign accent affect your hiring decision? Not with Interviewing.io, which runs interviews using voice-masking tools for tech candidates who pass rigorous mock interviews. Twitch, Lyft, and Asana are early embracers.

Test Their Skills, Not Their Talking Points

► You can set up coding interviews (even if you don't know how to write code) with Filtered's database of thousands of exercises, ranging from basic to advanced.

► GapJumpers steers job descriptions away from subjective filler like "passion" and "team player" and creates objective tests for candidates, pulling from more than 4,000 skill challenges. "This takes away the fear that hiring managers will lower the bar for quality, because they see the quality before they see the person," says CEO Kedar Iyer.

Pymetrics
Try to Clone Your Top Performers

Pymetrics leads your best employees through a series of neuroscience games to gauge traits—like risk-taking, focus, and fairness—and then candidates are put through the paces. Algorithms score how closely their traits align with those of top team members. Tesla, Unilever, and LinkedIn have jumped on this gamified A.I. platform.

Predict the Future

Other basic tools can scan a résumé. But Uncommon, which moved out of beta in February, has a predictive element: Using a candidate's previous experience—and redacting names, ages, and schools—the A.I. platform creates a merit-based profile. It ranks how well that person will meet or exceed job requirements, even if his or her résumé doesn't include a given skill. Before launching Uncommon, the team trained the platform on more than 50 million résumés and six million job descriptions. Then it had companies like Amazon, Lyft, and Etsy take it for a ride. When humans reviewed the platform's picks, they were in agreement 98 percent of the time.

62 Optimum line lengths

TWENTY PICAS IS A GOOD LENGTH to aim for when designing text type. Another common method for good legibility is to keep your measure between fifty-two and seventy characters per line (spaces and punctuation count as characters). This ensures that there will be enough words (and therefore word spaces) to accommodate justified type comfortably. Again, everything is relative, so optimum line length may vary based on typestyle, leading, tracking, and even the texture and tone of the printed surface.

spacing

line length

wider measure
needs more
leading

60 character
max

Four score and seven years ago our fathers brought forth on this continent, a new nation, conceived in Liberty, and dedicated to the proposition that all men are created equal.

Now we are engaged in a great civil war, testing whether that nation, or any nation so conceived and so dedicated, can long endure. We are met on a great battle-field of that war. We have come to dedicate a portion of that field, as a final resting place for those who here gave their lives that that nation might live. It is altogether fitting and proper that we

Four score and seven years ago our fathers brought forth on this continent, a new nation, conceived in Liberty, and dedicated to the proposition that all men are created equal.

Now we are engaged in a great civil war, testing whether that nation, or any nation so conceived and so dedicated, can long endure. We are met on a great battle-field of that war. We have come to dedicate a portion of that field, as a final resting place for those who here gave their lives that that nation might live. It is altogether fitting and proper that we should do this.

But, in a larger sense, we can not dedicate—we can not consecrate—we can not hallow—this ground. The brave men, living and dead, who struggled here, have

Four score and seven years ago our fathers brought forth on this continent, a new nation, conceived in Liberty, and dedicated to the proposition that all men are created equal.

Now we are engaged in a great civil war, testing whether that nation, or any nation so conceived and so dedicated, can long endure. We are met on a great battle-field of that war. We have come to dedicate a portion of that field, as a final resting place for those who here gave their lives that that nation might live. It is altogether fitting and proper that we should do this.

But, in a larger sense, we can not dedicate—we can not consecrate—we can not hallow—this ground. The brave men, living and dead, who struggled here, have consecrated it, far above our poor power to add or detract. The world will little note, nor long remember what we say here, but it can never forget what

Project
Single page

Design Director
David Curcurito

Art Director
Darhil Crook

Associate Art Director
Erin Jang

Design Assistant
Soni Khatri

Client
Esquire

This page (with its abundance of typographic "furniture") adheres in most places to the legibility guidelines for typographic measure. In two places, it violates those guidelines, but does so successfully: in the left margin, the callout has fewer than twenty characters per line, but the lines have been carefully ragged and tracked. And at the bottom of the page, the number of characters per line far exceeds the maximum number of recommended characters, but, because there are only two lines, legibility is not problematic.

THE SOUND & THE FURY

This Way In

THIS MONTH IN THIS WAY IN: *A letter from Rick Le Burkien! (page 42), new fiction (page 44), craft-beer suggestions from Rick Le Burkien! (page 46), things to do in Sandusky, Ohio (page 48), and a letter from a woman who might think we ruined her life (page 46).*

The January issue celebrated ten years of What I've Learned interviews. That's more than 180 notable minds, more than 1,000 pieces of wisdom, and, luckily, only one reference to Jimmy Kimmel's genitals.

WHAT YOU WROTE ABOUT:

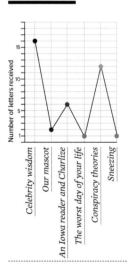

LESSONS LEARNED FROM WHAT I'VE LEARNED

Complementing new advice from Johnny Depp, Tim Burton, Michael J. Fox, and others in January were highlights from all ten years of What I've Learned, including a special interview with our mascot, Esky.

I do most of my reading in the sauna, and the January issue was no exception. I opened it up and couldn't put it down. Two hours later, I was a wrinkled prune.[1] Awesome. And thanks.

TOM J. INTIHAR
Brooklyn Park, Minn.

On December 22, I still had sixteen gifts to purchase. I was planning on giving things that would help my friends become better people in 2008—self-help books, mostly. Then I opened January's issue and discovered all the personal-growth, relationship, and career-building advice I wanted, from real people, shared in the most vulnerable and genuine way. For only $3.99.

RICK LE BURKIEN
Ukiah, Calif.

The photo that accompanied Michael J. Fox's What I've Learned interview is simply stunning. Alex P. Keaton is still there, but those are a man's fierce eyes looking out from the still-boyish face.

GREGORY TOD
Melbourne, Australia

I take great issue with your What I've Learned interviews. You always ask people who've already reached the pinnacle of their career for

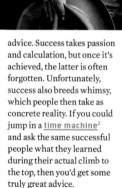

advice. Success takes passion and calculation, but once it's achieved, the latter is often forgotten. Unfortunately, success also breeds whimsy, which people then take as concrete reality. If you could jump in a time machine[2] and ask the same successful people what they learned during their actual climb to the top, then you'd get some truly great advice.

NEIL EDWARD ST. CLAIR
Martinsville, N.J.

A pox on you whipper-snappers who showed the much-revered Esky in such a dilapidated, indecent condition. Although he is only three years my senior, I respect him immensely. He led me to great writing, the fantastic art of Vargas, and sophisticated cartoons. My mustache, also over fifty, is based on his. To atone for this lack of respect, I suggest you bring this icon back to his rightful place on the cover, or, as a less acceptable alternative, as part of the masthead. On the spine, indeed.

LEE MALTENFORT
Savannah, Ga.

SURE, IT'S IMPRESSIVE, BUT SO IS READING
Convinced that he could identify the network responsible

HIGHLIGHT FROM A LETTER WE WON'T BE RUNNING "If I was going to have surgery, who knew how long I'd be out of the gym?"

---

(1) *The antioxidants in prunes may help reduce the risk of cancer. Luckily, whiskey has antioxidants, too. Some very good—and affordable—bottles are on page 77.*
(2) *H.G. Wells was twenty-nine when he published* The Time Machine *in 1895. We imagine he looked pretty young. For help doing the same, turn to page 80.*

PHOTOGRAPH BY MARC HOM

63 Increasing leading

SPACE BETWEEN LINES (LEADING) should be increased if the measure (line length) increases beyond the optimum range, or if the letterforms vary even slightly from a highly legible text face (designed to be read in quantity at small sizes). Even Bodoni, with its strong vertical strokes (in comparison to its horizontal strokes), may require a bit more leading to compensate. Increasing leading, even slightly, aids the eye in finding its place when it cycles back from the end of one line to the beginning of the next.

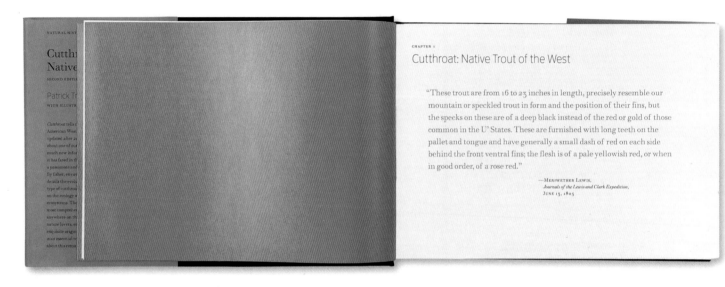

Project
Cutthroat: Native Trout of the West

Art Director
Charlie Nix

Designers
Charlie Nix and Gary Robbins

Client
University of California Press

The longish introductory quote is more legible (and more elegantly presented) with extra leading.

Project (opposite)
Single page

Creative Director
Donald Partyka

Client
Americas Quarterly

This airy text block has extra leading in keeping with the spacious graphic treatment and the other elements on the page.

Pisco

Chile 61.82%

Peru 38.18%

Rum

Barbados 24.94%

Jamaica 15.44%

Trinidad & Tobago 10.32%

Dominican Republic 8.55%

Anguilla 6.85%

Tequila

Mexico 99.99%

just the numbers

Liquor shelves in the United States are increasingly stocked with spirits from south of the Rio Grande. Tequila, pisco and rum imports have shot up in the last 10 years, reflecting U.S. consumers' thirst for some of our hemisphere's national drinks. AQ looks at the Latin American and Caribbean-produced spirits that Americans are drinking and where they come from.

Increases in Imports: 1997 and 2007

Pisco

1997 $127,715

2007 $521,566

Rum

$14,655,367

$53,408,547

Tequila

$129,379,228*

$595,249,921

*VALUES—NOT ADJUSTED FOR INFLATION—ARE ASSIGNED TO MERCHANDISE ENTERING THE COUNTRY BY THE U.S. CUSTOMS AGENCY. SOURCE: DISTILLED SPIRITS COUNCIL OF THE UNITED STATES (COMPILED FROM U.S. DEPARTMENT OF COMMERCE AND U.S. INTERNATIONAL TRADE COMMISSION DATA).

64 Tightly stacked lines

DECREASING LEADING and purposefully allowing ascenders and descenders to touch or even overlap should never be done with extended passages of text, but this can be used as a design device in limited quantities. Tightly stacked lines of capitals may be used to create a typographic mass without the worry of tangled extenders, but again, this is best when used only for a small quantity of text. Tightly stacking lines works against legibility, so care must be taken to employ this technique with restraint. When estimating just how much legibility may be affected, it is best to err on the side of minimally decreased leading.

Project
Cover

Creative Director, Designer
Maxine Davidowitz

Photographer
Firooz Zahedi

Client
More magazine

Tightly stacked and justified main cover lines are the hallmark of this cover aimed at older women; despite letters that touch, the text is eminently legible, partly due to differentiating each line with a distinct color. The touching lines set this text block apart from the other cover lines; this was intentional because the main lines contain the magazine's mission statement rather than highlighting specific content.

Project
Environmental graphics

Company
Pentagram

Art Director
Michael Bierut

Client
Museum of the City of New York

Part of a rebranding of the museum, this staircase was filled with quotes and images about New York City. The quotes are in a variety of weights of Titling Gothic, and they are all caps, and justified. The stacked lines and scale variations create drama and high impact in this vertical space.

65 Indicating paragraphs

THE MOST COMMON METHOD of indicating paragraphs is, of course, the indent. What is a matter of some debate is the length of the indent; however, at the very least, a minimum of one pica is needed to distinguish a new paragraph. A longer indent may be desirable depending on the column width. Other options include a line space between paragraphs—or somewhat less than a line space so there is less of a gap between lines and when scanning the text for color (one problem with this is that baselines will not align, and column lengths will vary). Another method is to set the copy so that the first line of every paragraph extends beyond the left-hand margin (also known as *outdents*). A more unusual method that preserves the flush look of the text block is to use paragraph ornaments to indicate new paragraphs.

Barbecue From Hell
The foam meat trays found in your local supermarket are made of expanded polystyrene, a petroleum product. *"Lighting it on fire is like burning gasoline,"* says Dennis Waters, a VP at insurance giant FM Global. The 1,500-degree inferno here was designed to find the best way of extinguishing a polystyrene blaze.

120   FAST COMPANY April 2008

Burn

This

An outsider might wonder how insurance giant FM Global stays in business. For one thing, staffers are constantly setting things on fire. Or blowing them up. Or swamping them. Some like to load pneumatic cannons with steel balls and launch them through plate-glass windows. "Our employees have no repression issues," says CEO and chairman Shivan Subramaniam. ¶ Things get even odder when you walk around the company's $80 million materials testing facility in West Glocester, Rhode Island, and realize

By **Paul Hochman**
Photographs by **Floto + Warner**

Project
Feature spread

Creative Director
Dean Markadakis

Designer
Jana Meier

Photographer
Floto+Warner

Illustrator
Reena de la Rosa

Client
Fast Company

The opening text block's first paragraph, set in a larger point size than the story that follows, begins with an extreme indent (it aligns vertically with the headline). Its second paragraph is indicated with a paragraph symbol in red, so that the text block can remain unbroken.

Project
Department page

Studio
Jeff Griffeth Creative

Creative Director
Jeff Griffeth

Designer
Jeff Griffeth

Client
Hallowed Ground
American Battlefield Trust

Ornate drop caps initiate text blocks while short paragraph indents indicate subsequent paragraphs.

Project
HotHouse exhibition catalog

Company
Studio of ME/AT

Art Director
Lucille Tenazas

Designer
Alexander Tochilovsky

Client
Cranbrook Art Museum

All lines are flush left with no indentations; paragraphs are indicated with line spaces. This works well with text that does not contain many short paragraphs and when there is sufficient space to accommodate line breaks.

66 Initial caps and drop caps

INITIAL CAPS MARK THE BEGINNING of a chapter or an article; drop caps may be used throughout the text to mark logical breaks in the text and to provide entry points for the reader. Drop caps may continue the style of the initial cap or be a variation of it. Drop caps and initial caps continue a long tradition that dates back to the earliest illuminated manuscripts (which often had entire scenes depicted within the counter spaces of the letterforms). There are many options for drop caps and initial caps: partial or full indents, partial or full outdents, tops flush with the body copy, baseline alignment with the first line of body copy, baseline alignment with any body copy, and baseline within the depth of the initial cap (these last two are called raised drop or initial caps). Some text does not lend itself well to an initial cap; most common are opening paragraphs beginning with a quote mark or punctuation, or when opening paragraphs are too short to accommodate the height of the cap.

Project
Feature spread

Design Director
Louis Fishauf

Designer
Louis Fishauf

Photographer
Pierre Manning

Client
Toronto Life

The initial cap is partially contained within the opening paragraph, and the wrap hugs its diagonal leg. Its vertical position matches the capital *A* in the headline, a nice touch of alignment.

Project
Feature spread

Design Director
Carla Frank

Designer
Erika Oliviera

Client
O, The Oprah Magazine

The initial cap sits partially within the text block and links into the photo; the top of its middle crossbar "kisses" the image. It intrudes upon the image, as does the pull quote at the top of the page.

Whether sweet or savory, a dish made with potatoes is just the most delicious part of any meal. Heavy on the starch, please.

There's something utterly simple and totally satisfying about red new potatoes smashed in a bowl and drizzled with nothing more than very good extra-virgin olive oil. A grind of pepper, a sprinkle of salt—and you're in heaven.

A little brown sugar and spice transforms a basic sweet potato into this scrumptious tart topped with a crunchy walnut streusel.

EVEN THE AIRLINES CAN'T RUIN POTATOES. "I THINK YOU could probably make them disgusting if you worked really, really hard," says Roy Finamore, author of the new cookbook *One Potato Two Potato*, "but you'd have to work with both hands for a week." So imagine the heights you can soar to with even the most minimal effort in the other direction. Here's one of Finamore's favorite potato recipes: Boil or bake; add salt. Sure, you can get fancy, preparing heirloom varieties with a bit more fuss, and the results can be incomparable—as O's recipe for fingerlings with asparagus, cherry tomatoes, and black olives proves resoundingly And, yes, those gorgeous purple Peruvians mashed with sour cream, spiked with pepper, and topped with sweet lime butter—can you *handle* that much pleasure? But potatoes aren't just a blank canvas. "As much as they accept almost any kind of flavor that you want to add to them," Finamore says, "on their own they're far from bland and innocuous, unlike, say, tofu." To him, the endless variety is "gravy"; the true glory of potatoes is in their democratic appeal. "The fact that there are really good potatoes that anybody can get from a grocery store is a great comfort," he says. "Potatoes are the people's food." ◆

210 OCTOBER 2001

Project
Feature spread

Creative Director
Donald Partyka

Photo Editor
Ramiro Fernandez

Photographers
Nicolas Villaume and
Aurora Seleet

Client
Americas Quarterly

This unusual version of an initial cap sitting on top of and aligning with the text column allows it to be scaled up; as an outline, it is lightweight and does not interfere with the overlapping headline.

Carlos Basombrio

:Re-Examine the War On Drugs.

Carlos Basombrio is a sociologist at the *Instituto de Defensa Legal* in Lima, Peru and a former Vice-Minister of the Interior Ministry. He is pictured here in Barranco neighborhood in Lima, Peru.

THE NEXT U.S. PRESIDENT HAS unique leverage to shape humanity's destiny. The disproportionate importance of the United States to the affairs of other countries creates a cruel paradox for those of us who are not U.S. citizens. We do not have the right to vote, but the outcome of the presidential elections will have a greater impact on Latin Americans—as well as on the citizens of other countries—than the outcome of our own local contests. We can only hope, therefore, that the policies which have caused such widespread damage over the last eight years will be replaced by significant and positive changes.

One area that calls for immediate re-evaluation is drug policy. It is time to discuss (together, instead of unilaterally) the anti-drug effort in the region. The United States has invested hundreds of millions of dollars to stop the flow of drugs to the north. The results are, to say the least, meager.

Recent figures show that the potential of Colombia, Peru and Bolivia to produce cocaine is even greater today than it was ten years ago. Any success against the drug cartels that can be claimed in Colombia is offset in Mexico, which has seen a great increase in drug trafficking. Moreover, Mexican society is now experiencing unprecedented levels of drug-

PHOTOGRAPH BY NICOLAS VILLAUME/AURORA SELECT

FALL 2008 Americas Quarterly 35

67 Opening paragraphs

THE APPEARANCE OF THE OPENING paragraph is as important as its content in drawing the reader into the text. There are myriad interesting ways to accentuate an opening paragraph that signals the beginning of a long passage of text. Some of these design directions may involve a different column width, a different point size (or mixing point sizes), leading, changing case, or some combination of the above. Small caps may be used as a transition from the initial drop cap to the body copy within the opening paragraph.

Project
Feature spread

Art Director
Francesca Messina

Designer
Donald Partyka

Client
Guideposts

An upside-down pyramid of text combines with the subhead, title, and byline to give an illusion of depth, tying in nicely with the facing photograph's runway perspective.

Our pilot opened the back doors
of the Bayflite 3 medical transport
helicopter and pushed aboard a stretcher.
I walked beside it, keeping a close eye on
the 10-day-old girl with weak lungs and a con-
genital heart problem who was in an isolette
on top. Beneath her was the equipment
monitoring her condition. Heartbeat.
Respiration. I checked the oxygen
saturation monitor. The
baby's levels were down...

A TRANSPORT NURSE,
A NEWBORN AND AN EMERGENCY
HELICOPTER RIDE GONE TERRIBLY WRONG

BAYFLITE DOWN

BY DIANE MUHL-LUDES, ST. PETERSBURG, FLORIDA

50 | GUIDEPOSTS

GOOD TO GO
Diane at the ready

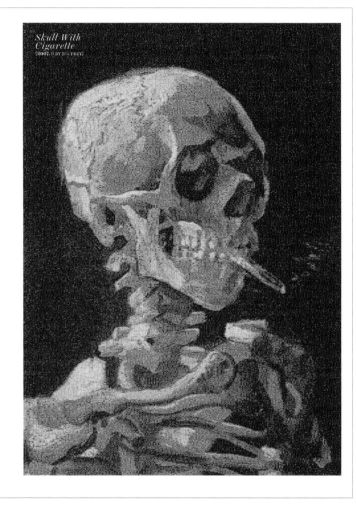

Skull With Cigarette
[2007, 6 BY 8¼ FEET]

Chris Jordan keeps his eyes open for staggering statistics, and the more alarming the better. What sets his 44-year-old heart racing is some new figure expressing American excess and neglect—the number of disposable batteries manufactured by Energizer every year (6 billion) or plastic beverage bottles used every five minutes (2 million) or children without health insurance (9 million). Think of him as the unofficial artist of the Harper's Index. ¶ The puzzle-like photographs he makes in response to these big numbers are designed to illustrate "the scale of consumption of 300 million people" and what such rampant profligacy, if unchecked, might mean for the future of the planet. He has completed 19 pieces for the sardonic series he calls Running the Numbers: An American Self-Portrait, and he has more in the works.

Figuring out how to translate what he calls the emotionless sums he finds in his research into visual metaphors that read on two levels is the challenge—a piece needs to be legible as one thing from afar and another up close. He recently finished a work dramatizing the 200,000 Americans who die every six months from smoking cigarettes. As you move toward the 6-by-8¼-foot print of a smoking skull—a macabre image lifted from Van Gogh—you realize it's as pixelated as a JPEG or a Chuck Close painting, with the kicker being that the portrait is composed of 200,000 cigarette packs. "When you stand back, you behold the collective, the forest," Jordan says. "But as you step closer, you see that it's made up only of individual trees. What I'm trying to suggest is that every individual matters. Our vote *does* count. If we do bad stuff, it *does* count."

After 10 years as a Seattle lawyer, Jordan opted out in 2003 to try his hand at large-format photography. He says one of his inspirations was *Powers of Ten*, the micro-macro picture of the universe by Charles and Ray Eames; another was staring at images from Google Earth. Despite his late start, he's doing well: His work is among the holdings of numerous museums and more than 100 private collectors.

The scale of his imagination is often defeated by the scale of what is feasible as a photograph. He has started a piece on the number of bullets fired in Iraq since the war began. But he calculates that even if he makes each bullet one-twelfth of an inch around, the work will have to be 60 feet high and 6,000 feet long. He would love to do a composition about oil or coal. "They deserve to be addressed brilliantly," he says. "But so far, nothing I've come up with honors the depth or complexity of the problem." Of course, as an industrial process dependent on chemicals and wood pulp, photography itself leaves a deep toxic footprint. "It's a question that I wrestle with," he says, sounding contrite. "It's hard to be a green advocate when I realize how deeply I'm implicated. But if I'm an alcoholic, we're all alcoholics. I'm like the guy who wakes up and asks, 'Hey, has anyone noticed the pile of empty vodka bottles in the corner?'" —*Richard B. Woodward*

Running Numbers →

200,000
Packs of Cigarettes

STANDS FOR THE NUMBER OF AMERICANS WHO DIE **every six months** FROM SMOKING

This piece was inspired by a news item. "Some diet pill caused the death of a baseball player," Jordan recalls. "An over-the-counter supplement had the potential to exacerbate a preexisting heart condition, and they immediately took it off the market. One person dies, and they pull it; more than 1,000 people died that day from smoking, and there's nothing done."

DETAIL

Project
Feature spread

Creative Director
Robert Priest

Designer
Jana Meier

Photographer
Chris Jordan

Client
Condé Nast Portfolio

This L-shaped opening paragraph "hugs" the following text; its slightly larger point size and wider leading, together with the bold lead-in and the large initial cap overlapping the text, leave no doubt as to where this story begins. Note the red paragraph indicator dingbat, which allows the text block to appear "solid," i.e., without a paragraph break that would not have filled out the space.

68   Orphans and widows

THESE REMNANTS ARE CARELESS and represent inattention to typographic niceties and detail. A good typographic "color" on the page is interrupted when a word or word fragment is alone on a line at the end of a paragraph or column (known as a *widow)* or, even worse, at the top of a column or page (known as an *orphan*). The reason an orphan is even worse than a widow is that it not only creates a gap in typographic color, but it also disrupts the horizontal alignment across the tops of the columns of text.

almost single-handedly transformed the school from a hidebound, traditional program into one that bred marketwise designers—just the entrepreneurial mind-set McComb was trying to instill at Liz Claiborne. A marketer to the marrow, he couldn't help but also appreciate that the Bravo breakout star was now a household name, gushed over by everyone from suburban moms to fashion plates like Sarah Jessica Parker. Gunn looked like money.

But Gunn was cautious. After nearly three decades as a college administrator, he had somehow landed on a hit TV show and become a pop-culture phenomenon. He routinely outshone the show's star—supermodel Heidi Klum—with his Victorian vocabulary, perfect posture, and prim Tim-isms ("Make it work!"

Tim Gunn's right eyebrow is shooting toward the sky like a boomerang. It's the signature gaze, filtered through a

pair of rimless glasses perched on his nose, that fans of reality television's *Project Runway* are used to seeing hurled at aspiring enfants terribles of fashion. But on this chilly morning in December 2006, Gunn's trained eye is on the suited businessman across the table. William McComb had invited Gunn to breakfast at Pastis, a bistro in Manhattan's Meatpacking District where pretty people with expense accounts linger *over oeufs* and brioches in an ersatz Parisian ambience. Now Gunn was waiting to hear what, exactly, the new CEO of Liz Claiborne Inc. was after.

Gunn had assumed McComb was just another new exec wedging his way into the anarchic and insular world of fashion. Two months earlier, McComb had left his senior post pushing orthopedic devices at Johnson & Johnson; no doubt he was reaching out for advice. But it turned out McComb had a different motive altogether. "I want you to be my first hire," the CEO proposed, nearly knocking the critic's designer socks off.

McComb knew that his $5 billion company had lost its creative juice. He wanted a chief creative officer, not to dictate product design but to put some meat on the bones of an atrophied design culture. The fact that Gunn ran Parsons's prestigious fashion program—the source of a good 70% of the designers on Seventh Avenue, from Anna Sui to Tom Ford—was key. He had a front-row seat to the industry's hottest emerging talent and a Rolodex that could be a serious weapon. What's more, McComb was intrigued by the Parsons turnaround story: Unknown to his TV fans, Gunn had

"Carry on!"). He was in the midst of writing his first book, *Tim Gunn: A Guide to Quality, Taste, and Style,* and by the fall would have his own fashion-therapy show on Bravo. "I was having the most fun I'd ever had in my life," says Gunn, 54. What's more, he had never worked for a company. "I had the greatest respect for the private sector, but I had never been part of it," he says, from his new office at Liz Claiborne headquarters in New York's Garment District. "The whole prospect of coming here was terrifying."

As it should have been. While Liz Claiborne the woman passed away last summer, Liz Claiborne the brand has been in a deep coma for years. Claiborne pioneered American women's wear in the 1970s; her impeccable designs, paired with her ability to reassess every aspect of the business—from merchandising to point of purchase—led her to become the first female founder of a Fortune 500 company. But by the time she retired in 1989, the company had plateaued. And by late 2006, the once-noble house had devolved into an unwieldy conglomerate that couldn't keep pace with newer, more stylish competitors. When longtime CEO Paul Charron retired, Liz Claiborne's board took a page from LVMH and Gucci, which had successfully imported consumer-products execs—P&G's Antonio Belloni and Unilever's Robert Polet, respectively—and brought in McComb, 45, to make radical changes. "I didn't come here because I love clothes," McComb says. "It's a business."

Whether McComb's hiring of Gunn in March 2007 was an act of desperation or inspiration is still unclear. Liz Claiborne stock is down sharply since McComb—one of the youngest CEOs in the industry—took over, despite his whacking jobs, shuttering brands, and reorganizing what's left. This January, he succeeded in luring another high-profile recruit: Isaac Mizrahi, the designer who jump-started discount mass fashion for Target and boasts his own shows on the Style Network and Oxygen (and even starred in his own one-man off-Broadway show, *Les Mizrahi*). He will become the Liz Claiborne brand's creative director this summer. With Gunn's help, McComb has also added fashion stalwart John Bartlett to reboot the Claiborne menswear line and acquired the critically acclaimed Narciso Rodriguez. Still, as Lori Holliday Banks, a senior fashion analyst at the Tobe Report, puts it, "There's no room for mistakes when a business is in the position that Liz is in right now." In mid-February, the company announced that earnings would fail to meet expectations, and the stock fell

---

F or one third of Esquire's seventy-five years, we've been heralding America's best restaurants—a chronicle of an era that saw France's nouvelle cuisine translated into New American cuisine, then fusion, global, and molecular cuisine. This year alone, we've chowed down fermented garlic, bacon-flavored peanuts, braised goat tacos, and soup for dessert. We've seen the rise of tea sommeliers and the near disappearance of tablecloths. And through it all, we've witnessed the emergence of American cooking as the most diverse and most innovative in the world. U.S. chefs born and schooled in every country in the world have mined their backgrounds and ingenuity to create a modern American food culture. Once again, after eating our way from coast to coast (hey, somebody's got to do it), we've narrowed it down to the twenty best new places to eat right now. Actually, make that twenty-one if you count your own dining room. (See page 92 to find out how.)

Zijp understands that when the strawberries are perfect, they need nothing more than a light marinade, a bit of meringue, and a small scoop of sorbet. All these dishes are richly satisfying, even homey. For all its modern white chicness, there is something comforting about Bar Blanc. And when you get up from the table, the owners seem really sorry you're leaving. *142 West Tenth Street; 212-255-2330; barblanc.com.*

BAR BOULUD
NEW YORK

Daniel Boulud grew up in Lyon, France, where his family ran a little café and his *maman* spoiled him with homemade charcuterie. Now,

BAR BLANC
NEW YORK

Sadly, enthusiasm and generosity of spirit don't always trump hype when it comes to a restaurant's endurance. But when you experience the kind of dedication and genuine hospitality of partners Kiwon Standen and Didier Palange at a jewel like Bar Blanc, you cheer it on (even if you'd prefer to keep it to yourself). Set in a former carriage house on one of the loveliest blocks in the West Village, Bar Blanc is a long sixty-seat dining room with white brick walls, white leather banquettes, and a twelve-stool white stone bar. Dutch-born chef Sebastiaan Zijp is a master at separating out the distinct flavors of each ingredient in a dish. Crispy sweetbreads lie on watercress made tangy with lemon vinaigrette and sweetened with sherry-poached cherries. Seared black cod is underpinned with spinach, roast sunchoke, and the anise scent of fennel, bathed in a saffron-mussel sauce.

Project
Single page

Creative Director
Dean Markadakis

Designer
Jana Meier

Client
Fast Company

Using a format with wide column measure means that partial line gaps left by widows are even more noticeable, so extra attention must be paid to filling out lines with text. This type-dense page with a wide measure carefully avoids widows and orphans.

Project
Single page

Design Director
David Curcurito

Art Director
Darhil Crook

Associate Art Director
Erin Jang

Design Assistant
Soni Khatri

Client
Esquire

The typographic color of this page is unbroken by widows or orphans. Note the presence of many rules, both double and single, color bars, elements that break out of the grid, and tiny directional arrows.

69 "Rivers" of space

GAPS THAT MOSEY THROUGH A PARAGRAPH of justified type link visually to form "rivers" of unsightly space, thereby ruining the evenness of tone (typographic color) of the text. The most common cause of rivers is a narrow column width combined with longish words. When the type is justified, word spacing increases to create the aligned edges, and when there are not enough words in a line to accommodate this adjustment comfortably, large gaps will occur. This decreases legibility; it is also a typographic eyesore.

spacing

line ⋯⋰ word
or
rivers

Four score and seven years ago our fathers brought forth on this continent, a new nation, conceived in Liberty, and dedicated to the proposition that all men are created equal.

Now we are engaged in a great civil war, testing whether that nation, or any nation so conceived and so dedicated, can long endure. We are met on a great battlefield of that war. We have come to dedicate a portion of that field, as a final resting place for those who here gave their lives that that nation might live. It is altogether fitting and proper that we should do this.

That, in a larger sense, we

Four score and seven years ago our fathers brought forth on this continent, a new nation, conceived in Liberty, and dedicated to the proposition that all men are created equal.

Now we are engaged in a great civil war, testing whether that nation, or any nation so conceived and so dedicated, can long endure. We are met on a great battlefield of that war. We have come to dedicate a portion of that field, as a final resting place for those who here gave their lives that that nation might live. It is altogether fitting and

Four score and seven years ago our fathers brought forth on this continent, a new nation, conceived in Liberty, and dedicated to the proposition that all men are created equal.

Now we are engaged in a great civil war, testing whether that nation, or any nation so conceived and so dedicated, can long endure. We are met on a great battlefield of that war. We have come to dedicate a portion of that field, as a final resting place for those who here gave their lives that that nation might live. It is altogether fitting and proper that we should do this.

Four score and seven years ago our fathers brought forth on this continent, a new nation, conceived in Liberty, and dedicated to the proposition that all men are created equal.

Now we are engaged in a great civil war, testing whether that nation, or any nation so conceived and so dedicated, can long endure. We are met on a great battlefield of that war. We have come to dedicate a portion of that field, as a final resting place for those who here gave their lives that that nation might live. It is altogether fitting and

Project
Inside page

Design Director
David Curcurito

Art Director
Darhil Crook

Associate Art Director
Erin Jang

Design Assistant
Soni Khatri

Client
Esquire

Mixing a variety of column widths skillfully, the text blocks on this page all have fine typographic color with no unsightly gaps or rivers.

Esquire's BEST NEW RESTAURANTS

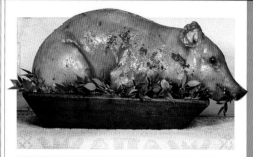

INGREDIENT OF THE YEAR

SUCKLING PIG

And that really means suckling: You can buy a young pig that has been weaned from its mother's milk, but it's just not the same. "The fat content isn't as high," explains Sal Biancardi of Biancardi Meats in New York. "A true suckling pig is chubby—the hindquarters are very fat, the color is pale white." During the cooking process, traditionally done slowly on a spit, the meat bastes itself, the fat oozes, the skin gets crisp as parchment. There's nothing wrong with that. But chefs across the country have been finding creative new ways to prepare and serve the pig, including the following from three of our best new restaurants.

CONFIT OF SUCKLING PIG, TERRA, NEW MEXICO
Charles Dale's version begins by rubbing the pork with Chinese five-spice powder and Spanish paprika, then simmering it in lard to make a soft confit, which is shredded, heated in pork stock, placed on a rice pancake, and dressed with a salad of pickled jicama, chives, chipotle hoisin sauce, and a paper-thin slice of Serrano ham—Peking pork, southwestern style.

SUCKLING PIG AL FORNO, SCAMPO, BOSTON
Lydia Shire pricks the skin with tiny holes, then rubs it with baking soda and vinegar. The meat is doused with a pomegranate-herb marinade. The pig is then splayed and roasted for an hour at a low heat, then blasted at 500 degrees for fifteen minutes to crisp the skin. Each plate is then loaded with thin slices of the leg, a whole large chop, and a big chunk of the shoulder—a Friday special.

MAIALINO DI LATTE, CONVIVIO, NEW YORK
Chef Michael White does a traditional Italian *maialino di latte*: He bones out a small twenty-pound Pennsylvania piglet, then grinds up the hindquarters meat and stuffs it into the body cavity, which is then rolled, tied, and roasted for two and a half hours, then sliced in generous slabs in its own juices.

MANSION RESTAURANT AT ROSEWOOD MANSION ON TURTLE CREEK
DALLAS

When chef Dean Fearing left the Mansion on Turtle Creek after twenty-one years to open his own namesake restaurant in the Ritz-Carlton (Esquire's Restaurant of the Year 2007), it nearly caused a management meltdown. Should they stick with the "New Texas Cuisine" style that Fearing pioneered? Or should the restaurant go in a completely new direction and risk alienating an already aging clientele? And should they allow…blue jeans? The final decision was to import veteran New York chef John Tesar and let him do his thing while revamping the dining room into three distinct spaces: a main à la carte dining room, a more luxe room offering prix-fixe menus, and a "Chef's Table" room, where Tesar cooks for six people according to his whim. And blue jeans are welcome, especially on the young Dallas women who now pack the place nightly for Tesar's cooking, which brings a New York edge to Texas swagger. Take his wagyu, caramelized in a red-hot skillet, then dressed with a truffle vinaigrette and raw fennel. He roasts guinea fowl until golden, then serves it with a casserole of seasoned French lentils, carrots, and bacon, and gilds it all with a potent reduction of foie gras and crème fraîche. Gamey rabbit is dressed up with fava beans, leeks, and tiny gnoc-

taurants have schlepped out to JetBlue's JFK terminal to cook—Italian (one of Mario Batali's crew), Mexican (a Rosa Mexicana vet), steak, tapas, and more—for the stopped-over, flight-delayed masses.

» LEAST ANNOYING LOCAL-FOOD MOVEMENT EXAMPLE
At the Healdsburg Bar and Grill, in northern California wine country, beyond the expected whites and reds on the list, one section offers wines produced within five square blocks of the restaurant, starting at thirty dollars a bottle.
» MOST UNNECESSARY BUT SATISFYING MANIPULATION OF AN INGREDIENT
At Foxtail, a lavish new place in West Hollywood, garlic is fermented in a bath of soy for a month, during which it turns tar-black, loses its spicy harshness, and takes on a molasses-y flavor. It then becomes

70 Eschew decorative type

SIMPLE, CLEAN, BASIC TYPESTYLING can be beautiful and effective; it is not necessary to embellish information in order for it to be appealing to the reader. Indeed, there is much to be said for leaving the bells and whistles to the display type, or to eliminate it altogether. Serious content is better served with a straightforward approach, and most informational text is best when treated simply. This creates good counterpoint: any accompanying images will be unencumbered by "noisy" typography.

Project
Poster

Company
Pentagram

Designer
Michael Bierut

Client
Yale University School of Architecture

Spare lines, minimalist typography, and plenty of wide-open spaces advance the architectural theme.

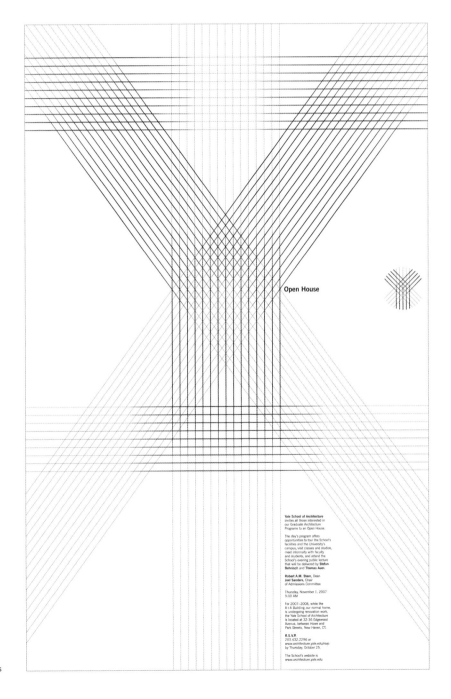

Project
Visual identity

Company
Remake Design

Design Director, Designer
Michael Dyer

Client
Art in General

Clean sans serif headlines and text are quietly authoritative.

04.17.08 – 05.03.08
High Risk Citizen **Video Program**
        The exhibition *High Risk Citizen* explores forms of political resistance and public engagement today, as considered by contemporary artists working in video. In this heated year of presidential electioneering, an ongoing, costly war in Iraq, and growing economic recession, both the precarity and possibilities of the moment are incredibly high. *High Risk Citizen* examines the stakes of active civic participation in an era of increased privatization and market- or wealth-driven access to state power. The works in *High Risk Citizen* move between depressed responses to the ways in which collective, political efficaciousness has been intentionally curtailed, and euphoric re-imaginings of sites of robust social and civic culture. While other forms of community affiliation (religious, military, or perhaps even consumer) are frequently invoked as possible substitutes, this exhibition revisits the role and affect of citizenship as one of potential tendentiousness, and questions how and what we are told about our relationship to government may be in conflict with how we constitute ourselves as a public.
        The program includes films by artists Peggy Ahwesh; Max Almy; Brian Boyce; Harun Farocki; Eric Fensler; Gabriel Fowler; Glass Bead Collective; Benjamin Gerdes; Neil Goldberg; Sabine Gruffat; Leopold Kessler; Emily and Sarah Kunstler; Les LeVeque; Jeanne Liotta; Van McElwee; Katherine McInnis; The Neistat Brothers; NYC Ya Basta; Mary Patten; Martha Rosler; Keith Sanborn; Shelly Silver; Brian Spinks, Eugene Mirman, and Bill Wasik; Daniel Tucker; The Yes Men; and Susan Youssef.

Exhibitions

04 05
04.17.08 – 09.13.08
Adrian Lohmüller Audio in the Elevator/Stairwell
        Adrian Lohmüller's practice spans a variety of media including video, film, site-specific interventions and performative events in public space. Much of his work plays with the borders of legality and requires him to attain an air of legitimacy by adopting the guises of construction worker, plumber, cleaning personnel, waiter, etc. According to these mimicries a flexible position can be found within institutional systems to encourage the de-automatization of habitual patterns. At the same time, subtle insertions of nonsensical components rupture this mimetic approach to prevent it from becoming a complacent, fail-safe methodology. Such interruptions incite hesitation in those who look closely, but without compromising the superficial appearance of authority established within the actions/artworks.
        Adrian Lohmüller was born in Germany and has traveled extensively in North and South America, Asia and the South Pacific. After completing his civil service in São Paulo, Brazil he moved to the United States and studied at the Maryland Institute College of Art (MICA) where he graduated with a BFA in 2006. During his studies, he acted as a curator in the artist-run space 5th story and began showing his work in diverse places such as Baltimore, Berlin, Innsbruck, Edinburgh, Chicago and New York. He now lives and works in Berlin.

Exhibitions

Project
Single page

Creative Director
Audrey Weiderstein

Art Director
Donald Partyka

Client
The Arthritis Foundation

A simple, justified text column, a subtle size shift leading into the body copy, and a modest headline treatment are appropriate for this serious medical information.

Juvenile Arthritis: A Primer

CHAPTER ONE
....

Getting Diagnosed: Steps and Obstacles

A nagging fatigue. A faint pinkish rash. A throbbing knee. A stubborn fever. A swollen hand.

Pain and swelling can flare unexpectedly one day, nearly immobilizing your once-active child as you shuttle between specialists, searching for answers. Or symptoms may be difficult to detect initially. Your child, particularly if she's quite young, may not recognize her discomfort as anything unusual. Or, she may adjust her activities and movements in ways that can be difficult to spot. She may rise more slowly from bed following a nap. You may one day realize that you can't recall the last time she jumped around the house, rattling the furniture. Something just doesn't seem... normal.

You are not alone.

Nearly 300,000 American children are currently diagnosed with a form of juvenile arthritis or an arthritis-related condition, living with some degree of pain and discomfort. That's more children than those affected by Type 1 diabetes, and many more — at least four times more — than those diagnosed with sickle cell anemia or muscular dystrophy, diseases that are much more widely known and discussed in the media. Children also can develop arthritis related to other autoimmune diseases, such as lupus.

ARTHRITIS FOUNDATION **3**

71 Celebrate decorative type

WHY NOT TAKE ADVANTAGE of all of the wild and wacky typefaces out there? Designers love to play, and decorative typography can be just the ticket to create something that is unique and memorable. Even a few splashy flourishes can demonstrate typographic virtuosity—a little "solo" or aria in the midst of sobriety might be just the touch that separates a design from its competition. Or a designer can choose the exuberant approach: pile on the style elements for effect—no limits to the excess!

Project
Halloween card

Designer, Illustrator
Marian Bantjes

Client
Marian Bantjes

Spot-varnished black-on-black typographic flourishes form a deep dark woods; in the "forest," we find a justified and underlined block of tightly packed text, an atmospheric frame for a spooky narrative about Halloween.

Project
Doyald Young Has Perfect Curves @80

Designer, Ilustrator
Marian Bantjes

Client
Marian Bantjes

A paean to fellow flourish-meister Doyald Young, this celebratory composition uses fluorescent inks for the roller-coaster ride of a message.

Project
Cover

Company
SpotCo

Art Director
Gail Anderson

Designers
Gail Anderson, Darren Cox, and Bashan Aquart

Client
STEP Inside Design

A collaged panoply of display forms, the cover provides engaging foreplay for a special issue on type.

72 Text overlapping images

LEGIBILITY ISSUES come into play when type overlaps images: the image demands our attention. To make the type stand out, type size and style, contrast with the background, and stroke weight all contribute to the important separation between the background and the foreground. Laying a few words of display type over an image can be complex enough, but where some designers go wrong is laying a quantity of text type over an image—this is sure to make reading a difficult task.

Project
Covers

Creative Director, Designer
Steven Hoffman

Client
Sports Illustrated

These covers demonstrate some good techniques for making sure that type is legible when overlapping complex details and many levels of contrast. The type must have enough weight and be large enough to stand apart from the images, but that is not always sufficient. A combination of outlines and hard and soft drop shadows provide separation and "lift" the text visually forward from the images.

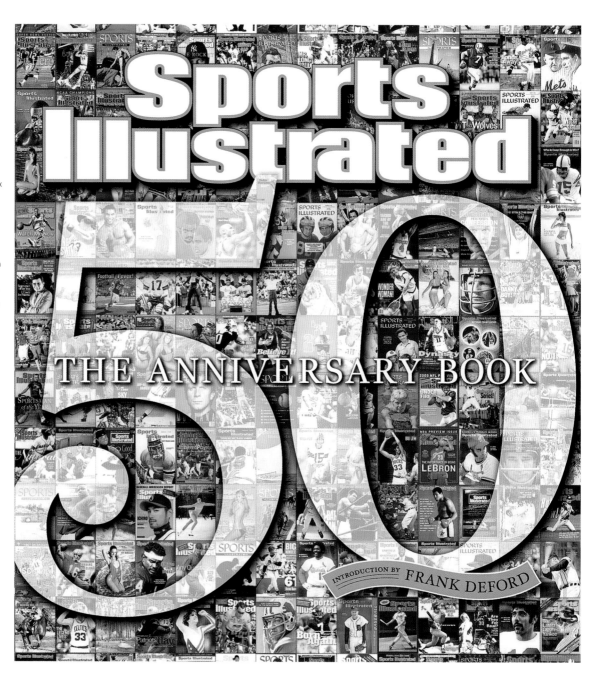

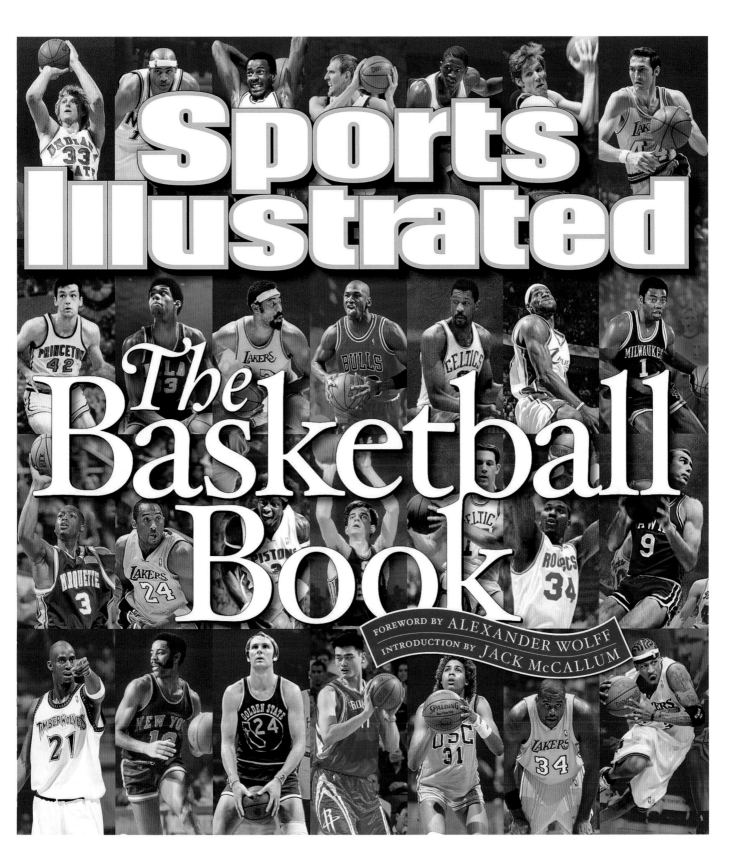

Sports Illustrated
The Basketball Book

FOREWORD BY ALEXANDER WOLFF
INTRODUCTION BY JACK McCALLUM

73 Text overlapping text

THE KEY TO SUCCESS when text overlaps text is differentiation, whether by scale, background and foreground contrast structure, or size. Again, legibility is paramount, so the designer must make certain that the overlap doesn't muddle the meaning. Separation can be accomplished using the same tools as just described for text overlapping images, but if all of the text is meant to be read, it is more difficult to maintain legibility than when part of an image may not be visible, however, its effect is still obvious.

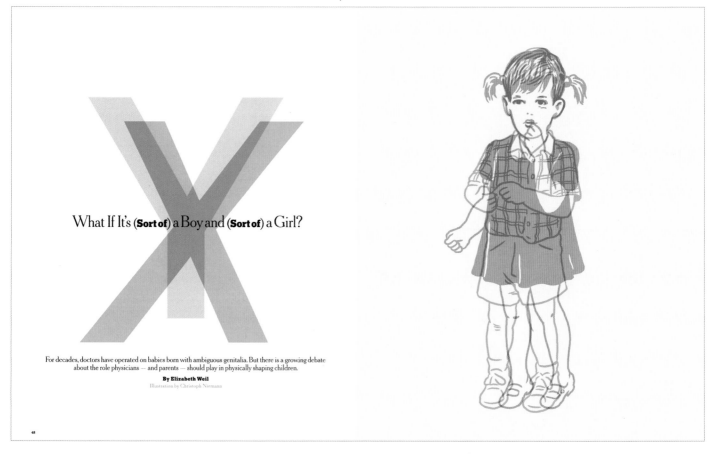

Project
Feature spread

Art Director
Arem Duplessis

Designer
Nancy Harris Rouemy

Client
The New York Times Magazine

Transparent letters representing chromosomes overlap and are bisected by the headline. This is a perfect marriage of meaning and type treatment for a story about hermaphrodites.

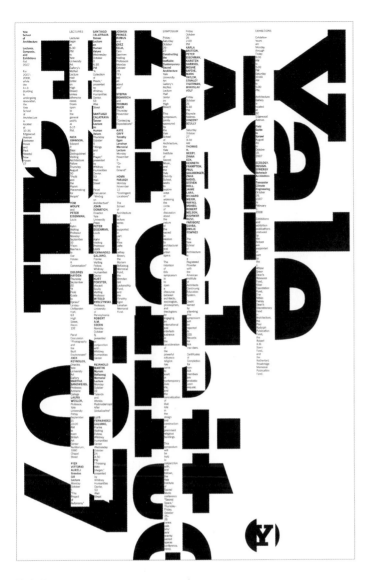

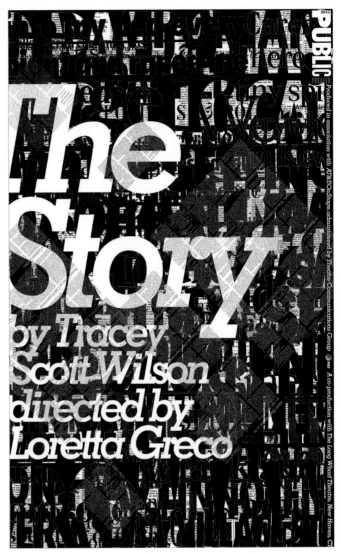

Project
Poster

Company
Pentagram

Designer
Michael Bierut

Client
Yale University School of Architecture

This poster uses a slicing technique with spaces running through the oversize text; the great disparity in size (the large type is still legible) makes this work. The bold slab serif provides visual punch and structure.

Project
Poster

Designer
Joe Marianek

Client
The Public Theater

The densely patterned backdrop of typography provides a strong, yet lively ground for the titling text (a weight slab serif) to be fully legible in reversed-out type.

74 The text block effect

WORDS BEG TO BE CLUSTERED TOGETHER to form chunks. One of the many arrows in a designer's quiver is the text block effect: look at the content and see how it can be packed inside a rectangle or square, aligned on all sides. Sometimes this can be accomplished by keeping the text all one size; other designs require massaging point sizes and varying weights and widths to achieve a solid shape. These efforts work best when the text is a single typestyle or type family.

Project
Cover

Company
Hopkins/Baumann

Creative Directors
Will Hopkins and
Mary K. Baumann

Designer
Preeti Menon

Photographer
Erik Vogelsang

Client
Kids Discover

Multicolored headlines stack up, interwoven with mini-illustrations, and are a lively static counterpoint for the "hair-raising" cover image.

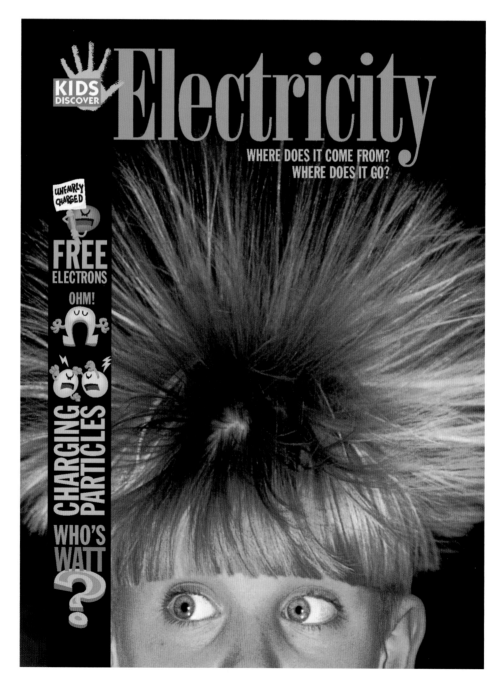

Project
Social media announcement

Art Director
Vera Naughton

Designer
Vera Naughton

No worries here about type families conflicting—using only one typeface (Helvetica Condensed) in light, regular and bold weights assures visual unification on the project; color and size add variety and hierarchy.

Project
Public Architecture

Creative Director, Designer
Jeremy Mende

Client
Public Architecture

Clean, balanced running text and contact information in all one size, style, and weight are headed up by the company name to form a tidy block, with contact info highlighted in red.

PUBLIC ARCHITECTURE
PUTS THE RESOURCES OF ARCHITECTURE IN THE SERVICE OF THE PUBLIC INTEREST. WE IDENTIFY AND SOLVE PRACTICAL PROBLEMS OF HUMAN INTERACTION IN THE BUILT ENVIRONMENT AND ACT AS A CATALYST FOR PUBLIC DISCOURSE THROUGH EDUCATION, ADVOCACY AND THE DESIGN OF PUBLIC SPACES AND AMENITIES. 1211 FOLSOM STREET, 4TH FLOOR, SAN FRANCISCO, CA 94103-3816 T 415.861.8200 F 415.431.9695 WWW.PUBLICARCHITECTURE.ORG

75 Theory of Relativity III

ALL TYPOGRAPHIC ELEMENTS within the paragraph have a relationship of each to every other, and all to the whole. The reader must see a clear hierarchy and elements must be legible. For a designer, balancing all of the typographic elements is one of the greatest challenges. Even slight adjustments in text characteristics (tracking, size, color, weight, slope, etc.) can clarify content.

Project
Single page

Creative Director, Designer
Steven Hoffman

Client
Sports Illustrated, The Baseball Book

A balanced, centered layout with elegantly fine-tuned typographic details, this single page packs information densely yet effortlessly. The small caps lead-in to the body copy is simple, yet it creates a clear entry point and does not compete with the restrained flourishes in the headline. Shifts in weight, case, and color clarify content and hierarchy in the player identification and the copy block below identifying the judges.

SI's ALLTIME ALL-STAR TEAM

WHO WOULD YOU RATHER HAVE: Mays or Mantle? Koufax or Spahn? Berra or Bench? Aaron or Williams? This is the classic baseball argument, sublime in its infinite variety. Gehrig or Musial? Robinson or Hornsby? Cobb or DiMaggio? ⚾ Any real fan could take either side of such debates and argue persuasively, but every real fan would also have an unshakable conviction about who was the better player. Wagner or A-Rod? Eckersley or Rivera? Young or Mathewson or Clemens? And though it is the nature of the game — indeed, a vital part of its appeal — that the debate will never end, SPORTS ILLUSTRATED polled a panel of current and former baseball writers and editors and distinguished outside experts to select our dream team. Voters received a ballot listing a total of 246 position players, pitchers and managers (along with a spot for write-in votes) and were asked to rank their preferences at each position to create a 25-man roster, plus a manager and two coaches. The resulting team, brought together for the first time in this portrait created by photo illustrator Aaron Goodman, is a pretty fair bunch of ballplayers. But so is the second team, the guys who didn't quite make the cut: Josh Gibson, Jimmie Foxx, Joe Morgan, Rod Carew, Ernie Banks, Cal Ripken Jr., George Brett, Brooks Robinson, Barry Bonds, Oscar Charleston, Roberto Clemente, Rickey Henderson, Bob Gibson, Grover Cleveland Alexander, Greg Maddux, Tom Seaver, Nolan Ryan, Bob Feller, Satchel Paige, Steve Carlton, Pedro Martinez, Rollie Fingers and Goose Gossage. ⚾ So who would you rather have?

PHOTO ILLUSTRATION BY AARON GOODMAN
UNIFORMS BY MITCHELL & NESS

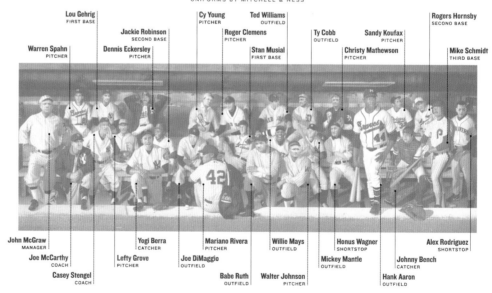

Lou Gehrig FIRST BASE · Cy Young PITCHER · Ted Williams OUTFIELD · Rogers Hornsby SECOND BASE

Jackie Robinson SECOND BASE · Roger Clemens PITCHER · Ty Cobb OUTFIELD · Sandy Koufax PITCHER

Warren Spahn PITCHER · Dennis Eckersley PITCHER · Stan Musial FIRST BASE · Christy Mathewson PITCHER · Mike Schmidt THIRD BASE

John McGraw MANAGER · Yogi Berra CATCHER · Mariano Rivera PITCHER · Willie Mays OUTFIELD · Honus Wagner SHORTSTOP · Alex Rodriguez SHORTSTOP

Joe McCarthy COACH · Lefty Grove PITCHER · Joe DiMaggio OUTFIELD · Mickey Mantle OUTFIELD · Johnny Bench CATCHER

Casey Stengel COACH · Babe Ruth OUTFIELD · Walter Johnson PITCHER · Hank Aaron OUTFIELD

THE JUDGES BILL JAMES *Author, Analyst, Boston Red Sox* ⚾ PETER GAMMONS *ESPN* ⚾ STEVE HIRDT *Elias Sports Bureau, Executive Vice President* TIM KURKJIAN, *ESPN* ⚾ STEVE WULF *ESPN the Magazine, Executive Editor* ⚾ DANIEL OKRENT *Author/Editor* ⚾ KEITH OLBERMANN *MSNBC, ESPN* JOHN PAPANEK *ESPN New Media, Senior VP/Editorial Director; former SI Managing Editor* ⚾ MARK MULVOY *former SI Managing Editor* ⚾ BILL COLSON *former SI Managing Editor* ⚾ ROBERT CREAMER *SI Special Contributor* ⚾ RON FIMRITE *SI Special Contributor* ⚾ DAVID BAUER *SI Deputy Managing Editor* ROB FLEDER *SI Executive Editor* ⚾ MICHAEL BEVANS *SI Executive Editor* ⚾ DICK FRIEDMAN *SI Senior Editor* ⚾ DAVID SABINO *SI Associate Editor* LARRY BURKE *SI Senior Editor* ⚾ TOM VERDUCCI *SI Senior Writer* ⚾ STEVE RUSHIN *SI Senior Writer* ⚾ RICK REILLY *SI Senior Writer* ⚾ ALBERT CHEN *SI Writer-Reporter*

spacing

letter
PROPORTIONAL TO

word
PROPORTIONAL TO

line spacing
(leading)
PROPORTIONAL TO

line length

Four score and seven years ago our fathers brought forth on this continent, a new nation, conceived in Liberty, and dedicated to the proposition that all men are created equal.

Now we are engaged in a great civil war, testing whether that nation, or any nation so conceived and so dedicated, can long endure. We are met on a great battlefield of that war. We have come to dedicate a portion of that field, as a final resting place for those who here gave their lives that that nation might live. It is altogether fitting and proper that we should do this.

But, in a larger sense, we can not dedicate—we can not consecrate—we can not hallow—this ground. The brave men, living and dead, who struggled here, have consecrated it, far above our poor power to add or detract. The world will little note, nor long remember what we say here, but it can never forget what they did here. It is for us the living, rather, to be

---

Project
Feature spread

Creative Director
Dean Markadakis

Designer
Jana Meier

Photographer
Howard Cao

Client
Fast Company

This spread contains a great deal of information, and its elements all support one another. For example, the serif weight on the initial cap matches the weight of the horizontal bar with dropout type, which introduces the sidebar. The black and yellow of the dotted rule is repeated in the dingbats illustrating the sidebar. The three-column, justified format has good weight and even color, and provides enough entry points to make certain the reader feels invited into the text.

Making cement without also making carbon dioxide seems impossible; the basic chemistry of the process releases the gas. But maybe that's not really true, Stanford University scientist Brent Contstantz began thinking last year. Of course, it was only a theory, he told himself, but the market for cement is so large—about $13 billion annually in the United States alone—and the pressure to reduce its effect on the environment so strong that he sent a 12-line email to venture capitalist Vinod Khosla.

"I have an idea for a new sustainable cement," Constantz wrote. "I'm sure you are already aware that for every ton of [standard] Portland cement produced, approximately one ton of carbon dioxide is released into the atmosphere. My cement wouldn't do that; in fact, it would remove a ton of carbon dioxide from the environment for every ton of cement produced."

Khosla, who knew Contstantz only casually—the two hadn't been in touch for 20 years—was on vacation. But after a discussion that lasted only an hour, he told the scientist, "I don't care about the rest of the business plan. You don't need to estimate costs. You don't need to do a cash flow. You don't need to do a presentation. Just hire five people, set up a lab, and go."

Contstantz was astonished. "What we're up to," he warned, "takes balls."

"Well, you've got the money now," was the response. "Get busy."

It was a classic performance from Khosla, a man who "enters any chamber believing he's the smartest man in the room," in the words of one longtime VC.

Over the past four years, Khosla has become the world's foremost investor in environmental start-ups. He has committed an estimated $450 million of his personal fortune to financing 45 ethanol factories, solar-power parks, and makers of environmentally friendly lightbulbs, batteries, and automotive components. These investments have made him the most prominent of an increasingly rare breed, the so-called angel investors who put their own funds into the youngest of companies—including outfits that are pursuing the most innovative, but not yet commercially viable, approaches to serious problems such as global warming.

"In 30 seconds, in one paragraph, I knew this was worth doing," Khosla says now, adding that the cement startup, called Calera, "may be our biggest win ever."

It's a kind of seed-stage investing that traditional venture funds have largely abandoned. And rightly so, Khosla says. "If somebody comes to you with a cold-fusion idea, you should not be funding it as an investor with other people's money. Funding it, if they're credible people, as a science experiment, as a hobby, is perfectly okay—as long as it's your own money."

Khosla's green investing has made him something of a celebrity, mentioned in the media with the likes of mogul Richard Branson, former President Bill Clinton, Hollywood producer Stephen Bing, and General Motors chairman and CEO Richard Wagoner. I've known Khosla since his days as a recent immigrant from India more than two decades ago but hadn't seen him in years until we met in his office in Menlo Park, California, earlier this year. Khosla Ventures is tucked away in an unprepossessing corner of a redwood complex of small offices. The decor is rental-furniture bland. The only reading set out for visitors is a four-month-old issue of *National Geographic* with a cover story on biofuels. Khosla's own office is spare, with 15 large black-and-white photographs of his four children on the walls. For others in the firm, office dress is Silicon Valley casual—jeans, fleece vests, and running shoes—but Khosla arrives more elegantly attired, in taupe slacks; a chocolate long-sleeve, zip-neck knit shirt; and slip-ons in luggage tan with leather bows and kilties. He's 53, a slender 5-foot-10, genial and looking relaxed despite the prominent dark circles under his eyes.

Although he lives near his office, this morning he has already driven one of his daughters to school in San Francisco, a 90-minute round-trip that he makes every weekday in order to spend time alone with her. Later, he'll review several business proposals, prepare to interview three new investments and the hiring of an operational manager for his firm, and polish his remarks for an appearance at the United Nations. To meet with me, he has taken a break from writing a position paper on where the world will get the biomass it needs for oil independence. He writes two or three such papers a month, averaging more than 100 pages a year. "Nobody wastes less of the time in his life than Vinod," says venture capitalist Roger McNamee, whose office at Integral Capital Partners was for a decade just down the hall from Khosla's, at the storied Silicon

---

Valley partnership of Kleiner Perkins Caufield & Byers.

During nearly two decades at Kleiner Perkins, Khosla lost far more often than he won. He wasn't responsible for the firm's best-known successes of his era—Amazon, Netscape, and Google. By any reckoning, he was most closely involved with 42 startups. Most were sold or closed, although a few still operate privately. Eleven, however, went public (mostly during the dotcom bubble). That's better than 25%—not at all bad in the VC world. And measured by return on invested capital, Khosla's record has been outstanding. His half-dozen best deals at Kleiner Perkins multiplied $314 million in investments into $15 billion in cash and stock—an increase of nearly fifty-fold, and five times more than all the money invested in all 42 companies.

It was at the peak of his success in late 2000 and early 2001—when *Fortune* named him the "most successful venture capitalist of all time" and he later appeared on the

covers of two other national business magazines in a single week—that he decided to change. Shares in his most successful company, Juniper Networks, were trading at more than 40 times their offering price a year and a half earlier. But he foresaw a bleak near future for optical networking equipment, in which he had made his name. Just as telecom stocks, including Juniper, were reaching all-time highs, he warned in a keynote at a Goldman Sachs conference that at least one of the industry's most famous companies would soon be bankrupt. "If I really believed what I was saying, I told myself, then it was time to look elsewhere," he recalls.

Around that time, a friend introduced him to a space-research scientist with a business idea unlike any Khosla had considered before: generating electric power from water, oxygen, and natural gas. Seven years later, the company, now known as Bloom Energy, has yet to introduce its first product, but Khosla marks

his initial support for it as a turning point in his career. "I knew then I wanted to go green," he says. In 2004, he struck out on his own. "I felt that energy needed more exploring than a responsible venture fund should do," he says.

At Khosla Ventures, he has put his own money into graphics-display, datacenter, and wireless technologies, but environmental startups are what excite him. He has been on a campaign to end American dependence on petroleum since oil was trading at a quarter of its present price. Unlike more famous former partner at Kleiner Perkins, the energetic John Doerr—who has choked up onstage recounting his daughter's worries about climate change—Khosla is unemotional about going green. He hopes to improve the world by developing, for example, cleaner-burning coal and cars that run leaner, but his more fundamental motivations seem to be the size of the potential market and, even

---

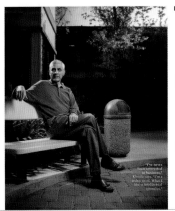

"I've never been interested in business." Khosla says. "I'm a techie in oil. What I like is intellectual stimulus."

khosla's green ventures

MOST OF VINOD KHOSLA's environmental startups are efforts to reduce our dependence on petroleum—both by making better use of oil and by finding other sources of liquid fuel. The rest address solar and geothermal power and desalination of seawater. Very broadly, his green-tech portfolio falls into three clusters.

 Fuel Efficiency: To lower the cost of driving, EcoMotors and Nanostellar are rethinking the diesel engine, Transonic Combustion is improving fuel injection, and Tula is at work on new versions of microprocessors that monitor the operations of today's cars.

 Alternative Fuels: Creating and refining ethanol are Cilion, Coskata, Ethos, Hawaii BioEnergy, LanzaTech, Mascoma, Praj, and Range Fuels. Amyris Biotechnologies, Gevo, KiOR, and LS9 are trying to commercialize other substitutes for petroleum.

Electric Power: Firefly Energy, Sakti3, and Seeo focus on batteries; Group IV, Kaai, Lumeta, Soexa, and Topanga, on lighting; Ausra, Infinia, and Stion do solar power; Altarock is in geothermal; and Great Point Energy aims to make clean-burning gas from coal.

94 FAST COMPANY July/August 2008

July/August 2008 FAST COMPANY 95

76 Legibility, legibility, legibility

'NUFF SAID. Like real estate's mantra (location, location, location), type exists to serve content, so its primary goal should be the ability to invite the reader to apprehend the content. Many factors can affect legibility, and the combination of factors also has an effect on legibility. Designers enamored with their own cleverness often underestimate the amount of time readers are willing to spend to get through the text. (Just because you design it does not mean they will come!) Once upon a time, blackletter (below) was considered legible. But it's a turnoff for our modern eyes.

Project
Feature spread

Creative Director
Robert Priest

Designer
Jana Meier

Illustrator
Tavis Coburn

Client
Condé Nast Portfolio

Complex stories need special clarity, not only in the legibility of the text type but also in every text element on the page. Providing mini-headlines, keying caption information using numbers or other identifiers, and highlighting important concepts all provide good service to the reader.

Decoding SPY-Speak

EX-AGENTS BRING *covert lingo* TO THE WORLD OF CORPORATE ESPIONAGE

PRETEXTING
Obtaining information by pretending to be someone else. Federal laws prohibit using a false identity to get someone's bank, financial, or telephone records, but claiming to be a reporter or job recruiter to extract other kinds of information is *generally legal.*

DATA HAUNTS
Methods for collecting electronically available information about someone *without leaving any trace.* These include intercepting emails by using secretly installed keystroke-logging software, illegally obtaining phone and bank records, and monitoring corporate-jet trips by identifying tail numbers.

SPY COUNTRY
An investment firm owned by Bill Gates (1) has used ex-C.I.A. polygraphers. Former F.B.I. and C.I.A. chief William Webster (3) advised two firms with former intelligence agents. The detective agency started by Jules Kroll (2) was one of the first to hire C.I.A. agents. Mississippi governor Haley Barbour (4) and ex-ambassador Richard Burt (5) were Diligence investors. Former federal agents working for Wal-Mart uncovered intimate emails from Julie Roehm (6).

MOST OF THE EX-AGENTS' activities, from surveillance to lie detection, are perfectly legal.

FALSE FLAGGING
Pretending that your client is the target of your investigation in order to *elicit candid comments* from business partners and rivals. This can help reveal who is bad-mouthing your client.

DUMPSTER DIVING
Recovering trash and other discarded material from a target's office or home. It's *pretty common* and is legal under most circumstances, such as when garbage is at the curb.

HARD SHOULDER
Digging up negative information as *leverage to persuade someone* to do what you want. Giving the hard shoulder was originally coined by Israeli intelligence agents.

(continued on page 145)

87

GAA MEDAL

This gold medal was presented to a Limerick player, P.J. Corbett, a member of the team that won the first all-Ireland Gaelic football championship final. On 1 November 1884, at Hayes's Hotel in Thurles, Co. Tipperary, Michael Cusack convened the first meeting of the 'Gaelic Athletic Association for the Preservation and Cultivation of National Pastimes'. Cusack had been an enthusiast for rugby and cricket. Another of the prime movers, Maurice Davin, was an accomplished all-round athlete. In the atmosphere of the 1880s, they and others were now determined that Ireland should have its own distinctive sporting culture. The GAA thus set out to take control of Irish athletics, to codify the ancient sport of hurling and to develop Gaelic football, a version of the game influenced by both rugby and soccer. Indeed, in its first two or three years, it was the GAA's athletics events that were its most popular aspect.

In one sense, the GAA was a very 'British' development, part of the great Victorian drive to codify all kinds of games and turn them into popular spectacles. Thus, although it found its greatest support among the growing class of 'strong farmers', the GAA was in many ways a typical product of nineteenth-century modernisation. All over Europe, a new popular nationalism looked to culture as the basis for a collective identity that could bind together an increasingly literate and mobile population.

In Ireland, these notions had a particular appeal. After the fall of Parnell, the parliamentary Irish party was bitterly split and Home Rule was a more

Project
Tablet app

Creative Direction
Joe Zeff Design

Client
A History of Ireland in 100 Objects

A single justified column of a roman (book) weight of sans serif with generous margins provides a comfortable on-screen reading experience. Generous leading, margins, and sizes are even more important for legibility of screen-based media (light-emitting devices).

77 Legibility taking a back seat

THERE ARE REASONS WHY legibility might not be a designer's primary concern. When type is treated as an image, it can communicate on a different level. Type can be manipulated or used in such a way that it is difficult or impossible to read and still play a pivotal role in the reader's understanding of the text.

Project
Feature spread

Creative Director, Designer
Dirk Barnett

Photographer
Rennio Maifredi

Client
Blender

This artist's appearance was clearly the inspiration for the opposite text treatment; a youthful audience of music lovers will undoubtedly be more interested in appearances than content (as it takes a great deal of effort to decipher this text).

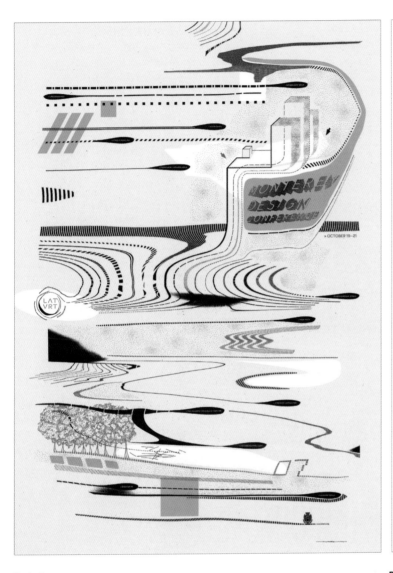

Project
Lateral + Vertical

Design Director
Jeremy Mende

Designers
Amadeo DeSouza, Steven Knodel, and Jeremy Mende

Client
American Institute of Architects, California Council (AIACC)

This poster for a design conference does provide some basic information, but it must be searched out amid the woozy graphics; since the readers are likely an audience of designers, they are probably willing to make the effort.

Project
Poster

Company
Henderson Bromstead Art Co.

Client
Triad Health Project

The text is so embedded in the gridded imagery that we can scarcely make it out, but it is repeated at the bottom left. The poster is coveted as memorabilia from the event, but it "pushed the decorative envelope," says the designer.

78 Limiting typefaces

WHEN WE CHOOSE DIFFERENT TYPEFACES to work side by side in the same document, every pairing has the possibility for conflict; do these typefaces, designed by different designers, from different historical classifications, with different characteristics, work together? Is there really a need for each of them, i.e., do they perform essential functions? Is there enough difference between them to justify employing them? These are some of the questions that designers must ask themselves. Too many (unnecessary) choices can result in "type soup."

Project
Dino-Rama

Art Director, Designer
Charlie Nix

Client
Barnes & Noble

This project uses just one condensed display typeface, always in the same weight and always all caps. The choice works well with the very lengthy dinosaur names, allowing the text to have a large x-height and presence on the page.

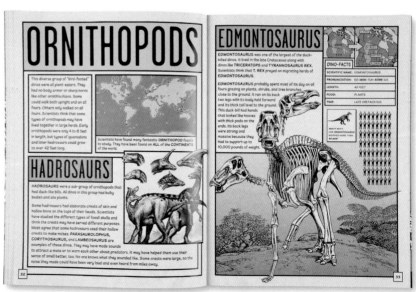

Project
T-shirt

Art Director
Aaron Belyea

Designer
Chris Piascik

Client
Big Honcho Media

One typeface does double duty when filled with a pattern.

Project
Book cover

Art Director
Roberto De Vicq

Designer
Roberto De Vicq

Illustrator
Roberto De Vicq

Client
Memoria Visual

No worries here about type families conflicting—using only one typeface, PF Regal, assures visual unification on the project; color and size add variety for a lively and fun effect. An especially charming detail: the use of different colors within single letters.

79 One type family

SOME TYPE FAMILIES ARE BROAD and contain within them a hearty bounty of options, useful for a wide variety of typographic needs. And the inherent benefit to sticking with one family is that the type designer has already created a harmonious grouping of proportion and shape. We do n[ot] need to guess whether these variations belong together; t[hey] are designed to be familial and therefore comfortable wit[h] one another.

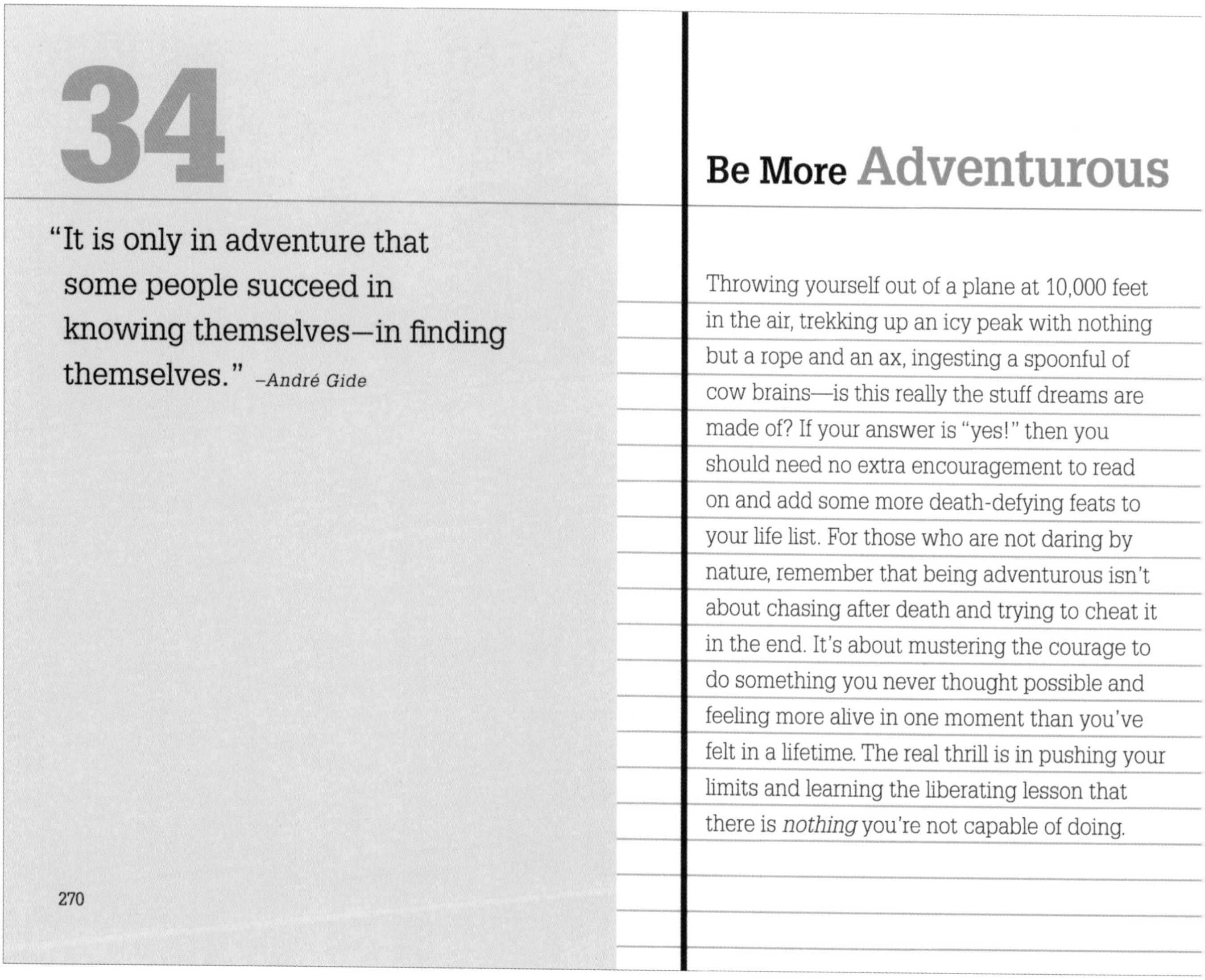

34

"It is only in adventure that some people succeed in knowing themselves—in finding themselves." *—André Gide*

270

Be More Adventurous

Throwing yourself out of a plane at 10,000 feet in the air, trekking up an icy peak with nothing but a rope and an ax, ingesting a spoonful of cow brains—is this really the stuff dreams are made of? If your answer is "yes!" then you should need no extra encouragement to read on and add some more death-defying feats to your life list. For those who are not daring by nature, remember that being adventurous isn't about chasing after death and trying to cheat it in the end. It's about mustering the courage to do something you never thought possible and feeling more alive in one moment than you've felt in a lifetime. The real thrill is in pushing your limits and learning the liberating lesson that there is *nothing* you're not capable of doing.

Project
Book spread

Art Director, Designer
Francesca Messina

Client
Workman Publishing

A text-weight slab serif is used for body copy; weightier versions in the family are employed for display.

Project
Battle of Amsterdam 2008

Creative Director, Designer, Illustrator
Donald Beekman

Client
Amsterdam City Council

This lively graphic campaign uses just one family. Note the green-on-green background pattern of letterforms.

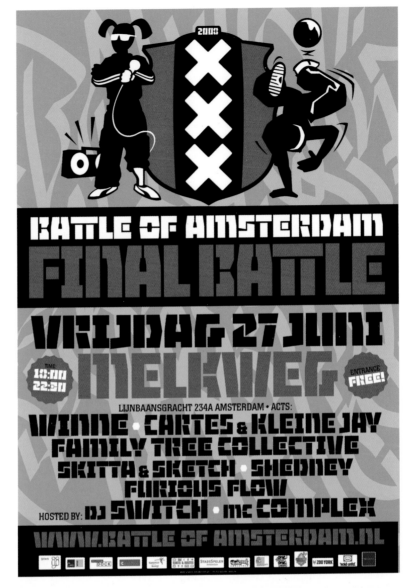

80 Six necessary typefaces

THE MORE TYPOGRAPHIC CHOICES WE HAVE as designers, the harder it is to practice restraint. But imagine a time when typefaces were made of metal, and they were so laborious to produce and to use that the choices were very limited. It is reminiscent of the early days of broadcast television, when a few networks had a monopoly on our viewing attention. Now, with digital and cable television technology available almost everywhere, with hundreds of choices, we often feel there is nothing of interest to watch. Similarly, a few typefaces may be all we really need in our repertoire.

Some well-known and highly regarded designers have advanced the argument that perhaps as few as six typefaces might be enough for every possible design contingency. Those typefaces would certainly include widely used and highly recognizable classics such as Caslon, Garamond, Baskerville, Helvetica, Futura, and Gill Sans. Depending on the designers and their personal preferences, the six typefaces might vary somewhat (but the notion of six "necessary" typefaces should be considered a viable one).

Project
The Dictionary of Love

Company
Hopkins/Baumann

Creative Directors
Will Hopkins and
Mary K. Baumann

Client
Avon Books

Bodoni and Gill Sans—two of the typefaces on most short lists—are on this cover.

Project
Exhibition design

Design Director
Jill Ayers

Designers
Rachel Einsidler and Christine Giberson

Client
The One Club for Art & Copy

The entire exhibition was done with Futura, one of the six useful typefaces that would make even a minimalist's cut.

81   A need for every typeface

NO MATTER HOW BIZARRE or how extreme its forms, somehow, somewhere, there is a purpose for every typeface under the sun. The tricky part is knowing where and how to use a typeface for the very purpose that suits it. The vast universe of available typefaces can be daunting when searching for just the right style to advance the meaning of the text. Ideally, an appropriately designed typeface will do dual service as an image and to convey information. The best typographic designs advance the message on many levels. Some display faces are so specific that they almost demand a unique use, and to try to force them into doing and saying something that they were not meant to do is practically impossible.

Project
Paper Expo poster

Designers
Tiziana Haug and Steve Rura

Client
The Art Directors Club

The typeface, custom-designed for this project, intended to capture the feeling of paper unfurling. Haug calls it, "a study of the interaction between light and paper, and the transformation of a 2-D to a 3-D object. The poster originated through a joined effort between Steve Rura and myself. We took turns drawing and redrawing letterforms until we achieved the right balance between the visual consistency of a typeface and the looser, less predictable qualities of curling paper."

Project
Guide for Living 2008

Designer
Jianping He

Client
Publikum Calendar

The typeface for this calendar page emulates stenciled spray-painted graffiti-style forms; the numbers merge seamlessly with the asphalt signage embedded in the imagery. This is perhaps the only perfect use for these letterforms.

82 Text typefaces versus display typefaces

TEXT TYPEFACES HAVE BEEN DESIGNED with legibility and beauty as their twin goals. Most text typefaces have stood the test of time and usage as appropriate for lengthy passages of text under a variety of reading conditions and with the expectation of a broad reader demographic. Display typefaces, designed less urgently for legibility (although some are eminently legible), are more about style, so the level of legibility may be very minimal. But their raison d'être is a unique stylistic expression of content.

Project
Birds of the World

Art Director
Charlie Nix

Designers
Charlie Nix, Whitney Grant,
and May Jampathom

Client
University of California Press

This body copy is both legible and beautiful, not only due to the letterform details, but also in the way the text has been set. The proportions of the column width, leading, and margin spaces all contribute to the harmony of its presence on the page.

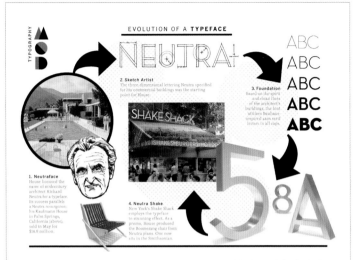

Project
Cover

Creative Director
Scott Dadich

Design Director, Designer
Wyatt Mitchell

Illustrator
The MarkMakers

Client
Wired

Letterforms that have been chosen to emulate data are a fine display choice for the cover, but they are appropriate only for use at large sizes and with a limited amount of text.

Project
Single page

Creative Director
Dean Markadakis

Designer
Jana Meier

Client
Fast Company

This excerpt from a story about a type foundry shows text type is used for the body copy, with a sidebar infographic about the creation of Neutra, a display typeface.

83 Organized entry points

READERS ARE BESET BY DISTRACTION, and unless they are highly motivated, they will take the path of least resistance (which might mean ignoring the text completely). Much has been written about the decline in attention spans and the competition for attention from all sides. So the successful typographic designer will offer up an appetizing smorgasbord of options for the reader, offering many places where the text may be entered and consumed in bits and pieces that can be easily digested. This layering and compartmentalization may also signal that there is something for everyone: more perceived value because there is a lot of content constrained in a confined space.

Project
The Culturati Caucus

Design Director
Chris Dixon

Art Directors
Randy Minor and
Kate Elazegui

Designer
Robert Vargas

Client
New York

Spectacular in its complexity, this four-page cultural survey section pulls off a tour de force of organized entry points by using a mixture of strong grids, the restraint of two colors, and the simplicity of two type families. Segments include an intro, seventeen infographics, and eight sets of survey quotations, plus all of the attendant credits and other "utility" text. Subtle changes in width, weight, and slope, as well as the use of small but essential chunks of white space, demonstrate a masterful handling of detail and an awareness of how readers enter and absorb the content.

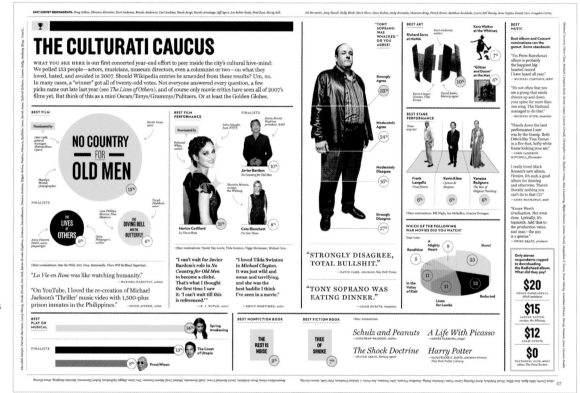

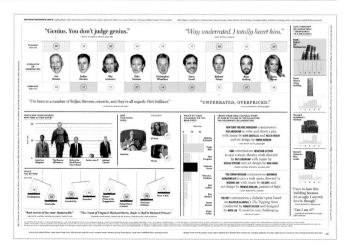

The delicate interplay of hierarchy has an important role: relationships of bold and light, roman and italic, small and large, and caps and lowercase should faithfully represent the relative importance of the content. Typographic hierarchy cues the reader to evaluate the content in relation to the whole. Variety in typographic presentation is the key to directing the reader to pierce the typographic veil. Even modest adjustments in size, weight, width, color, and slope can signal shifts in the content to provide entry points. Overall balance must be maintained simultaneously, making these pages among the most complex to design well.

Project
Single page

Creative Designer
Donald Partyka

Designer
Cathy Yun

Client
Americas Quarterly

Eighteen different sizes, styles, weights, and colors of type populate this deceptively simple single page. The overall effect is clean, compartmentalized, and organized, so readers may easily enter the text at many points and choose bite-size info bits. Infographic options include a map, a poll with percentages, sound-bite quotations, and a pie chart.

STAT BOX

Support for democracy in Latin America and the Caribbean fell to

53%

in 2017, the lowest level since 1995.

source: Latinobarómetro

QUOTES

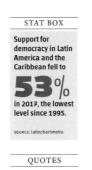

"I think this is another step in visibility, knowing that it's not just the whim of some people, but it's the progress of a whole society."

—**Enrique Sánchez,**
Costa Rica's first openly gay congressman

"How many more will have to die for this war to end?"

—**Marielle Franco,**
Rio de Janeiro councilwoman, on March 13, the day before her assassination

ELLIS RUA/AP PHOTO; JESS MARQUEZ GASPAR; MIGUEL TOVAR/ LATINCONTENT/GETTY

UP CLOSE: MEXICO

As Mexico's presidential race heats up ahead of a July 1 vote, so do the allegations of corruption involving top candidates. This has helped anti-establishment front-runner Andrés Manuel López Obrador. Concurrent legislative elections, however, are unlikely to secure his party a congressional majority.

GDP Growth	Approval	Homicides
2.0% 2017	**22%** FIRST QUARTER OF 2018	↑ **23%**
2.3% 2016	FIRST QUARTER OF 2017 19%	25,339 IN 2017 / 20,547 IN 2016

What's Next?

ELECTIONS With his two closest challengers duking it out for second place, López Obrador remains ahead. The March poll from Consulta Mitofsky gave him an eight point lead over Ricardo Anaya. In the same poll 12 years ago, López Obrador held a similar lead over eventual winner Felipe Calderón. He claimed his subsequent loss was fraudulent.

CORRUPTION WATCH Legislators from the ruling PRI party voted in March to block an investigation into contract irregularities between Brazilian construction firm Odebrecht and Mexico's state oil company. A lack of accountability for Mexican officials implicated in the Odebrecht corruption scandal continues to incite frustration among voters.

NATIONWIDE POLL

GEA-ISA asked 1,782 Mexicans: Will elections be clean or will there be fraud?

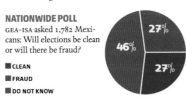

27%
46%
27%

■ CLEAN
■ FRAUD
■ DO NOT KNOW

Source: México: Política, Sociedad y Cambio, GEA-ISA, MARCH 2018

What's Up

MARINE CONSERVATION
After Mexico created North America's largest marine reserve last November, Brazil announced plans in March to protect two offshore areas equivalent to a quarter of the country's ocean waters. Chile, meanwhile, will protect nearly 450,000 square miles of water. These are encouraging steps to protecting biodiversity, though governments can do more to protect the coastal waters where species spawn and feed.

What's Down

ARGENTINE CROPS
Analysts predicted Argentina's worst drought in three decades would cost its economy over $3.4 billion, or 0.5 percent of total GDP. The dry spell has produced the worst harvests since 2009, particularly battering soy and corn. A leading grains exchange estimated the 2017-2018 soy and corn crops would be down 14 and 6 percent, respectively.

84 Systematizing hierarchy

WHEN A DOCUMENT HAS A REPETITIVE hierarchy, an important function of the design is to make that hierarchy clear to the reader. The trick is to make the system work in all possible iterations within the document. The designer must assess all of the text and identify the worst-case scenarios (usually in terms of length) to make the hierarchy systematically cohesive.

Project
Menu design

Company
Mucca Design

Creative Director
Matteo Bologna

Designer
Andrea Brown

Client
Morandi

A menu can be a tricky piece of design; many levels of hierarchy must be identified and fit into a fairly compact, yet highly legible form. In addition, the typical low lighting of a restaurant environment may present a challenge to the reader.

Project (opposite)
Single page

Design Director
David Curcurito

Art Director
Darhil Crook

Associate Art Director
Erin Jang

Design Assistant
Soni Khatri

Client
Esquire

This formatted monthly magazine page uses a flexible grid to accommodate more than a dozen pieces of text. Every month the vocabulary changes, but the complex repetitive hierarchy is always apparent to the reader through shifts in weight, case, size, and style. Note this example of "the rule of three typefaces"; even using only two colors, there is a wide range of possible typographic effects.

Man at His Best

THE VOCABULARY

Terms and ideas you will encounter in the pages that follow. Great for conversation.

● **the great bedraggling** *n*: A PERIOD THAT BEGAN IN THE MID-2000s WITH THE PROLIFERATION OF EASILY UPLOADED WEB VIDEOS, WHICH HAVE MADE FAMOUS PEOPLE SEEM UNATTRACTIVE AND NONFAMOUS PEOPLE REALLY UNATTRACTIVE. (SEE PAGE 50.)

● **UNREAL DEATH** *n*: A manner of death so unlikely, shocking, and brutal that it overshadows the life of the deceased. (SEE PAGE 42.)

FIG. 2

● **CHILI** *n*: Fundamentally, a stew comprising bits of spiced meat and sometimes beans. Easily corrupted. (SEE PAGE 59.)

● **DUMP** *n*: A blend of chili spices added at precise moments in the chili-cooking process. Done either two or three times, depending on the chef. (SEE PAGE 62.)

● **engineered helplessness** *n*: SURREPTITIOUSLY PLACED INFORMATION IN A CONVERSATION THAT SUGGESTS A FLAW AND BAITS A WOMAN INTO SYMPATHETICALLY ATTEMPTING TO FIX A MAN. (SEE PAGE 70.)

● **BARREL PROBLEM** *n*: The effect that the heat in the tropics (as opposed to the heat in, say, Scotland) has on liquor stored in wooden casks, like rum (as opposed to, say, Scotch). Often results in rum tasting significantly less wonderful than other aged liquors (like, say, Scotch). (SEE PAGE 66.)

● **HOLD THE MONKEYS** *n*: 1. A request made by a bar patron that specifies his cocktail should come without tiny umbrellas, ornamental fruit, or small plastic monkeys. ("I'll take a daiquiri. Hold the monkeys.") 2. A euphemism for any request to eschew unnecessary accoutrements. ("I'll take the Sebring. But hold the monkeys.") (SEE PAGE 66.)

FIG. 3

● **RESTRAINED** *adj*: An increasingly rare quality among modern architects characterized by not designing a ridiculous building just because one can. (SEE PAGE 46.)

FIG. 1

● **MOLIAN SNUB** *n*: The puzzling phenomenon whereby beautiful, talented, charming actresses (e.g., Keri Russell, Leelee Sobieski, Gretchen Mol) are not in more things. (SEE PAGE 48.)

GOOD IDEAS FEATURED IN THIS SECTION:

- GO SEE *MILK*. (PG. 42)
- ROAST AND GRIND WHOLE SPICES YOURSELF. (PG. 62)
- SHOW SOME HUMILITY EVERY NOW AND THEN. (PG. 70)
- TRY SIPPING RUM, NEAT. BUT FOR THE LOVE OF GOD, MAKE SURE IT'S THE GOOD STUFF. (PG. 66)
- AND BY "GOOD," WE MEAN SOMETHING OTHER THAN THE STUFF YOUR COLLEGE GIRLFRIEND USED TO "PRE-PARTY" WITH. (PG. 66)
- HAVE ANOTHER BOWL. EAT! (PG. 62)

"When it gets warmer, it turns green." *(—ITALO ZUCCHELLI, PAGE 77)*

"This is chili you want to keep coming back to." *(—DANIEL BOULUD, PAGE 64)*

ILLUSTRATIONS BY JOE McKENDRY

85 Using justified type

ALIGNMENT OF THE LEFT AND RIGHT SIDES of the column, known as justified type, imparts a cool, clean, considered look to the text. It is a more formal and even a more authoritative look, so this convention is highly favored for books and newspapers but less so for magazines and other documents, which may use a mix of justified and unjustified type within their pages to indicate different types of content formats. If not well planned and tailored during editing, justified type has the potential to be "gappy" between words, as typesetting software adjusts the word spaces to achieve justification (see pages 118–119, Hyphenation and Justification.) If there are too few words in a column, there may not be sufficient opportunities for the software to apportion the spaces in a way that will retain an even typographic color throughout the passage of text.

Project
Feature spread

Creative Director
Robert Priest

Designer
Jana Meier

Illustrator
Bryan Christie

Client
Condé Nast Portfolio

Using only two colors and an uneven column grid, this layout uses justified type to create a clean edge around the infographic and as a way of balancing special blocks. Note the use of an off-center headline and subhead to create counterpoint, and the centered text above the infographic to set it apart from the body copy.

the markets be available solely by subscription. Instead, companies would pay to be rated. "That was the beginning of the end," says Rosner.

It might come as a surprise, but rating credit is a heck of a business to be in. In fact, Moody's has been the third-most-profitable company in the S&P 500-stock index for the past five years, based on pretax margins. That's higher than Microsoft and Google. Little wonder that Warren Buffett's Berkshire Hathaway is the No. 1 holder of Moody's stock.

McGraw-Hill's most recent financial report shows that S&P has profit margins that would put it in the top 10. Fitch Ratings, owned by the French firm Fimalac, is a distant third in market share but nevertheless has an operating margin above 30 percent, about double the average for companies in the S&P 500.

In 2006, nearly $850 million, more than 40 percent of Moody's total rev-

loans and slicing them up into differently rated pieces called tranches. The investors in the lowest-rated—and potentially most-profitable—tranches take on the most risk, because they're on the hook for the first losses. The tranches can then be sliced up again into new bundles. By this alchemical process, risky loans, such as subprime mortgages, can be converted into triple-A-rated securities. An investment bank's goal is to have the highest percentage of its deals rated triple-A and to keep returns high for the investors who take on the lowest, riskiest tranches.

If the ratings agencies prevent the creation of a high percentage of triple-A paper, the deal won't sell. The ratings agencies' customers—the investment banks—will be unhappy, and the ratings agencies' bottom lines will suffer. "Bankers get paid a lot of money. The ratings-agency people get pushed," says a hedge fund manager who is betting that the securitization market will continue to sour. The agencies "never stopped to question" this, he says, "because they had zero economic risk."

While the agencies haven't entirely

$1.1 trillion in 2002. Today, the securitization market as a whole is worth about $11 trillion, according to the Japanese securities firm Nomura.

At an investor presentation in June, Moody's showed that in 1992, it provided ratings on only three credit-derivative products. By 2006, that had soared to 61. And 23 of those had been introduced in the past two years. "This business enabled loans that have never been made before," says Simon Mikhailovich, who runs a fixed-income hedge fund. "There's fairly little ability to second-guess or independently establish whether the ratings are correct, because the complexity is so high."

✳✳✳✳✳✳✳

So HOW DID THE AGENCIES help create the securities that are now causing so much trouble? A 2001 lawsuit sheds some light. In 1999 and 2000, the American Savings Bank of Hawaii asked PaineWebber,

what firms do in such cases: It sued.

In defending itself against A.S.B.'s accusations, PaineWebber made an interesting claim: It said that Fitch had been intimately involved in the structuring of the deal and that it had relied on Fitch's representations for assumptions about the performance of the underlying assets. The U.S. Court of Appeals for the Second Circuit agreed, writing that A.S.B. had discovered that "PaineWebber and Fitch had extensive communications about the structure of the transactions [that] concerned what PaineWebber needed to do to earn an investment-grade rating from Fitch." The ruling also said the claim that "Fitch plays an active role in structuring the transaction is extremely credible."

The case is notable in part because ratings agencies are rarely sued or even ensnared in other parties' lawsuits. In the A.S.B. case, Fitch refused to turn over documents, claiming protection under the New York State shield laws that allow journalists to guard their sources and methods—a claim the court didn't buy. Credit-ratings agen-

damage could spread to other markets, such as the high-flying private equity world, which depends on the agencies to stamp dependable ratings on the bonds of companies that private equity firms want to acquire. "The reason this works is because the ratings agencies have said it works," said Bill Ackman, a hedge fund manager who has about $6 billion under management, in a speech at a charity-investment conference in May. "The big point here is that everyone in the chain gets paid up front. The rating agencies get their fee…if they say the deal works. If they say the deal doesn't work, well, you just go across the street" to another agency to get the rating you want.

✳✳✳✳✳✳✳

The 2006 VINTAGE of subprime mortgages was troubled from the start, coming as it did when real estate prices began their descent. Consumers were offered loans that, at

The recent crisis has led the agencies to make a series of embarrassing tweaks. In April, Moody's said it would start doing what it should have done long ago: more aggressively scrutinizing new mortgage loans. The company acknowledged that its models, created in 2002, were out-of-date. "Since then, the mortgage market has evolved considerably, with the introduction of many new products and an expansion of risks associated with them," a Moody's report said. In hindsight, it seems astounding that the most influential rater of mortgage bonds wouldn't be upgrading its models regularly to account for the growth in exotic mortgages.

The changes may be too little, too late. Last year, President Bush signed a law to have the S.E.C. monitor and regulate credit-ratings agencies, taking what has been a free-market free-for-all and putting it under the microscope. The S.E.C. formalized its rules this summer.

Other ideas for reform are flowing in. Rosner suggests that ratings for structured securities use a different scale—say, numbers instead of letters—to differentiate them from ratings for corporate and municipal bonds. He believes the agencies need to step up the training for analysts and should be compelled to re-rate transactions regularly rather than monitor them haphazardly. Furthermore, he thinks efforts should be made to distance the agencies from Wall Street. He proposes that any ratings-agency employee involved with a structured-finance deal for a Wall Street firm should have to wait a year before being able to join that firm. Such a waiting period already exists for auditors.

Murphy, the ex-Moody's executive, doesn't blame the ratings agencies alone. "But in the end," she says, "it's supposed to be the ratings agencies that are the purest of them all. They should be held to the highest standard. Maybe we should fundamentally rethink their position in the markets." ●

Write to JEISINGER@PORTFOLIO.COM.

enue, came from the rarefied business known as structured finance. In 1995, its revenue from such transactions was a paltry $50 million.

The agencies argue that most investors still see them primarily as information providers. "I think it's fine that people actually rely on ratings, but it's not a recommendation to buy or sell.… We are just looking at the credit," Clarkson says. And Moody's claims that it has strong systems in place to prevent conflicts of interest. "There is no transaction or line of business that's worth our reputation," Clarkson says. S&P and Fitch, through their spokespeople, contend much the same thing.

But the agencies know that if they crack down too hard, by toughening standards, it won't be good for business—theirs or their customers'. Securitization is the art of bundling

neglected the investors who ultimately buy these complex products, "the ratings agencies were very banker-, manager-, and market-friendly," says Eileen Murphy, who, before taking a job on Wall Street, worked at Moody's for five years, including three years as co-head of structured derivatives. "They spent a lot of time developing new methodologies. We can argue how that turned out. It was enlightened self-interest. They created a huge moneymaker for themselves."

That's putting it mildly. The value of new structured-finance deals hitting the market has grown 27 percent a year for the past four years, to more than $3 trillion in 2006, up from about

now owned by UBS, to create a product that would generate a higher return than it was getting through its typical, safe investment choices like municipal and corporate bonds. PaineWebber created a structure called a collateralized loan obligation, made up of the risky portions of other transactions. A French insurance company guaranteed A.S.B.'s principal. The bankers worked with Fitch, the ratings agency, to put the deal together. Moody's also vetted it.

A.S.B. bought $83.5 million worth of the securities, but then federal bank regulators disallowed the purchase, unconvinced by the ratings that the investments were safe. A.S.B. tried to return the securities to Paine-Webber, but the investment bank refused them. So A.S.B. was forced to sell the securities at a loss. It then did

cies still maintain that their ratings are simply published opinions, which investors are free to heed or ignore.

But as a result of the subprime-mortgage mess, pressure is building to rein in the agencies. Mason and Rosner, for instance, are convinced that the agencies are hopelessly conflicted. They argue that there are "fundamental flaws" in the rating process for mortgage-backed securities, suggesting that the entire world of structured finance could be suspect.

Mason estimates that direct losses from mortgage securities and other complex structures called collateralized debt obligations are already between $70 billion and $100 billion. And the

times, exceeded the entire value of the homes they were about to buy. Some borrowers didn't have to verify their income before receiving mortgages. These are denigrated as "liar loans" in the industry, and not surprisingly, they are going bad at a rapid pace.

While the agencies say they have tightened up their standards in recent years, the data suggest otherwise. The ABX index, which tracks the subprime business, shows that, beginning in the last half of 2005—long before the scope of the crisis became widely known—subprime securities were already starting to get shaky. The amount of protection for the riskiest investment-grade tranches was going down. Yet the agencies continued to assign high ratings to a big percentage of subprime deals, collecting fees along the way.

While the **ratings agencies have profited** from the mortgage boom, it's not at all clear **enormously** they have their arms around the business.

Project
Feature spread

Creative Director
Robert Priest

Designer
Jana Meier

Client
Condé Nast Portfolio

This second spread creates counterpoint to the formality of justified columns by intentionally misaligning them vertically and slicing through the columns and the gutter with a callout.

86 Using flush-left, rag-right type

THE COMMON ALTERNATIVE to justified type is flush-left type: since we read from left to right, it is important, especially for reading long passages of text, that the eye of the reader can return to an easy-to-locate place when beginning every line of text. The added advantage of this unjustified type alignment is that the word spaces are consistent, unlike those of justified type, thereby aiding legibility.

Project
Single page

Creative Director
Dirk Barnett

Art Director, Designer
Claudia de Almeida

Client
Blender

The more informal flush-left format works well for this letters page and with the demographic of the audience. Note the use of blue and black "bullet" shapes echoing the letter shapes of the headline display type; they work as content bearers and as navigational symbols.

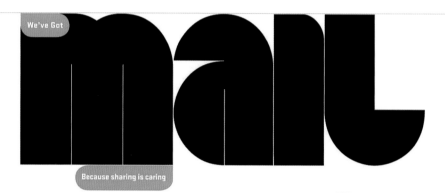

We've Got **mail**

Because sharing is caring

Readers were much kinder to July's cover subject, British good girl **Leona Lewis** ("Leona Lewis Wants a Cuddle ... But Not the Way You Want To"), than they were to the previous month's, American naughty girl Tila Tequila. One reader, Craig Brabant of Yuma, Arizona, praised Lewis for her "stunning" looks and for having a "voice like a choir of angels." He also insisted that her hit "Bleeding Love" is directed to him: "When she sings, 'But I don't care what they say, I'm in love with you,' anyone can tell she is singing to Craig Brabant of Yuma, Arizona." Um, whatever you say, Craig Brabant of Yuma, Arizona.

LEONA LEWIS CAN'T LOSE
I loved your article on Leona Lewis. Leona is gloriously talented. She is a devout vegetarian because she loves all of God's creatures. She never insults other performers and is devoted to her family. Leona Lewis is a saint who sings like an angel!
BRIEN COMERFORD, GLENVIEW, IL

LEONA LEWIS CAN'T WIN
Should Mariah Carey "look out" for Leona Lewis, as your July cover suggests? Hmm, let's see. Mariah Carey: 20 years in the music business, 18 No. 1 hits, 11 studio albums. Leona Lewis: Debuted this year, one No. 1 hit, one album. I think Leona Lewis is very talented, but if Christina Aguilera couldn't knock Mimi off her throne, what makes you think Leona can?
ANGELA LOPEZ, STOCKTON, CA

BEET IT!
Dwight Schrute is my hero! I loved Rainn Wilson's picks for best fictional rock bands ("Fakin' It!" July) in your Summer Movie Special. The only thing that would be better? His picks for best beets at Schrute Farms. Beets rock!
TAYLOR HAWKINS, OTTAWA, CANADA

Beets do indeed rock! Personally, we dig a good Burpee's Golden, but Detroit Dark Reds are nice, too.

SHINE ON, YOU CLASSY DIAMOND
Blender, the articles about Vince Clarke of Yaz ("Station to Station") and Neil Diamond ("Dear Superstar") made the July issue for me. Rob Sheffield's overview of Clarke's musical and personal growth was truly engaging and, at times, very amusing. And Neil Diamond's answers to readers' questions were both classic and classy.
AARON TAP, LOS ANGELES

SEXUAL-METAPHOR ALERT!
You would not know good music if it walked up, introduced itself, took you out for an expensive dinner, and then invited you in for a nightcap and a happy ending. There wasn't a single thing in the July issue, besides the Sub Pop oral history ("Going Out of Business Since 1988!"), that wouldn't immediately put someone to sleep, and even that story was clearly there for "underground cred" that you don't deserve.
BRIAN ELLIS, LOS ANGELES

Wait, music can buy you dinner *and* give you a hand job? To think, we've wasted all this time just writing about it.

IF POP STARS WERE DOGS ...

IGGY POP
THE POP STAR

ROCKY
THE DOG

Send us a photo and tell us which music celebrity your pooch resembles. If we print it, you'll win **Yamaha's RH10MS Professional Monitor Headphones.**

WIN ME!

LISTEN UP
BLENDER READERS:
We want to hear from you! So write and tell us how you really feel.

SEND ALL CORRESPONDENCE TO:
your2cents@blender.com, or Blender, 1040 Sixth Avenue, 15th Floor New York, NY 10018.

POP: SIGI TISCHLER/AP PHOTO.

Man at His Best

1. THE CULTURE » Robert Downey Jr. in blackface, the Hold Steady.
2. THE INSTRUCTIONS » Absinthe, New Orleans, sex. And GPS!
3. STYLE » What a little color can do for a man. Not blackface.

THE VOCABULARY
Terms and ideas you will encounter in the pages that follow. Great for conversation.

● **EXTRARACIAL** *adj*: Marked by an innate coolness that mutes an expected discussion of race. As exemplified by Barack Obama, Stevie Ray Vaughan, Lando Calrissian, and Robert Downey Jr. (SEE PAGE 28.)

● **purification through violence** *n*: A CATHARSIS CAUSED BY CONFLICT AND PAIN, AS SEEN IN CORMAC McCARTHY NOVELS, GRAND THEFT AUTO IV, AND YOUR CHILDHOOD. (SEE PAGE 38.)

PANTONE®
2603 C

FIG. 1

FIG. 2

● **WETTING THE SUGAR** *n*: 1. An exotic cocktail preparation whereby something is melted, dissolved, set on fire, juggled, etc. 2. A euphemistic expression for any kind of exotic preparation a man might undertake. (SEE PAGE 41.)

● **LIQUORS OF MYSTERY** *n*: Alcoholic beverages that one has heard of, is intrigued by, but is not quite sure what to do with, such as absinthe, mescal, grappa, Armagnac, "malt." (SEE PAGE 41.)

● **PURPLE** *n*: A color with a fluctuating but ever-present position within the Hierarchy of Tricky Hues for Men. It's currently in first place but being challenged by orange. (SEE PAGE 49.)

● **physical abnormality** *n*: A MOMENT OF FRISKINESS IN AN OTHERWISE SEXUALLY STAGNANT RELATIONSHIP, FACILITATED BY THE EFFECTS OF OXYTOCIN (DEFINED BELOW). (SEE PAGE 46.)

CONTEXT-FREE PIECES OF ADVICE IN THIS SECTION:

● YOU WOULDN'T GO WRONG IN CHECKING OUT THE FOLLOWING: *AMERICAN TEEN, THE ROCKER, GENERATION KILL, BOY A, PINEAPPLE EXPRESS.* (PG. 31)

● UPGRADE YOUR GPS SYSTEM. (PG. 43)

● NEW RESTAURANTS IN NEW ORLEANS: YES. NEW BARS IN NEW ORLEANS: NO. (PG. 42)

● LIGHT PURPLE: YES. DARK PURPLE: NO. (PG. 49)

FIG. 3

● **OXYTOCIN** *n*: A hormone released during intimate physical contact, such as when you kiss your beautiful wife or when she hugs your good-looking friend. (SEE PAGE 46.)

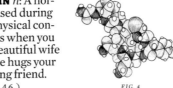

FIG. 4

● **ICELANDIC** *adj*: Accessible but nuanced. Northern but vibrant. Cold but green. Fun but intellectual. Björk but normal. (SEE PAGE 36.)

● **SUPPORTING VOCALIST** *n*: A music fan who publicly and energetically expresses his faith in, love for, and allegiance to a band, indiscriminately encouraging others to listen as well. Common among enthusiasts who are no longer concerned with "image" or being "cool." (SEE PAGE 34.)

 "You'll have as much fun with the trolls as with the blonds." *(—ANITA BRIEM, PAGE 36)*

"These things go down easy. If you overdo it, all bets are off." *(—DAVID WONDRICH, PAGE 41)*

ILLUSTRATIONS BY JOE McKENDRY

25

87 Using centered, asymmetrical, and flush-right type

THESE LESS-COMMON FORMS of alignment are fine when used with limited quantities of text. The flush-right setting may be a good choice for a caption that sits to the left of a photo, so there can be a neat column of space between image and text, for example. Centered text works well with announcements, as long as there are not too many line turns for the reader to navigate, and as long as the line breaks occur logically. With centered or asymmetrical text, the designer should turn the lines for sense and appearance, with an awareness of the shape of the ragged text. Try to avoid line breaks that create a shape (unless that is the designer's intention—for example, type that fills a polygon).

Project
Feature spread

Design Director
Carla Frank

Designer
Kristin Fitzpatrick

Photographer
Hugh Hales-Took

Illustrator
Neil Gower

Client
O, The Oprah Magazine

The shape of the fruit in the illustration is reprised in the shape of the type. Note the headline's stylistic reference to early fruit box labels.

Project
Single page

Creative Director, Designer
Steven Hoffman

Client
Sports Illustrated, The Baseball Book

This complex mix of lists is well crafted using a combination of centered, flush-left, flush-right, and justified type. Note its subtle use of rules and typographic hierarchy (weight, slope, case, size) to clarify the text.

1950S CULTURE

MUSIC: *Elvis' Christmas Album* (Elvis Presley), *Kind of Blue* (Miles Davis), *Tutti-Frutti* (Little Richard); *Mona Lisa* (Nat King Cole)

MOVIES: *Lady and the Tramp, Rebel Without a Cause, Singin' in the Rain, On the Waterfront, Sunset Boulevard*

TELEVISION SHOWS: *I Love Lucy, The Ed Sullivan Show, The Honeymooners, Dragnet, What's My Line?*

BOOKS: *The Catcher in the Rye* by J. D. Salinger; *From Here to Eternity* by James Jones; *The Power of Positive Thinking* by Norman Vincent Peale; *Lolita* by Vladimir Nabokov; *Atlas Shrugged* by Ayn Rand

ACHIEVEMENT: In 1956, President Eisenhower approves funding for interstate highway system, spurring commerce and the population shift to the suburbs.

INVENTIONS: pacemaker, cordless TV remote control, bar codes, microchip.

SEX SYMBOLS: Marilyn Monroe & James Dean

VILLAIN: Sen. Joseph McCarthy (R-Wis.) held congressional hearings that became a witch hunt for communists in government, the military and the entertainment industry.

PERSONALITY OF THE DECADE: Elvis Presley

< MARILYN MONROE

>NICKNAMES<

Bill [Moose] Skowron ∧
Willie [the Say Hey Kid] Mays
Lawrence [Yogi] Berra
Henry [Hammerin' Hank] Aaron
Edward [Whitey] Ford
Billy [the Kid] Martin
Orestes [Minnie] Minoso
Ernie [Mr. Cub] Banks
Don [Popeye] Zimmer
Wilmer [Vinegar Bend] Mizell
[Puddin' Head] Willie Jones
James [Dusty] Rhodes
Luis [Yo-Yo] Arroyo
Sal [the Barber] Maglie
Frank [Taters] Lary
Harvey [the Kitten] Haddix
Roy [Squirrel] Sievers
Joe [Goofy] Adcock
Felix [the Cat] Mantilla
Frank [Pig] House
Norm [Smiley] Siebern
Mickey [the Commerce Comet] Mantle

BORN		DIED
Lance Ito	1950	George Bernard Shaw
Sting	1951	William Randolph Hearst
Bob Costas	1952	Evita Peron
Hulk Hogan	1953	Josef Stalin
Oprah Winfrey >	1954	Enrico Fermi
Bill Gates	1955	Albert Einstein
Larry Bird	1956	Jackson Pollock
Spike Lee	1957	< Humphrey Bogart
Michael Jackson	1958	Tyrone Power
Sarah Ferguson	1959	Frank Lloyd Wright

> **NEWS OF THE REAL WORLD** 1950: The Brink's bank job in Boston nets 11 thieves more than $2.7 million in 17 minutes 1951: The 22nd Amendment to the U.S. Constitution, limiting Presidents to two terms, is ratified 1952: They like Ike: Gen. Dwight Eisenhower elected president; he travels to Korea seeking end to conflict there 1953: Francis Crick and James Watson discover the double-helix structure of DNA 1954: British runner Roger Bannister runs the mile in 3:59.4 1955: Rosa Parks arrested in Montgomery, Ala., after refusing to give up her seat on a bus to a white man 1956: Fidel Castro and Ché Guevara mount the insurgency in Cuba that will eventually overthrow regime of Fulgencio Batista 1957: The U.S.S.R. launches *Sputnik I* and *II*, the first man-made satellites 1958: U.S. aircraft accidentally drops atom bomb on Mars Bluff, S.C.—but it's a dud 1959: Alaska and Hawaii become 49th and 50th states.

Project
Holiday card

Company
We Made This

Design Director, Designer
Alistair Hall

Client
Royal Borough of Kensington and Chelsea Transport, Environment and Leisure Services

This asymmetrical arrangement works in two ways: first, when the fold is closed, the title reads *The Snow and the Frost;* second, the line breaks amplify the cadence of the poetry.

88   The multicolumn text grid

GRID SYSTEMS FORMATTED TO CONTAIN TEXT and images can take many forms and be multifunctional. They should be flexible enough to accommodate all possible situations in the case of a complex document or project. Grids are invaluable in organizing text and other visual elements and in creating a comfortable environment for the reader. Depending on the size of the vessel (page or screen) and the size, leading, and weight of the text, multicolumn grids may contain as many as twelve columns (as in the well-known grid used by Willi Fleckhaus for the German magazine *Twen*) or as few as two columns. The width of the column may vary, but principles of legibility (optimum line length and character count) should be observed.

Project
Feature spread

Creative Director
Donald Partyka

Client
Americas Quarterly

The end of one story in a three-column format and the introduction of a second story on the same spread are neatly separated by the use of a new column grid for the second story (as well as a tint box, with the clear beginning indicated with a large initial cap, large weighty title, and red cap leading into the body copy).

The North Bridge
Minute Man National Historical Park
Concord, Ma.
VATH SOK

TRUST ASSUMES LEADERSHIP ROLE
for America's 250th anniversary

REPARATIONS are underway for the nationwide 250th anniversary commemoration of this country's founding, and the American Battlefield Trust has been selected as the official nonprofit partner (referred to as the "administrative secretariat") for the United States Semiquincentennial Commission.

The Trust's proposal was chosen by Secretary of the Interior Ryan Zinke following a competitive process and the unanimous recommendation of a selection panel. As the official nonprofit partner of the federal commission, the Trust will raise funds for its work and prepare reports to the White House and Congress on progress and activities.

The Commission was established by unanimous votes in both houses of Congress in 2016. It will serve as the primary body to coordinate and facilitate activities to commemorate the 250th anniversary of American independence. The Commission includes 24 appointed members — four U.S. senators, four U.S. representatives and 16 private citizens — as well as a variety of ex officio members, including the secretaries of the interior, state, defense and education; the U.S. Attorney General; the librarian of Congress; secretary of the Smithsonian; archivist of the United States, and the presiding officer of the Federal Council on the Arts and Humanities.

In announcing his choice of the Trust, Zinke noted that the organization "has distinguished itself in fundraising and managing high-profile commemorative events, and that expertise will be invaluable to the U.S.A. 250th Commemoration planning efforts."

Trust leadership celebrated the news, with President Jim Lighthizer declaring, "It has long been our desire to be involved in the Revolutionary War's 250th anniversary, ensuring that the battlefields where the lofty ideals of the Declaration of Independence were secured play a key part in the commemoration.

"To be selected as the nonprofit partner for such a momentous occasion is possibly the greatest honor in the field of historic preservation. We embrace this challenge and the opportunities to advance the cause of battlefield protection and high-quality history education, while remaining firmly committed to our ongoing Civil War mission." ★

TRUST NAMED OUTSTANDING "FRIEND OF HISTORY"
by prestigious Organization of American Historians

T ITS APRIL annual meeting in Sacramento, Calif., the Organization of American Historians (OAH), the largest professional society dedicated to the study and teaching of this nation's past, presented the Civil War Trust (now a division of the American Battlefield Trust) with its 2018 Friend of History Award, recognizing outstanding contributions to the field made outside a typical academic environment.

Accepting the award on behalf of the organization, longtime Trustee and chair of the education committee Dr. Mary Munsell Abroe reflected on the evolution of our mission. "I have seen the Trust's educational efforts evolve over the past 20 years into a rich tapestry of outreach programs that employs multiple media to engage audiences," she said. "Those programs operate on the principle that preservation and education are flip sides of the same coin — and that learning is a lifelong process. Whether these educational activities are geared toward teachers, students or battlefield visitors of whatever age or background, they all use battlefields as outdoor classrooms that challenge us to find America's Civil War past."

Trust President James Lighthizer agreed, noting he was "gratified to receive this prestigious award from the OAH, but, more importantly, to be viewed as a friend of history — not only through our land acquisitions, but through our work to transform these historic places for K-12 teachers and students, as well as adult learners, into outdoor classrooms."

In selecting the Trust for this honor, the OAH cited the variety of media we employ to reach numerous audiences, from our suite of digital programing to the Traveling Trunk, which supplies reproduction artifacts to classrooms, making the past tangible for students. Also cited were our free continuing education opportunities for teachers and our acclaimed Field Trip Fund, which provides competitive grants to help K-12 teachers pay for class visits to historic sites.

Since its origination in 2005, recipients of the Friend of History Award have included Colin G. Campbell, chairman emeritus of the Colonial Williamsburg Foundation, and two former members of our Board of Trustees — Lonnie G. Bunch, III, founding director of the Smithsonian Institution's National Museum of African American History and Culture, and Dr. Libby O'Connell of The History Channel.

Founded in 1907, the Organization of American Historians seeks to promote excellence in the scholarship, teaching and presentation of American history, and wide discussion of historical questions. Its 7,800 members include college and university professors, pre-collegiate teachers, archivists, museum curators, public historians, students and scholars working in government and the private sector. ★

FIELD TRIP FUND SENDS 20,000TH STUDENT TO HISTORIC SITE
Impressive milestone reached in just four school years

OW BETTER to comprehend our nation's history than to follow in the footsteps of those who made it?

Early exposure to historic places has prompted many of the nation's best historians to devote their lives to investigating and writing about America's past. To give that opportunity to the next generation of budding scholars, the Field Trip Fund idea — scholarships designed to help underwrite school expeditions to these "outdoor classrooms" — was born in late 2014 to instant acclaim.

On April 10, 2018, students from Michigan's Grand Rapids Christian Middle School arrived in Gettysburg, Pa., and the 20,000th student sponsored by the Field Trip Fund set foot on a battlefield. Teachers from more than 200 schools in 39 states have used the Fund to visit historic sites in 26 states.

"It's great to get kids out onto a battlefield," said Trust President James Lighthizer. "Their visits are thought-provoking and can be life-changing."

Garry Adelman, the director of history and education who envisioned the program and oversees the application process, agrees. "I do not know whether any of these kids will become the next Bruce Catton or the next James McPherson, but my hope is that they become better citizens by understanding their history better and knowing it more personally."

Educators almost universally agree that venturing beyond the classroom — often called experiential learning — is tremendously helpful for students. So, in an era when schools' budgets for field trips keep shrinking, it is no surprise that they deeply value these competitive grants.

"Without the Field Trip Fund, my classroom could never have made the trip from Wisconsin to Gettysburg and Antietam," said Dave Wege, a teacher at Waucousta Lutheran School in Campbellsport, Wisc. "This 'Best Field Trip Ever' allowed my students to walk hallowed ground and connect in a way that textbooks, videos and discussions just cannot do. What an experience for my kids!"

Grants from the fund may be used for transportation, meals, site admission and/or guide fees, and recipients are asked to respond with "enthusiasm equity" in activities like taking photos, writing an article or participating with their students in Park Day, the Trust's annual community cleanup event. The Field Trip Fund is entirely administered using contributions designated specifically for educational activities; no donations toward land-acquisition efforts are redirected.

Classes that receive grants from the Field Trip Fund are asked to furnish the Trust with testimonials, photos, videos or other means of showing that they seized the opportunity afforded them by visiting historic sites.

The Trust's education goals and resources employ delivery methods appropriate to different age groups and skills. Some specifically target students, others teachers and still others the broader universe of lifelong learners online. Learn more about these outstanding — and typically free — resources at *www.battlefields.org/education*, and consider making a targeted gift to further these efforts. ★

Project
Spread

Studio
Jeff Griffeth Creative

Creative Director
Jeff Griffeth

Photographer
Vath Sok

Client
Hallowed Ground
American Battlefield Trust

The two sidebars depart from the standard three-column page grid to accommodate related but distinct content. Note that the second column of the tinted sidebar aligns with the column above to preserve visual organization.

89 The uneven text grid

AN INTERESTING TREND that goes against conventional practice is the use of uneven-width columns on the same page or within the same story. This is a step beyond the opening paragraph treatment, and it can be seen in a number of mainstream high-circulation magazines that are breaking out of the usual formats with some hits of "subversive" typography.

Project
Single page

Creative Director
Scott Dadich

Design Director
Wyatt Mitchell

Designer
Christy Sheppard

Illustrator
Kerry Roper

Client
Wired

Adding a bit of extra interest to the page, this short piece of text exists in two distinct column widths. Note the extra-wide white space to the right of the narrower column and the super narrow column under the broken, overlapped, and stacked headline "Jargon Watch" at right (that headline is as much a piece of art as a headline; it adds a wonderful color blast topping off the column, which has no other room for art).

Prefabs Sprout
Instant suburb hits New York.

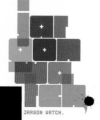

JARGON WATCH.

× **Tourists press up** against the construction fence on the corner of 53rd and Sixth, staring speechless as a giant crane lifts an entire bathroom into the air and deposits it in what will be a master bedroom. Cellophane House is five stories tall, with floor-to-ceiling windows, translucent polycarbonate steps embedded with LEDs, and exterior walls made of NextGen SmartWrap, an experimental plastic laminated with photovoltaic cells. Its aluminum frame was cut from off-the-shelf components in Europe, assembled in New Jersey, then snapped together in 16 days on a vacant lot next to the Museum of Modern Art—joining four other full-size houses onsite through October as part of the exhibit *Home Delivery: Fabricating the Modern Dwelling*. It looks as if a suburban cul-de-sac took a wrong turn at the Holland Tunnel.

Prefab is "modernism's oldest dream," curator Barry Bergdoll says. Since the industrial revolution, architects have been in thrall of the idea that houses could be built in factories, like any kind of widget. But reality hasn't been extremely cooperative. Whether because of conservative public tastes, unachievable economies of scale, or designers' less-than-stellar business acumen, their utopian visions have mostly remained fantasies.

Frank Lloyd Wright, Buckminster Fuller, and Charles and Ray Eames each had compelling concepts of housing for all, most of which turned out to be housing for a few. Modernist masters Walter Gropius and Le Corbusier were among hundreds who patented replicable designs that never materialized. Thomas Edison eked out a hundred units using his "single-pour concrete system"—which formed whole houses, down to the bathtub, from a single mold—before his company folded. Prefab's only success stories have been far from museum-quality: Sears, Roebuck sold more than 100,000 kit houses between 1908 and 1940, and the steel half-moons of World War II's Quonset huts stubbornly squat on military bases worldwide. (To say nothing of the nearly 100,000 ›

× **Green crude**
n. A new kind of crude oil harvested from genetically engineered algae. The dark-green syrup thrives on CO_2, which could be funneled from coal-burning power plants, and can be made into gasoline or diesel in conventional refineries. The results burn cleaner than petroleum fuels.

× **Popcorning**
v. A chain reaction in which the accidental explosion of one nuclear warhead causes others in the vicinity to detonate, releasing lethal radiation for miles in every direction. Newly declassified documents reveal that dropping a Trident missile while loading it onto a submarine could ignite a Jiffy Pop Nagasaki.

× **Edupunk**
n. Avoiding mainstream teaching tools like Powerpoint and Blackboard, edupunks bring the rebellious attitude and DIY ethos of '70s bands like the Clash to the classroom.

× **Hairy blobs**
n. pl. Prickly prehistoric microorganisms that once lived in acidic, saline lakes chemically similar to ancient Martian waters. The recent discovery of fossilized hairy blobs in North Dakota lake beds could help in the search for microbial chia pets and other exotically hirsute life-forms on Mars and beyond.
—Jonathon Keats
jargon@wired.com

0 5 0 OCT 2008

ILLUSTRATION BY **Kerry Roper**

RICHARD BARNES/MOMA

Project
Feature spread

Creative Director
Scott Dadich

Design Director
Wyatt Mitchell

Designer
Margaret Swart

Photo Editor
Zana Woods

Photo Assistant
Sarah Filippi

Photography
Jeff Mermelstein

Client
Wired

This one-pager creates some extra visual interest by using a text block (in a larger point size but with a tighter leading to match the leading of the rest of the story) that is wider and wraps around the remainder of the text, plus an outsized initial cap floating in white space, aligned with the top of the text block.

TEST

Steven Levy The Thingamapod

The chunky, funky Chumby wireless device was built to feel more like a pet than an iPod.

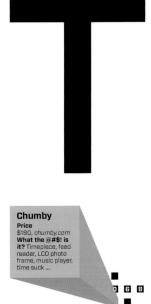

Chumby
Price
$180, *chumby.com*
What the @#$! is it? Timepiece, feed reader, LCD photo frame, music player, time suck ...

0 6 8

T he Chumby didn't have to look like a mashup of a beanbag, a TV, and a Birkenstock sandal. It didn't have to come wrapped in a woven pouch like a pound of pistachios. It didn't even have to have a fanciful moniker that trips off the tongue and cutely embeds a synonym for *friend*. But because Chumby does all these things, this gizmo, which hit the market in February, has a shot at overcoming its greatest failing—that it's really hard to explain exactly what it is. (Here's my attempt: Chumby is a $180 Internet-widget device that uses Wi-Fi to grab Flash video, RSS feeds, Net audio, and other mini apps. In other words, it's a clock radio for the Twitterati.) By sheer force of personality, Chumby gets you to stick around long enough to discover its virtues. ¶ How do you get people to relate to a thing as if it were a pet? One way is to shape it like an animal, as Nabaztag, a Chumby competitor, does: Its Wi-Fi gadget is molded to look like a rabbit, complete with twirling ears. Much better, though, to work a more subtle magic. The auto industry long ago mastered the technique of using form to evoke speedy, violent wildlife— even when standing still, a Jaguar looks like it's chasing down prey. "We touch people's emotions by using a certain shape," explains Peter Horbury, head of Ford's North and South American design team. ¶ The Chumby people wanted to mess with our heads as well. "Make the anti-iPod," company founder and CEO Steve Tomlin told industrial designer Thomas Meyerhoffer. "I thought *soft*," Meyerhoffer says, "so the user is emotionally attracted." ¶ That wasn't easy. Manufacturing a Chumby combines some unusual materials—a flat glass screen, a somewhat rigid skeleton to protect the electronics, a layer of padding for pliancy, and a smooth coat of Italian leather for sensuality. In fact, the company had trouble finding an electronics factory in China that also had the fashion skills to stitch the leather. But the final product nicely »

PHOTOGRAPH BY **Jeff Mermelstein**

Typographic "furniture"

THE TERM *FURNITURE* IN TYPOGRAPHY refers to all of those bits and pieces that support and separate the text elements: rules, boxes, dotted and dashed lines, ornaments, and the like. These may represent signature elements for a recurring publication or project, or they may help form an important structure for the content. They can be decorative or functional, or both. Column rules and scotch rules in particular seem to go in and out of fashion—they are generally considered more traditional; however, they may also be used in an untraditional way.

Project
Editorial page

Art Director
Roger Black

Designer
Roger Black

Image
Atelier Marge

Client
Type magazine

Thick horizontal bars and strong column rules position the text in space and create a muscular structure for the story. At bottom right, "scotch rules" frame the pullquote. Interestingly, the page design pictured within the page also exhibits the use of thick horizontal rules as typographic furniture.

SHAKING THE WALLS

Design and type working together

Old-style meets the nouvelle vague *with work from Atlier Marge and Long-Type*

By Lucas Czarnecki

ATELIER MARGE took inspiration directly from Théâtre de la Bastille's Director, Jean-Marie Hordé, when designing the theater's 2017–2018 season promotion: "The theater is a democratic experience in this first, I believe, if it aspires to a common recognition, it does not yield on the real fragmentation of looks."

The quote is translated from an impassioned editorial written by Hordé in April, which gave Atelier Marge all they needed to craft the strikingly original collateral for the trend-setting Parisian theater. Their designs employ the idea of fragmentation, cutting together shards of red, black, and white to create attractive and surprising mosaics for posters, banners, programs, and more.

The theater, which has been a cinema and vaudeville theater at times through its history, began operating as Théâtre de la Bastille in 1982 and came under the leadership of Hordé in 1989. In the near-30 years since, the Hordé has set the two-room theater apart as an international leader in both dance and theatre. The gravity of working for such a landmark was not lost on stafff at Atelier Marge, which makes no claim that their designs have had an impact on the theater's position.

TO BUILD the typographic palette, Atelier Marge collaborated with its close partner LongType, ⅔which develops fonts exclusively for "real-life graphic design projects." The resulting designs juxtapose two styles: early Modernist typography and Dadaist collages.

Typographic, textural collages, reminiscent of Kurt Schwitters in form but not color, draw the pedestrian's eye and echo another line from Hordé's editorial: "Faces are lost, words and images blur." These loud and often dense graphics appear to move and fall in place—exactly the kind of effect needed on crowded walls in Paris.

The color scheme, frequent horizontal rules, bold sans-serif type, flush left treatment, and use of all-caps harken back to 1920's modernist typography à la Jan Tschichold. Considering the similar style and subject matter, Tschichold's "Musik der Zeit, Wort der Zeit, Tanz der Zeit" poster could have been an inspiration for Atelier Marge.

According to Jean François Porchez, founder of Typofonderie in Paris, Atelier Marge "are story-telling graphic designers who believe that the expressiveness of typography is a determining factor in their work. Designing their own typefaces is a natural exten-

"Our work is a typo-graphic and colorful radicality—in the service of expressive and paradoxically figurative compositions."
—Mathieu Chévara
Atelier Marge

They create a demanding visual language which prolongs, emphasizes and questions.

18

The privileged status given to Cuban nationals under the 1996 Cuban Refugee Adjustment Act of 1966 can be rescinded at any time by the president.

The Act says that "any alien who is a native or citizen of Cuba [...] who has been physically present in the United States for at least one year, may be adjusted by the Attorney General, in his discretion, [...] to that of an alien lawfully admitted for permanent residence." All it takes to end the present policy is a directive from the president to the attorney general ordering him or her to cease granting permanent residence to Cubans who enter the U.S. without visas.

A president can exercise his or her pardon powers set out in Article II, Section 2 of the U.S. Constitution to end the incarceration of the three remaining Cuban intelligence officers.

Commutation of sentences (reducing them to time served) is inherent in the president's power to pardon. In the case of the three remaining members of the original "Cuban Five" who are still in prison, a commutation of their sentences would, at this date, mean they will have served 16 years in prison. An additional advantage, apart from addressing the Cuban people's sense of injustice, is that a commutation could help facilitate the release of USAID contractor Alan Gross, who is jailed in Cuba and not yet one-third of the way through a 15-year prison sentence.

And yes, the president can also resolve Cuba's grievance over the continued U.S. presence in Guantánamo Bay.

The right of the U.S. to establish and occupy a naval base at Guantánamo Bay dates to 1901, with modifications in 1903 and 1934. In the latter year, the U.S. and Cuba signed a treaty stipulating that, "So long as the United States of America shall not abandon the said naval station at Guantánamo or the two governments shall not agree to modification of its present limits, the station shall continue to have the territorial area it now has [...]".

The U.S. Constitution gives the president the power to make treaties on behalf of the U.S., but says nothing about the power to terminate treaties. That power is nevertheless held by the president. Article II, Section 1, provides the president with the "executive power" of the United States. That power finds its principal application in the execution of the nation's laws. Under Article VI of the Constitution, treaties are considered laws of the United States. Should the president decide, in the language of the 1934 treaty, to "abandon" Guantánamo,

his execution of that prerogative of the treaty would, at the same time, terminate the treaty itself. Legal precedent supports the conclusion that Congress would be powerless to overturn such action. In *United States v. Curtiss-Wright Export Corp.* (1936), the Supreme Court said:

"It is important to bear in mind that we are here dealing [with...] the very delicate, plenary and exclusive *power of the President as the sole organ of the federal government in the field of international relations*—a power which does not require as a basis for its exercise an act of Congress [...]" [emphasis added].

Relying on that authority, then-President Jimmy Carter was able in 1980 to terminate the mutual defense treaty with Taiwan following his recognition of the Chinese government in Beijing. Similarly, President George W. Bush in 2001 gave Russia notice and withdrew from the Anti-Ballistic Missile (ABM) Treaty ratified by the Senate in 1972.

3: MOVE TO FULL NORMALIZATION OF RELATIONS

Trade

Cuba and the U.S. are founding members of the World Trade Organization (WTO). When the WTO was established in 1995, both the U.S. and Cuba accepted the General Agreement on Tariffs and Trade (GATT) as binding on all members. Article I of the Agreement prohibits signatories from discriminating among signatory nations when extending trade benefits. For example, if a nation grants another nation a lower customs duty rate on a product, it must extend that rate to all WTO members. This means both the U.S. and Cuba must extend Most-Favored-Nation (MFN) treatment to other members' exported products, with the result that Cuban goods must be allowed into the U.S. on terms as favorable as those extended to other WTO members' goods.

However, in 1962, the U.S. invoked the Article XXI exemption of GATT when Kennedy issued Proclamation 3447 (referred to above) to establish the current embargo on Cuba. Under this article, any nation can opt out of its obligations under the GATT by claiming such action "necessary for the protection of its essential security interests." All it will take for MFN status to apply to Cuba-origin products is a presidential rescission of the U.S. invocation of Article XXI.

Intellectual Property Protections

Currently, intellectual property protections between the U.S. and Cuba are covered by an 85-year-old agreement, the General Inter-American Convention for Trademark and Commercial Protection. A number of developments in intellectual property (cybernames, etc.) have occurred in the intervening years. One of the more useful first steps in restoring normal relations with Cuba would be to negotiate a new agreement that reciprocally protects the intellectual property of each country's nationals.

Environmental Cooperation

The U.S. and Cuba share the Caribbean. As an element of normalized relations, it makes sense for the two countries to enter into agreements ensuring reciprocal cooperation to protect Caribbean waters and the fragile environments of its islands.

CONCLUSION

Some aspects of normalized relations—although very few—require Congress to act. For example, any ambassador the U.S. president appoints to Cuba would require confirmation by the U.S. Senate. The current representation by heads of the Interests Sections degrades bilateral relations. The U.S. maintains diplomatic relations with Russia, Nicaragua, Venezuela, and other countries while having no fondness for the governments of those nations. It can do the same with Cuba. Another area in which Congress would play a role is the enactment of investment protection measures for U.S. investors in Cuba. Congress has a role in this because such protections are most often secured by bilateral investment treaties that require Senate rat-

ification. But again, the role of Congress in the normalization process is a small one.

It is clear that a president, using the inherent authority of the office, can take the United States there. When the moment arrives, there remain a series of steps that the U.S.—and Cuba—must take to truly establish normal relations between the one-time Cold War enemies that go beyond just lifting the embargo. However, some of the most punitive elements of the embargo could become the tools of creative, focused diplomacy by executive action. The question is when, not how.

Robert Muse is a Washington DC-based lawyer.

FOR SOURCE CITATIONS SEE: WWW.AMERICASQUARTERLY.ORG/MUSE

Project
Editorial spread

Creative Director
Donald Partyka

Designer
Kathy Yun

Client
Americas Quarterly magazine

Typographic furniture is used here to create the illusion of tradition, as in the style of an old dictionary. The discreet use of ornament, the modern caps, traditional typefaces, the en dashes on either side of the letters of the alphabet, the column rules, and the boxes framing the pages all contribute to the effect.

91 Decks, callouts, and pull quotes

THESE FUNCTION AS ENTRY POINTS to the text for the reader who is still undecided about whether to commit to a complete article or passage of text. They can be playful or dramatic: this is a chance for the designer to take some liberties and create some typographic focal points that leap out of the background textual tonality of the content. Callouts and pull quotes may be lifted out of their context within the text and repositioned to maximize the page design, or they may be left in place and highlighted; either way, the quotes should be carefully chosen to represent the best of the body copy.

Not bam bam bam bam bam bam,

but *bama bampa barama bam bammity bam bam bammity barampa* FIRE! was the first thing she thought of because nobody ever banged on your apartment door in a building like this nobody would be so impolite as to even rap on your door with his knuckles unannounced in a building like this much less bang on it with both fists for this was not one fist pounding on the door but both fists *bama barampa bam bam bammity barampa bam bam*—

FIRE! she rose from the 18th-century burled-wood secretary, her grandmother's, where she always wrote her thank-you notes and hurried out of the study and across the living room toward the entry gallery absolutely by herself in all these rooms not one soul to look to for help because it was Sunday and her husband was still down in Palm Beach and none of the help, not even the Filipino, came in on Sundays—BAMMITY BAM BARAMPA terribly loud now that she was approaching the door, and an entirely new fear stopped her in her tracks. Whoever was on the other side of that door was not yelling "Fire!" or anything else. A PUSH-IN ROBBER! She could feel her heart start hammering away in her rib cage. In all their years in this building, nothing even close to a push-in robbery had ever occurred. She had never heard of any such thing at any other co-op on Park Avenue, either. Push-in robberies happened out on Long Island in places like Hempstead and Roslyn or was it North Babylon, the last one she read about? in the *Times*? more likely the *Post*.

Now she was in the entry gallery no more than two feet from the door. In what she meant to be a loud, strong voice, she said, "Who is it?"

The banging stopped. With that slow syllable-by-syllable pronunciation most people would save for a cabdriver or some other servitor for whom English was not his first language, he said his name.

She let out her breath and immediately felt her runaway heart get hold of itself. It was merely the new tenant, the man who had the hedge fund with the whimsical name and "more money than God," as her husband had put it, but why on earth was he creating such a ruckus?

Ever so gingerly, she opened the door. He was a meat-fed man wearing a rather shiny—silk?—and rather too vividly striped open shirt that paunched out slightly over his waistband. The waistband was down at hip-hugger level because the lower half of his fortyish body was squeezed into a pair of twentyish jeans—prefaded? distressed?—were those the right terms?—gloriously frayed at the bottoms of the pant legs, from which protruded a pair of long, shiny pointed alligator shoes. They looked like weapons.

"Oh," she said. She started to add, "Please come in," but the look on his face made her worry that he might do just that.

Without any preamble, no "Excuse me" or even "Hello," much less "How do you do?"—and they had never had any communication other than a nod once on the elevator—he said, "I need to speak to your husband." It was the sort of commanding voice that makes it clear that I *need* what I *want—now*.

Meekly: "He's not here."

Accusingly: "Where *is* he?"

It was none of his business, but he was so overbearing she heard herself confessing, "Palm Beach."

The big man in the ridiculously tight jeans looked at her with his mouth open and his eyebrows squeezed together as if she had just told him something not only astonishing but implausible, beyond the boundaries of reason.

"I'll probably be talking to him later on. If you'd like, I could tell him—"

"Ahhh … no," he said in a lower, calmer voice. He suddenly turned his head away from her. Something had caught his eye. "Nice *vaz*. Tiffany, right?"

It took her a moment to realize he meant "vase," the vase on a little table in the entry gallery. Why he had pronounced it the French way she couldn't imagine. She answered in a toneless voice, "No, I don't think so." In fact, it was older and considerably more precious than a Tiffany, but she hadn't the faintest desire to prolong the conversation with any discussion of the higher ceramics.

"Looks like a Tiffany," he said. He turned as if to leave but then swung back. "Maybe you could pass along one thing—for when he comes back from *Palm Beach*." He gave the *Palm Beach* a certain edge, as if her husband's being in Palm Beach were a pretentious or perhaps slothful and decadent act on his part. "Tell him I hope he's having a good time. What's the name of that club they have there, the Everest or something?"

"The Everglades"—and as soon as the words passed her lips, she knew she should have feigned ignorance.

"Well, tell him I hope he's having a nice time at his club in Palm Beach, because my wife and I are having a lousy time in our apartment in New York."

"My goodness. What's happened?" She immediately regretted asking that too.

He took a deep breath … and then … a red storm blew.

"What's happened? What's happened is, I just spent $200,000 on a state-of-the-art positive-pressure HVAC system in our apartment, and I've gotta put in new windows to make it work right, and I gotta put four vents, four lousy little vents, through the walls of this building, which nobody's ever gonna notice—and THE WAY IN UP TO YOUR ARMPITS, AND YOU CAN'T MOVE! AND I'LL TELL YOU ANOTHER THING: IT'S NO USE TRYING TO BE NICE AND ACCOMMODATING AND REASONABLE IN THIS BUILDING! WE TRIED THAT, AND YOU CAN SEE HOW FAR IT GOT US! NEW WINDOWS, WHICH WOULD IMPROVE THE FREAKING BUILDING, AND FOUR LOUSY LITTLE DUCTS IS ALL WE'RE TALKING ABOUT. LOOK, WHETHER ANY OF YOU PEOPLE LIKE IT OR NOT, WE *LIVE* HERE. I PAID A FREAKING FORTUNE FOR THAT APARTMENT! OKAY? THAT'S WHERE WE LIVE, AND YOU PEOPLE ARE RUINING IT FOR US! TELL HIM *THAT*! Okay?"

She shut the door in his face. She was indignant, but that wasn't the reason she shut the door. She shut the door because she was afraid. The man was beginning to sizzle like a fuse, and she didn't want his face to be in hers when he exploded.

For men making, in many cases, tens of millions and up per year, they qualify as young. They talk about business in young-warrior metaphors: "pulling the trigger" (making huge risky bets on the market); "mowing them all down" (overpowering companies that try to block your strategies); "This is war!" (get out of my way—or else I'll make you suffer); "Surrender your booty!" (I'm a corporate raider poised to take over your company); "We don't eat what we don't kill" (if you, the investor, don't make a profit, then we in the hedge fund's management don't take a profit ourselves, something oddly true in spirit although, as we shall soon see, not in fact). *These people* tend to be bright and well educated, many at Harvard, Princeton, and other top-ranked colleges. They come from well-educated

He strikes a BLACKBEARD THE PIRATE *pose right out in the open— Blackbeard, who took what he wanted and* WAS ACCOUNTABLE TO *no one.*

I've gotta put it *now*—AND THE BOARD IN ALL ITS AUGUST WISDOM IS BREAKING MY— OBSTRUCTING ME EVERY INCH OF THE WAY!" He paused. "Nawwww … don't tell him that. Just let him enjoy himself in *Palm Beach … at the club*."

"Well. I don't—"

"Of course you don't. Why should you? Right? He's the one who's president of the board, and so why should—" He stopped abruptly.

"Well, in any event—"

He trampled the *any event* too.

"When we moved into this building, we were told this was a first-class building. We were told this building was 'prewar.' That's all we kept hearing, 'prewar,' and they don't build them like this anymore. Okay? But they didn't tell us it also has a bunch of obsolete rules that are prewar too. *Prehistoric* is more like it, if you want my candid opinion."

"I'm afraid that's not—"

The *that's not* got flattened. "The board of this building is like quicksand. You put one toe in"—he lifted one of his weapons and pointed the toe down with a mock prissiness—"and it SUCKS YOU ALL

A few days later, she happened to be sitting in her study recounting this story to an acquaintance. She asked him, "What do you suppose he meant by all this 'you people' business? It's like they all have a big chip on their shoulder. What is it that makes these people so angry and nasty?"

These people are hedge fund managers such as the bratwurst in blue jeans we just met, private equity fund managers (who have become increasingly indistinguishable from hedge fund managers), stock and bond traders (but nobody else in the investment banking firms they work for—especially not that pathetic creature the C.E.O.), and various lone-wolf entrepreneurs such as real estate developers. Everybody who cares at all knows their occupations, but what's their *problem*?

There are some heavy-hitting Medicare-qualified hedge fund managers, notably Carl Icahn, 71, and the home run king, T. Boone Pickens, 78, who made $1.5 billion—personally—in a single year, 2005. But most of *these people* are in their late thirties and early to mid forties.

families. They still enjoy the virgin animal health of youth. They are flush with optimism and confidence, as well as money. With all that going for them, what inna nameagod *is* their problem?

THE BATTLEMENT REACHES ITS PEAK IN New York City's Connecticut commuter towns, Stamford, Norwalk, Westport, and especially Greenwich. With its manicured-bucolic wilderness-less-woodsy rolling hills and arboreal dells, all ornamented by mansions and irrigated by cash flow, Greenwich is now headquarters for more than 100 hedge funds handling just about $100 billion, nearly one-tenth of all hedge fund money in the world. This town of 62,000 has become the Wall Street of hedge funds.

The collision of new money and old money or, to be more accurate in our American context, slightly older money, has been a recurring drama. At the turn of the 20th century, Edith Wharton established herself as perhaps America's greatest female novelist by focusing on

---

Project	Designer	Client
Feature spread	Jana Meier	*Condé Nast Portfolio*

Creative Director	Illustrator	
Robert Priest	Kagan McLeod	

Stacked repetitive large words are certainly a way to draw the reader in; on the opposite page, the pull quote is made more interesting by shifts in typographic case, slope, and color (as well as the use of an illustration). Note the use of text overlapping an initial cap to indicate a break in the story.

THE RUSSIAN
CONNECTION
The investigation
firm run by Yuri
Koshkin (таят) hires
ex-K.G.B. agents to
advise U.S. companies.
*Photographed in
Arlington, Virginia,
on November 18.*

SPY
vs.
SPY

They're
leaving "the
Company"
to snoop on
your com-
pany. How
C.I.A. agents
are pushing
*corporate
espionage* to
ominous new
extremes

BY
Douglas
Frantz

PHOTOGRAPHS BY
Matt *Hoyle*

Project
Feature spread

Creative Director
Robert Priest

Designer
Jana Meier

Photographer
Matt Hoyle

Client
Condé Nast Portfolio

The treatment of the deck of this opener
is quiet and surreptitious, as befits the
imagery and the headline treatment.

92 The "birth and death" of the text

JUST AS WE ARE BORN AND WE DIE, so the text begins and ends. Mark these seminal events well; regard the text as a discrete entity and plan its unfolding as you would a lifetime. The birth and death of the text should be related to one another visually. Some of us lead boisterous, flamboyant lives; others, lives of quiet simplicity. As always, evaluate the nature of the content and make your typographic decisions accordingly.

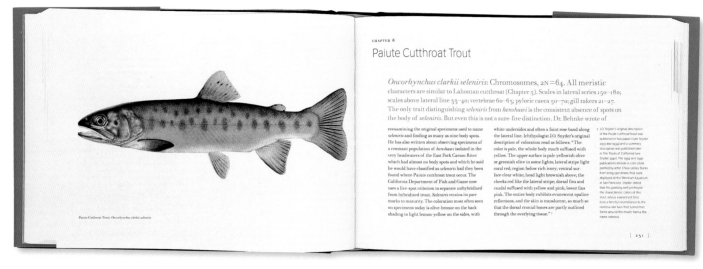

Project
Cutthroat: Native Trout of the West

Art Director
Charlie Nix

Designers
Charlie Nix and Gary Robbins

Client
University of California Press

The elegant text treatment elevates the content of this book and is consistent from beginning to end.

Andrónico Luksic Craig

Mr. President-elect, it is time for the U.S. to present a "New Deal" to the international community, one which restores the integrity of multilateralism and the precedence of global institutions.

You have pledged to inspire change in the administration of the domestic matters that confront you. I hasten to encourage you, at the same time, to address the global impact of your election and the possibilities that new, distinct and modern U.S. policies might represent to nations around the world and this hemisphere.

You must provide very clear and powerful signs that a new era has opened, in which things will be different, when the U.S. is willing to reach out to the world with a friendly, open hand.

As an entrepreneur and businessman from Chile, I would like to offer three suggestions for your global policy that I feel are most relevant to Latin America but which may also provide a clear message to the world.

It is fundamental that you conduct an extensive review of the current U.S. trade embargo of Cuba, with the intention of ending it. This antiquated policy, marooned in the Treasury Department, has produced a very negative image throughout the Americas. The embargo is not only demonstrably inefficient; it lacks economic rationale. All attempts to blockade commerce are vulnerable in one way or another and, at the end of the day, they are counterproductive. The recent change of government in Cuba, as well as the start of a new administration in the U.S., provide an opportunity to re-think a policy which may have made sense in the past under different conditions—but now no longer does.

Second, it is important that you play an active role in advancing multilateral trade agreements. Further trade liberalization will deliver a significant economic boost and a powerful impetus to speed the recovery from the current global economic slowdown. This is a more reasonable alternative than allowing the trajectory of inflation and recession to continue and imposes a lower cost upon the Americas in both economic and social terms, namely by attacking unemployment and poverty.

Despite the recent failure of the Doha Round, the U.S. can still push for trade liberalization initiatives at the World Trade Organization . Alternatively, such liberalization schemes can be achieved at the APEC level or indeed even at regional or sub-regional levels.

Third, you must address immigration early in your tenure. It will undoubtedly be a politically volatile subject. But it may also be the first opportunity you have to demonstrate to the world the goodwill of the U.S. and, as such, would become the cornerstone of your global policy. This matter is of preeminent concern to the entire Latin American region as it affects most of our nations either directly or indirectly.

On these three issues, we anxiously await your leadership, with the same hope for real change that so many citizens of your nation believe you represent. I look to your administration to be the author of real change for global policy, but especially hope that you will focus due attention on normalizing policy toward Latin America, a region that has long been either too prominent in U.S. policy or almost entirely neglected. ●

Andrónico Luksic Craig is the Vice Chairman of the Board of Directors of *Banco de Chile*.

> **Further trade liberalization will deliver a significant economic boost and a powerful impetus to speed the recovery from the current global economic slowdown.**

PORTRAIT BY CHRIS LYONS

AMERICASQUARTERLY.ORG

María Teresa Ronderos

:Develop a New Hemispheric Vision.

OR MANY YEARS MOST LATIN AMERICAN PRESidents favored maintaining close relations with the United States. The best university students coveted scholarships to attend graduate school in the U.S., and thousands of the more than 190 million poor in our region migrated to the U.S.—sometimes at great personal risk.

But "the times, they are a-changin'." Today, many Latin American leaders—and their people—are trying to establish some distance and develop their own world views while at the same time work together toward achieving a more permanent autonomy. President Hugo Chávez in Venezuela and a few others hurl heavy verbal artillery at the U.S. every day. While other socialist Presidents in the region may not be as offensive, the recent creation of the South American Security Council lead by Brazilian President Luiz Inácio Lula da Silva, in which even Colombia, the closest ally of the U.S. is participating, is symptomatic of the change.

It's not so much that the region has become anti-American. But a feeling of disillusionment with what the United States represents has emerged.

The next U.S. president must take these changes into account as he develops new policies towards the region. Latin America has come a long way in the last decade. Its democracies are maturing. As Salvadoran ex-guerrilla leader Joaquin Villalobos once said: "In this region social and political actors who had no participation are now seated at the table of power; with elections and democracy, violence has no reason to exist."

Its economies have matured as well. In the longest and greatest expansion in the region since the 1970s, average Latin American GDP grew around 4.8 per cent each year between 2002 and 2007. At the same time, many Latin American cities such as Rosario in Argentina, Curitiba in Brazil and Bogotá in Colombia are proposing new and creative urban models for the world, in which the car is no longer the paradigm. These are cities of parks and public libraries, of exclusive bicycle lanes and brand new public schools in the poorest neighborhoods designed by prominent architects.

In spite of these transformations, U.S. policies do not seem to reflect that someone is taking note of the change. Too often we find the same disdainful look at our countries and the same narrow-minded approach guided by short-term U.S. interests in the region: open markets for American business and fighting illegal drugs.

Hence my first recommendation to the

Project
Feature spread

Creative Director
Donald Partyka

Illustrator
Chris Lyons

Client
Americas Quarterly

This related family of stories has repeating elements that link them together as a package. The type treatment is fitting for the serious content, which aims at influencing political policy makers.

93 Chaos versus order

OPPOSITES ATTRACT AND CAN COEXIST. Sometimes we crave structure; other times, we want nothing more than to break free from that very structure. As long as the designer's intention is clear, either approach may work well—or, in some cases, both can work together, playing o one another. Type, whether it's individual letters or passa of text, has the plasticity to accommodate chaos as well a the inherent structure that allows it to be well organized.

Project
Influence chart

Designer, Illustrator
Marian Bantjes

Client
Marian Bantjes

An infographic of methods, mentors, places, and graphic movements that influenced the artist is a masterful blend of organic organization. Its items are contained within a free-flowing and rococo framework that is orderly, yet wild.

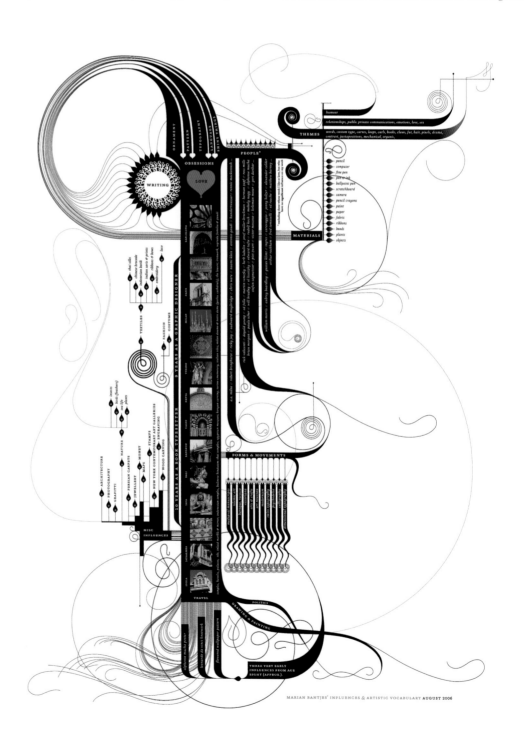

Cyber-Neologoliferation

In the age of
the Internet, the Oxford
English Dictionary is coming
face to face with the boundlessness of the English language.
By James Gleick

When I got to John Simpson and his band of lexicographers in Oxford earlier this fall, they were working on the P's. *Pletzel, plish, pod person, point-and-shoot, polyamorous* — these words were all new, one way or another. They had been plowing through the P's for two years but were almost done (except that they'll never be done), and the Q's will be "just a twinkle of an eye," Simpson said. He prizes patience and the long view. A pale, soft-spoken man of middle height and profound intellect, he is chief editor of the Oxford English Dictionary and sees himself as a steward of tradition dating back a century and a half. "Basically it's the same work as they used to do in the 19th century," he said. "When I started in 1976, we were still working very much on these index cards, everything was done on these index cards." He picked up a stack of 6-inch-by-4-inch slips and riffled through them. A thou-

Typography by Sam Winston

54

Project
Feature spread

Art Director
Arem Duplessis

Art Director, Designer
Gail Bichler

Client
The New York Times Magazine

Here we can see order on one side, disorder on the other, achieved solely through the creative use of type as illustration as well as information.

94 Commentary, marginalia, and alternate languages

AS EARLY AS THE HEBREW TALMUD, commentary on the main text—indeed, layers of commentary not unlike the text threads that are everywhere online—needed to be accommodated on the page. The Talmud, a marvel of typographic structure and hierarchy, employed many ingenious techniques for incorporating commentary, which ran around the central text. More common is the practice of allowing an extra-wide margin outside of the primary text area (henc the term *marginalia*). In order to set the text apart even further and to respond to the narrower measure, margin is usually set in a smaller point size with correspondingly proportional leading; sometimes its color or slope are als different from the main text.

Project
Birds of the World

Art Director
Charlie Nix

Designers
Charlie Nix, Whitney Grant, and May Jampathom

Client
University of California Press

An elegant treatment of marginalia is used here to provide some info-bits about the species.

Project

*Blow-Up: Photography, Cinema
and the Brain*

Company

Pure+Applied

Client

Distributed Art Publishers (D.A.P)

Offsets in body copy relieve the density of
the text of this scholarly work and provide
a framework for the narrow text blocks
used for footnotes (typically relegated to
the bottom of the page).

Project

Karsonwilker's 12 Days in Serbia

Creative Director

George Mill, aka Stanislav Sharp

Client

Publikum Calendar Project

This unusual exposition of a dual-language
text uses alternating lines of language
in opposing colors. The reader slides an
acetate insert to cover one of the two
languages, so that only alternating lines
are visible at any one time.

ПУБЛИКУМ КАЛЕНДАР ФЕНОМАН
PUBLIKUM CALENDAR PHENOMAN

неким страницама осетио да се нешто догодило, нешто што сам и тражио, а то је нека
mixture of the East and West. Something like your handwriting which is modern, trendy in New
мешавина Истока и Запада. Нешто налик на ваш рукопис, који је модеран и у тренду у
York and you were using the stuff from Serbia … And the usage of different things from Serbia
Њујорку, а користили сте ствари из Србије… А коришћење различитих ствари из Србије
was kinda very unusual and funny, especially the thing with the arch in which you put all these
било је на неки начин врло необично и чудно, посебно она ствар са кружницом у коју сте
different objects. So, I was happy with that because it was different… I don't think that any
убацили све те различите предмете. Био сам задовољан јер је било другачије… Мислим
Serbian designer would do something like that and I thought it was also going to be a different
да ниједан дизајнер из Србије не би направио тако нешто и мислио сам да ће то бити
experience for the Serbian people viewing it. What I was looking for was to have some sort of
исто тако другачији доживљај за српску публику. Оно што сам тражио било је нека врста
a nice product bearing characteristics of both cultures. I think I gave the same answer to Bata
доброг производа са карактеристикама обе културе. Мислим да сам тако исто одговорио
and Srdjan, the documentary director, when they asked me what I thought about it… and be-
Бати и Срђану, режисеру документарца, када су ме питали за мишљење… А поред тога,
sides, working with Bata is a very nice experience because he is so open-minded to new ideas.
рад са Батом је лепо искуство зато што је он увек отворен за нове идеје. У ФЕНОМАН
The Phenoman project is about ideas, not too much about design, and I saw some good ideas
пројекту ради се о идејама, а не толико о дизајну, а на вашој презентацији видео сам пар
there at your presentation. I think that was why Bata liked it, too because he really likes clever
добрих идеја. Мислим да је зато и Бати допало, јер он заиста воли занимљиве идеје. Да,
thoughts. Yeah. Let's go then to the party. So, what did you expect from this party? Was it a
да. Идемо сад на журку. И тако, шта сте очекивали од те журке? Да ли је била изненађење
surprise or not? W. Since some of your comrades couldn't hold these things to themselves, we
или пак није? W. Пошто неки од твојих другара нису могли то да задрже за себе, тачно
already knew exactly what would happen and when (laughs). And I think as soon as I heard that
смо знали шта ће се и када десити (смеје се). И мислим да сам, чим сам чуо да ће бити
there would be a karioke machine, and karioke is not very common in Belgrade, I was like - Oh,
караоке, што није баш уобичајено у Београду, помислио: О, Боже, морамо то да урадимо,
my Gosh, we have to do this, because otherwise they will be very angry if we don't do this
јер ће се сви јако љутити ако то не урадимо (смеје се). К. Очекивао сам неки брод са
(laughs). K. I expected some sort of a boat with lots of lights, everybody's just sitting there and
пуно светиљки, да сви седе, а да нас двојица морамо да идемо и певамо пред свим тим
the two of us would have to go and do this song in front of all these people! So, I was like - No,
људима! И зато сам се осећао као: Човече, ово ће бити грозно! W. Мислим да је првих
man, this is going to be horrible! W. I think the first ninety minutes was for the press people, so
деведесет минута било за новинаре, па тада није било караока. Разговарао сам са много
there was no karioke. I talked to many people you were so kind to introduce me to. Also, I loved
њих са којима си био љубазан да ме упознаш. Исто тако допала ми се вода, допао ми се
the water, the boat, and this smell of water and blue sky. I think it was beautiful. There was
брод, и тај мирис воде и плаво небо. Мислим да је било предивно. Прво је био званични
first the official part and I think Stan had about three or four sliwowitz. S. Well, I don't remember
део и чини ми се да је Стан попио три до четири шљивовице. С. Па, ја се доста тога не
too much, I remember we joked like - Let's drink as much as we can - so, I had to be a good host.
сећам, сећам се да смо се шалили у стилу: Хајде да пијемо колико год можемо, тако да
When the boat ride started it was nice with music from the CD and then suddenly these guys - a
сам морао да будем добар домаћин. Кад је брод кренуо, била је добра музика са CD-а
live music band started to play like Bata wanted. So I said - Let's take the microphone and give
и онда су ти момци, музичари, почели да свирају како је Бата желео. После сам рекао:
some sort of speech and try to break all this noise… W. When the official part was over, it was
Хајде да узмемо микрофон, одржимо неки говор и покушамо да разбијемо ту буку… W.
the karioke time. It was like - Now you guys (KW), you wished for this, you wanted to have this
По завршетку званичног дела дошло је време за караоке. Било је као: Е, сада ви момци
and we all know that you love karioke, so show us now what you can do. It was - Oh, my
(KW), то сте тражили, хтели сте то и сви знамо да волите караоке, сада нам покажите
God, so unfair, this is so unfair. Why we? …And I feared that no one had ever done this so Hjalti
шта знате. И то је било … о, мој Боже, тако неправедно, то није било фер. Зашто баш
and I just decided to pick a song. S. I don't remember what we were talking about when Jan
ми? … И плашио сам се да то нико није пре тога радио тако да смо Хјалти и ја одлучили
came and insisted on doing this karioke thing with me, and then Hjalti came over and the three
да изаберемо неку песму. С. Не сећам се о чему смо причали када ми је Јан пришао и
of us had this song. It was really an unusual experience for me because first I had never done

КАРЛССОНВИЛКЕР ВС. СЕРБИЯ
KARLSSONWILKER VS. SERBIA

СТРАНА 66 ДАН 5 И 6
PAGE 66 DAY 5 AND 6

INFOGRAPHICS (also known as data visualizations or information architecture) should be typographically related to the body copy with which they coexist. There are a number of excellent texts and online courses specializing in designing tabular material. This type of design work is a specialty all its own. However well-designed tables and charts—and all infographics—may be, the typography m[...] be carefully crafted with an eye toward proportional rela[...] tionships and a stylistic compatibility with the surroundi[...] text. Clarity and legibility are paramount when conveyin[...] this detailed information.

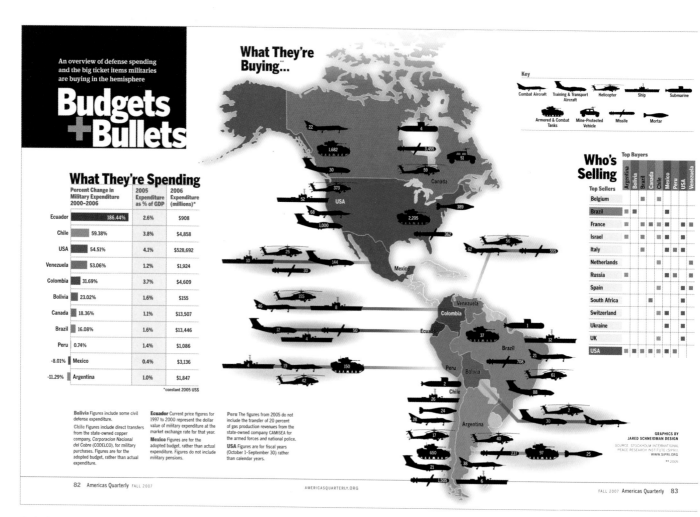

Project
Feature spread

Creative Director
Donald Partyka

Illustrator
Jared Schneidman

Client
Americas Quarterly

This complex infographic combines a number of tables and charts in a very straightforward and legible manner, using simple typestyles and plenty of space to lay out the charts, tables, and diagrams.

Project
Single page

Design Director
David Curcurito

Art Director
Darhil Crook

Associate Art Director
Erin Jang

Client
Esquire

To analyze the characteristics of the subjects of a story, this infographic, set at a vertiginous tilt, slices and dices using a composite of profiles. It is stylistically in keeping with the entire issue's package of profiles.

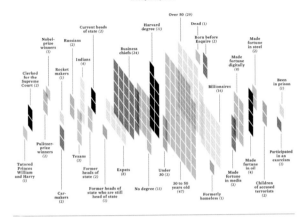

Project
Feature spread

Creative Director
Dean Markadakis

Designer
Jana Meier

Photographer
Jonathan Worth

Client
Fast Company

Lists of statistics (which can otherwise be visually boring) have been enlivened here by the use of simple graphics, changing the scale, color, orientation, and expression of numbers and text.

96 Navigational devices

PAGE NUMBERS, FOLIOS, and other navigational devices are mission critical for designers; time-challenged readers have little patience for finding their own way. Though small and shunted off to remote areas like page bottoms and corners, these bits of text provide the important service of navigation. Whether located in a prominent spot or a lowly one, readers depend on their guidance.

Other navigational devices include any directional signals that assist the reader: arrows, dotted lines, section heads, and any and all typographic or related glyphic elements that serve this purpose. Designers of mobile and tablet apps must integrate UI/UX design elements including taps, swipes, pinches, and other ever-evolving gestural navigation markers, indicating them on-screen.

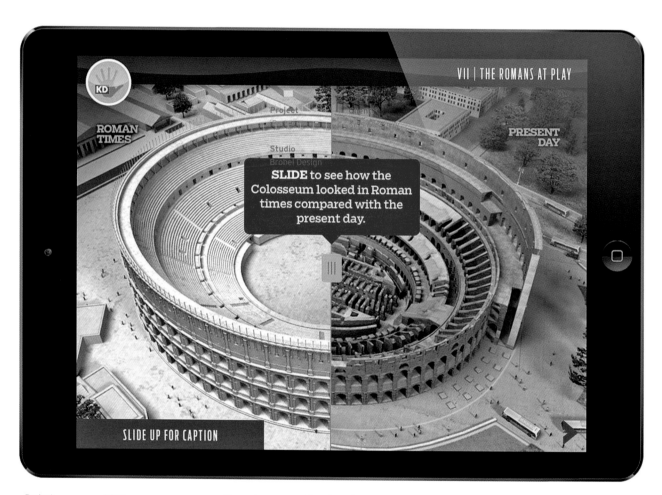

Project
iPad app

Studio
Brobel Design

Client
Kids Discover
magazine

Viewers have many options to navigate this screen; they may slide horizontally to change the timeframe of the image, they may slide up from the bottom for a caption, and an arrow at the bottom right directs them to the following screen.

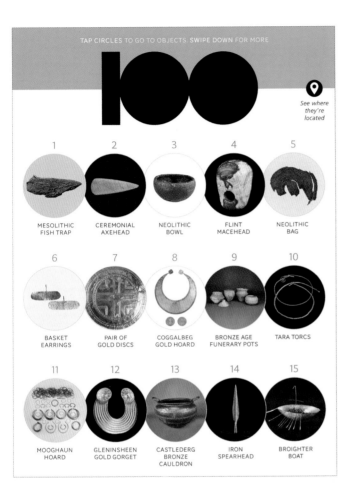

TAP CIRCLES TO GO TO OBJECTS. SWIPE DOWN FOR MORE

100

See where they're located

1 MESOLITHIC FISH TRAP

2 CEREMONIAL AXEHEAD

3 NEOLITHIC BOWL

4 FLINT MACEHEAD

5 NEOLITHIC BAG

6 BASKET EARRINGS

7 PAIR OF GOLD DISCS

8 COGGALBEG GOLD HOARD

9 BRONZE AGE FUNERARY POTS

10 TARA TORCS

11 MOOGHAUN HOARD

12 GLENINSHEEN GOLD GORGET

13 CASTLEDERG BRONZE CAULDRON

14 IRON SPEARHEAD

15 BROIGHTER BOAT

Project
Tablet app

Studio
Joe Zeff Design

Client
Joe Zeff Design

Each image links to a descriptor of the object, as we are directed by the info line at the top of the screen. We can also "swipe down for more." An additional navigation button (top right) will tell where each object is located.

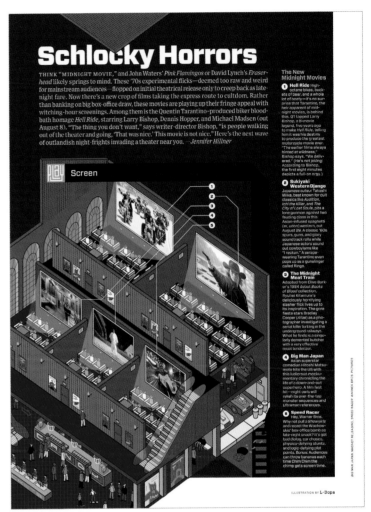

Schlocky Horrors

THINK "MIDNIGHT MOVIE," and John Waters' *Pink Flamingos* or David Lynch's *Eraserhead* likely springs to mind. These '70s experimental flicks—deemed too raw and weird for mainstream audiences—flopped on initial theatrical release only to creep back as late-night fare. Now there's a new crop of films taking the express route to cultdom. Rather than banking on big box-office draw, these movies are playing up their fringe appeal with witching-hour screenings. Among them is the Quentin Tarantino–produced biker bloodbath homage *Hell Ride*, starring Larry Bishop, Dennis Hopper, and Michael Madsen (out August 8). "The thing you don't want," says writer-director Bishop, "is people walking out of the theater and going, 'That was nice.' This movie is not nice." Here's the next wave of outlandish night-frights invading a theater near you. —*Jennifer Hillner*

The New Midnight Movies

1 Hell Ride High-octane bikes, buckets of beer, and a whole lot of booty—it's no surprise that Tarantino, the heir apparent of midnight movies, is behind this. QT tapped Larry Bishop, a B-movie legend, five years ago to make *Hell Ride*, telling him it was his destiny to produce the greatest motorcycle movie ever. "The earlier films always hinted at wildness," Bishop says. "We delivered." (He's not joking; the first eight minutes depicts a full-on orgy.)

2 Sukiyaki Western Django Japanese auteur Takashi Miike, best known for cult classics like *Audition*, *Ichi the Killer*, and *The City of Lost Souls*, pits a lone gunman against two feuding clans in this Asian-infused spaghetti (er, udon) western, out August 29. A classic '80s spurs, guns, and glory soundtrack rolls while Japanese actors sound out cowboyisms like "I reckon." A serape-wearing Tarantino even pops up as a gunslinger called Ringo.

3 The Midnight Meat Train Adapted from Clive Barker's 1984 debut collection, *Books of Blood*, Ryuhei Kitamura's deliciously horrifying slasher flick lives up to its inspiration. The gore fiesta stars Bradley Cooper (*Alias*) as a photographer investigating a serial killer lurking in the underground railways. What he finds is a singularly demented butcher with a very effective meat tenderizer.

4 Big Man Japan Asian superstar comedian Hitoshi Matsumoto hits the US with this ludicrous mockumentary chronicling the life of a down-and-out superhero. A film fest hit—night owls will relish its over-the-top monster sequences and *Ultraman* references.

5 Speed Racer Hey, Warner Bros. Why not pull a *Showgirls* and recast the Wachowskis' box-office bomb as late-night snack? It's got bad dialog, cor chases, physics-defying stunts, and logic-defying plot. Bonus: Audiences can throw bananas each time Chim Chim the chimp gets screen time.

ILLUSTRATION BY L-Dopa

Project
Single page

Creative Director
Scott Dadich

Design Director
Wyatt Mitchell

Designer
Margaret Swart

Illustrator
L-Dopa

Client
Wired

The illustration incorporates screens keyed to the list at right; numbered indicators help readers navigate to the screen matching the text.

The Page 199

Margins and gutters

THE SPACES WITHIN AND BETWEEN areas of text are places where the eye can rest; they also help define the tenor of the content. Books have a more leisurely pace and the margins and gutters reflect that pacing; magazines and newspapers are "busier" and more urgent in their appearance, so the space around the text is lessened.

Gutters and the space they require depend on the width of the project and the binding (as well as the weight and flexibility of the stock). A saddle-stitched project will fall open to the page more easily and therefore need less space across the gutter; a perfect-bound project, stiffer in the middle, will need more gutter space so that the text does not get "swallowed up" in the middle.

Project
Cutthroat: Native Trout of the West

Art Director
Charlie Nix

Designers
Charlie Nix and Gary Robbins

Client
University of California Press

This classical horizontal book format lies fairly flat when open, so the gutter has sufficient space to accommodate readability. Spaces between columns and overall page margins are generous but not wasteful.

Project
Editorial spread

Creative Director
Blake Taylor

Art Director and Designer
Sarah Garcea

Client
Inc.

The four-column grid is used with three different typographic weights, styles, color, and leading. Because the text is set rag right, the columns have plenty of space between them. Note the "hanging" length of the numbered text blocks, a more casual approach than the first two columns, which are bottom aligned.

This magazine is perfect-bound, so it requires a generous gutter to separate the pages.

98 Framing the text

LOOKING AT THE TEXT as a unit, how much space should be allowed around the edges of the page, and between two pages? Classical proportions such as the golden section rectangle are often used in book design, and magazines and newspapers have conventions all their own (generally there is not as much space devoted to framing the text in these). In web design, space is even at a greater premium, with margins that are almost nonexistent.

Project
Open Studio

Company
Studio of ME/AT

Designer
Alexander Tochilovsky

Client
Cranbrook Academy of Art

This novel turning ribbon of paper forms a frame within a frame and provides multiple surfaces for text; it works neatly with the photography opposite with its unfolding spaces.

Project
Editorial spread

Design Director
Roger Black

Client
Type magazine

Circumscribed by a panoply of vertical, horizontal, and scotch rules, the text blocks seem tidier and more organized as they float within generous margins.

99 Floating in space

THINK OF THE TYPOGRAPHY as a person, who needs a certain amount of personal space to feel "comfortable." How much space should be left so that there is a feeling of enough separation? This may depend as much on the circumstances as on the type of person (or content).

PREVIOUS SPREAD
Untitled (peasant militia),
Eitaro Ishigaki, oil painting,
as reproduced in New Masses,
December 15, 1936 (detail).

ABOVE, FIGURE 1
Bombardment, 1937-38,
Philip Guston, oil on canvas.

NEW YORK VISUAL artists with leftist sympathies strongly supported efforts to preserve Spain's democratic government when it came under attack by Franco's troops in 1936; they continued to agitate for its survival and for an end to America's embargo on military assistance to the embattled Spanish defenders through fundraising campaigns, exhibitions, and potent visual images until the Republican government surrendered in 1939. The energy to undertake such activism was generated by their recent successes in gaining federal work-relief for artists through the establishment of the Works Progress Administration's Federal Art Project (WPA-FAP) in 1935, and in developing several militant organizations to demand fair treatment for these new federal workers and to promote democracy and artists' rights in the larger society.

The national Artists' Union (AU) was formed in New York in 1935 by the same artists who agitated to gain work-relief programs and then found employment on the WPA-FAP. Along with efforts to institute permanent federal support for the arts and more secure conditions for federal artist-workers, Union members discussed current politics and rallied to support Republican Spain. The Artists' Union raised funds to send two fully equipped ambulances, with its logo emblazoned on their sides, to the American base hospital outside Madrid. [1] Thirty-five national AU members went to Spain as fighters, translators, drivers, and nurses, and more than half were killed; among the New York contingent were Paul Block, who died in Spain in 1937, and Phil Bard, Mildred Rackley, and Joseph Vogel, who all returned to continue organizing and making art. [2] Bard was sent back to America after an incipient heart attack. Rackley worked as a secretary-translator for Dr. Edward K. Barsky, head of the American Medical Bureau, and as a hospital administrator; on her return to New York, she was elected the only woman vice-president of the Artists' Union in 1938. [3] Vogel, like many other leftists, went on his own initiative (most likely with Communist Party clearance) and was circumspect later in discussing his experiences with interviewers. [4] The Artists' Union produced its own newspaper, *Art Front*, which published news, essays, and photographs from the Spanish front; this became a significant source of information for artists who wanted to make art that addressed the war's heroism and suffering.

105

Project
Facing Fascism: New York and
the Spanish Civil War

Company
Pure+Applied

Client
Museum of the City of New York

This handsome page of body copy with its massive initial cap, with the image on the opposite page of the spread, feels balanced on the page.

Project
Feature spread

Company
FB Design

Creative Director
Florian Bachleda

Photographer
Ian Spanier

Client
Private Air

Enfolded by typographically aero-dynamic brackets, the centered text of the opener floats in harmony opposite the centered close-up of the plane's curved hull.

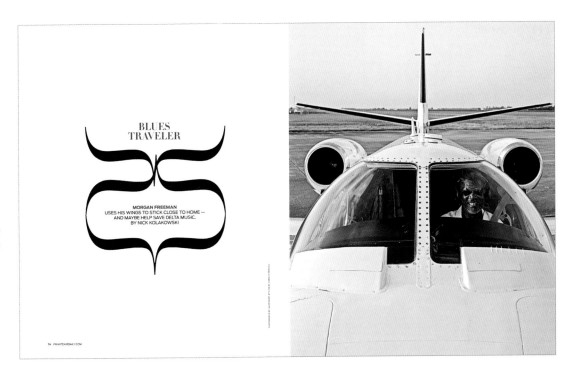

BLUES TRAVELER

MORGAN FREEMAN USES HIS WINGS TO STICK CLOSE TO HOME — AND MAYBE HELP SAVE DELTA MUSIC. BY NICK KOLAKOWSKI

74 PRIVATEAIRDAILY.COM

Project
Birds of the World

Art Director
Charlie Nix

Designers
Charlie Nix, Whitney Grant, and May Jampathom

Client
University of California Press

Classical page proportions with an extra bit of space added to accommodate marginalia make for a handsome and comfortable format, with plenty of breathing room for the eye.

Cockatoos occur in almost all terrestrial habitats within their ranges, from forests (including the margins of rainforests) to shrublands and even in desert regions—wherever they can find food and places to roost and nest. Like other parrots, cockatoos are highly social, usually foraging and roosting in flocks. They eat fruits, nuts, seeds, flower parts, and some insects; some use their strong bills to extract insect larvae from wood. Using their powerful feet to grasp branches and their bills as, essentially, a third foot, cockatoos clamber methodically through trees in search of food. Just as caged parrots do, they will hang gymnastically at odd angles and even upside down, the better to reach some delicious morsel. Cockatoo feet, with their powerful claws, also function as hands, delicately manipulating food and bringing it to the bill. Cockatoo tongues, as in other parrots, are thick and muscular, used to scoop pulp from fruits and hold seeds and nuts for the bill to crush. Although many species feed primarily in trees, some, pursuing seeds, such as Galahs, forage mainly on the ground. Some of the corellas use specialized bills to dig in the ground for roots.

Monogamous breeders, cockatoos form long-term pairs that generally remain together all year. Most species breed in cavities in live or dead trees; nests are lined with wood chips. The female only or both sexes incubate; in the former case, the female may be fed on the nest by her mate. Young are fed, as nestlings and fledglings, by both parents. In some species, the young stay with the parents until the next breeding season.

Cockatoos, generally, are threatened because they nest in tree cavities, and the large trees they breed in are increasingly scarce owing to such human activities as logging and land clearance. Also, they are persecuted by farmers and orchardists because they eat seeds and fruit crops, and are pursued for the pet trade. In Australia, cockatoos such as the Galah, Cockatiel, Red-tailed Black-Cockatoo, and Western Corella, have long been poisoned or shot to protect crops. Sulphur-crested Cockatoos are considered to be real pests; they damage trees in orchards, and apparently exercising their powerful bills, tear up car windshield wipers and house window moldings. The Galahs, taking advantage of agriculture and artificial water supplies, now occur throughout Australia in large numbers and are as much a part of the landscape as kangaroos. Two cockatoo species are considered vulnerable and three are endangered (one each in Australia, Indonesia, and the Philippines).

158 · BIRDS OF THE WORLD

Turacos

TURACOS are large, colorful, arboreal birds of sub-Saharan African forests, woodlands, and savannas. They are known for their brilliant plumage and have long been hunted for their feathers; turaco feathers are commonly used in ceremonial headdresses of various African groups, including East Africa's nomadic Masai people. Being large and tasty birds, turacos are also pursued for the dinner table. Visitors to African forests and savannas are made quickly aware of these birds by their raucous, often repetitive calls, some of the most characteristic sounds of these habitats. The twenty-three turaco species are all confined to Africa; they are known as louries in southern Africa. The family, Musophagidae, although its classification is controversial, is usually placed in order Cuculiformes with the cuckoos. (*Musophagidae* refers to banana or plantain eating, but despite being fruit-eaters, turacos rarely eat wild bananas.). Some of the turacos are formally called plantain-eaters and others are known as go-away-birds, for their loud distinctive "g'way, g'way" calls.

Turacos, all with conspicuous, sometimes colorful crests, are 16 to 29 inches (40 to 74 cm) long and have short, strong bills; short, rounded wings; and long, broad tails. Many have bare, brightly colored patches of skin around their eyes. Most species are primarily a striking glossy blue, green, or purplish. Studies of turacos show that their bright coloring at least partially reflects the foods they eat. Some fruits in their diet provide copper, and a red copper-based pigment (turacin) unique to turacos provides the brilliant reds in their plumage. Similarly, the deep greens of some species

Distribution:
Sub-Saharan Africa

No. of Living
Species: 23

No. of Species
Vulnerable,
Endangered: 1, 1

No. of Species Extinct
Since 1600: 0

TURACOS · 159

100 Theory of Relativity IV

LAST BUT NOT LEAST, once again and always, it is the typographic relationships that exist on the page, screen, or document that are the ultimate arbiters of the success of the designer. Clarity of intent, clear separation of elements, typographic harmony, beauty, and legibility must reign together to form a satisfactory whole.

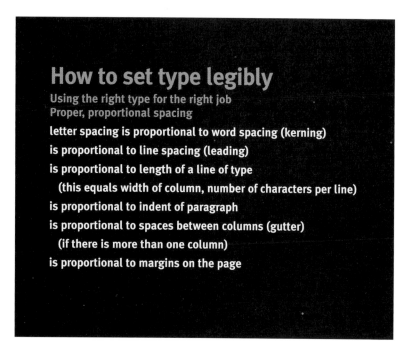

How to set type legibly
Using the right type for the right job
Proper, proportional spacing
letter spacing is proportional to word spacing (kerning)
is proportional to line spacing (leading)
is proportional to length of a line of type
  (this equals width of column, number of characters per line)
is proportional to indent of paragraph
is proportional to spaces between columns (gutter)
  (if there is more than one column)
is proportional to margins on the page

Project
Cover

Design Director
Robert Priest

Art Director
Grace Lee

Photographer
Sacha Waldman

Client
Condé Nast Portfolio

A clear sense of hierarchy, harmonious type choices, excellent legibility, and elegantly tailored type fit together with an arresting image and a strong main cover line to create a memorable and stylish design.

Project
Single page

Creative Director
Scott Dadich

Design Director
Wyatt Mitchell

Designer
Margaret Swart

Photographer
Todd Tankersley

Client
Wired

Playful and dramatic, this modern page with multiple text blocks manages to keep all the plates spinning in the air; the text is accessible and inviting, and the information feels organized and structured.

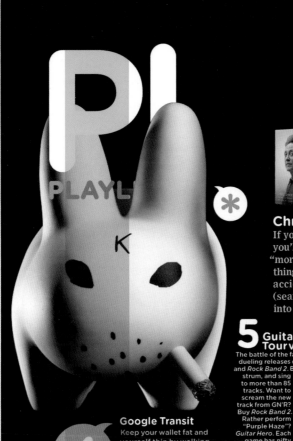

PL
PLAYLI

3

Christopher Walken A to Z
If you already have the More Cowbell iPhone app, you'll love this encyclopedia. If you don't know what "more cowbell" refers to, you *need* it. Inside is everything we ever wanted to know about the actor whose accidental second life as a twisted YouTube hero (search "walken impersonations") has turned him into a high-haired cultural meme—the new Lebowski.

5
Guitar Hero World Tour vs. Rock Band 2
The battle of the fake bands erupts with the dueling releases of *Guitar Hero World Tour* and *Rock Band 2*. Both let four players drum, strum, and sing to more than 85 tracks. Want to scream the new track from GN'R? Buy *Rock Band 2*. Rather perform "Purple Haze"? *Guitar Hero*. Each game has nifty new functions: *World Tour* lets you create your own instrumentals; *Rock Band 2* has a drum training mode (and an optional $300 controller from Ion that converts into a real kit). Bonus: The instruments from the original *Rock Band* work with both titles.

6

Ferrari F1 Lego car
This 1/9-scale model of Ferrari's iconic Formula One racer is made out of everyone's favorite building blocks—nearly 1,000 of them. The 20-inch-long stallion is not the fastest build, but from the functional steering and removable front spoiler to the authentic branding, it's the perfect nexus of gearhead obsession and toy nerddom.

4

Google Transit
Keep your wallet fat and yourself thin by walking and taking public transit. Thanks to Google engineers who used their "20 percent time" to pore over bus, subway, and train schedules from 70 metro areas, Google Maps now offers step-by-step instructions for *not* driving from point A to point B.

7

CybeRacers
Next time you need a weirdo blocker on your commute, pop in the earbuds and flip your cell to the new phone-based series *CybeRacers*. The futuristic animated serial tracks a rogue scientist whose hobby seems to be setting off a natural disaster whenever a car chase ends in a crash. Part extreme sports spectacle, part *Matrix*, *CybeRacers* delivers flying cars, giant man-eating sharks, and a bikini-clad surfing heroine. Creator Gun Ho Jang—who produced effects for films like *Hollow Man* and *Mission to Mars*—dispenses enough eye candy to prop up the absurd story line.

8
Mix Tape USB Stick
MP3s killed the mix tape, and a disc full of dragged-and-dropped tracks just doesn't show the same dedication. Fake that old-school aesthetic with this cassette from SuckUK. The hollowed-out cartridge conceals a 64-meg USB stick, and a blank insert hosts your scrawled track list and schmoopy cover art. ($38 each. John Cusack and boom box not included.)

10

9
Incase KRINK sleeve
When product design firm Incase needed to make a splash, it tapped niche mag *Arkitip* to curate a line of arted-up gadget sleeves. For the first quarterly installment, *Arkitip* chose street artist and drippy paint entrepreneur Craig "KR" Costello. Incase scanned his work, then foil-stamped the flowing abstraction onto the case. Up next: sky-inspired computer and iPhone armor from Dutch artist Parra.

KORG DS-10
Being a pretend guitar hero with your game console is so five Playlist items ago. Be a real rock star with your Nintendo DS (between *Mario Kart* sessions, natch). The DS-10 game card turns any DS into a six-track, 16-step sequencer—a pro-grade sim of the KORG MS-10 synth, first released in 1978 and now beloved by the likes of Autechre and the Chemical Brothers.

*Continued from Playlist Item 1: Smorkin' Labbit, by Frank Kozik

0 9 8 OCT 2008

PHOTOGRAPHS BY **Todd Tankersley**

Contributors index

Special thanks to Donald Partyka for the infographics on pages 38, 40, 52, 103, 117, 118-119, 130, 142, 144, 157, 158, and 204.

About the author

INA SALTZ is an art director, a designer, an author, a photographer, and professor of digital design at the City College of New York, whose areas of expertise are typography and magazine design. She is the author of seven online courses, focussing on typography, for Lynda.com/LinkedIn Learning.

Previously, for over twenty-five years, Saltz was an art director, at *Time* magazine (International Editions) and other publications, including *Worth*, *GOLF*, *Golf for Women*, *Businessweek,* and *WorldBusiness*.

Saltz was on the design faculty of the Stanford Professional Publishing Course, and she has also taught virtually for Stanford via webcast. She lectures on topics related to magazine design and typography (most recently in Calgary, Toronto, Atlanta, Minneapolis, Denver, Moscow, and Amsterdam). She has written over fifty articles for various design magazines including *Graphis* and *Print.*

Saltz's two books documenting typographic tattoos, *Body Type: Intimate Messages Etched in Flesh*, and *Body Type Two: More Typographic Tattoos*, were published by Harry N. Abrams Books (www.bodytypebook.com). She is also a contributing author for Phaidon's *Archive of Graphic Design*, and a co-author of *Typography Referenced: A Comprehensive Visual Guide to the Language, History, and Practice of Typography*, published by Rockport Publishers.

Acknowledgments

My passion for the glorious things that are letterforms was first ignited by my calligraphy teacher at Cooper Union, Donald Kunz, who had studied under Lloyd Reynolds at Reed College in Portland, Oregon. A few years later, as president of the Society of Scribes, I had the privilege of inviting and hosting Lloyd, who was a gurulike spiritual leader to our lettering community as much as a scribe, to visit and teach in New York City. Other calligraphers taught and inspired me in the years that followed: Donald Jackson (Queen Elizabeth's scribe), my great mentor Hermann Zapf, Alice Koeth, Lili Wronker, Paul Standard, Jeanyee Wong, Sheila Waters, Ewan Clayton, Peter Thornton, and many others. I engaged in lengthy (and beautifully written) correspondences with calligraphers in far-flung corners of the globe and enjoyed the artistic company of a large and generous extended family of fellow scribes. To this day, calligraphy and my comradeship with all calligraphers occupy a deep place in my heart and soul, and reminds me of the source of all design principles.

A love of words and letterforms led me to a rewarding career as an editorial design director. My first job in publishing was at *Cue* magazine (now defunct), which was still being set in hot metal on linotype machines, with headlines set by hand on composing sticks. There I experienced the tail end of hot type in the mainstream of mass media. A whirlwind of short-lived technologies followed, and now we are firmly ensconced in the age of digital typography, with approximately two million (!) typefaces available (as of this writing) for our delectation.

I am indebted to many authors who have written eloquently about typography, none more so than Robert Bringhurst, in his magnificent work, *The Elements of Typographic Style*. His erudition, sensitive phraseology, and abiding respect for letterforms and their use may never be surpassed.

Many colleagues in the design world have given generously of their time and talent to contribute to this book, especially Joe Zeff, Bonnie Siegler at Eight and a Half, and Luke Hayman at Pentagram. I thank Donald Partyka and Mirko Ilic, who, for many years, have provided me with guidance and wise counsel. I thank my editor, Emily Potts, for inviting me to write this book and for her encouragement along the way.

Finally, I thank my wonderful husband, Steven Beispel, whose humor, understanding, patience, and love have sustained me throughout this and all of my endeavors.